A VOICE AT TWILIGHT

A VOICE AT TWILIGHT

Diary of a Dying Man

TESSA LORANT WARBURG
based on material by
JEREMY WARBURG

PETER OWEN · LONDON

ISBN 0 7206 0706 X

PETER OWEN PUBLISHERS
73 Kenway Road London SW5 0RE

First published in Great Britain 1988
© Tessa Lorant Warburg 1988

Photoset and printed in Great Britain by
Redwood Burn Limited Trowbridge Wiltshire

To the memory of
Jeremy Fredric Warburg
and to the future of
Jeremy Hillier Warburg

Ashes to ashes,
Dust to dust;
If the drugs don't get you,
The cancer must.

A paraphrase of Jelly Roll Morton's New Orleans Jazzmen's
'Oh, didn't he ramble' funeral march. From a 78 rpm record,
vocalized by Will Handy.

FOREWORD

by The Bishop of Leicester

Jeremy Warburg wanted his wife to publish this diary of his last few months 'to help the many people in my situation'. Since we must all die, we are all in his situation.

Three months before the end he could still, in spite of increasing helplessness, 'look forward to the beautiful, the funny, the interesting, the fascinating, the wonderfully curious and the fair side of life'. As he found himself more and more at the mercy of others, the diary makes it clearer that the process of dying is what frightens us, not death itself. Even his loving family often failed to understand him. Occasionally he quarrelled with his wife. This account of it all is searingly honest, and Tessa is courageous in letting it all be told. Their joint honesty validates Jeremy's conviction that their marriage was all that a marriage could and should be.

The same honesty shows bitter resentment against those whom society appoints to help the dying. Doctors, nurses, undertakers and priests collectively make a poor showing in this diary. They are nearly all themselves unable to face death, and refuse to talk to the dying man about death, even when that is what he most needs to talk about. Thus they dehumanize him. Their subterfuges and self-deceptions can be tortuous. 'Just because one is reasonably intelligent, and asks to be told the truth, doesn't mean one is ready for it when one hears it' is an elaborate ploy of self-protection by a member of a 'caring profession' caring for self.

The physical humiliations of Jeremy's illness; the mental humiliations caused by insensitive people around him; the distress of a man who needs his wife's presence more than anything else, but realizes how he is taxing and draining her by staying with her – all this makes disturbing reading. Yet, so long as the reader does not try to make excuses for himself as he reads, this book is a comfort to the reader. Dying with Jeremy, we face our own death; and thus learn more about the care of the dying.

PREFACE

The diagnosis of an incurable, progressive and ultimately fatal illness, in particular cancer, is held in dread by every patient seeking medical advice. This prospect is equally unwelcome to the medical adviser. How much more satisfactory it would be to tell a patient that there is 'nothing to worry about', especially when rapid cure or relief of symptoms can be effected by competent surgery, than to ask him to face the reality of almost certain death. Surgeons are by nature confident and optimistic, usually with justification, thanks to modern technology. However, the management of malignant disease – cancer – can and does tax the physical, emotional and psychological reserves of any surgeon who genuinely cares about his fellow man. Perhaps this is why the medical profession may appear at times to distance itself from patients and their relatives.

When I first met Jeremy Warburg I realized immediately that I had no easy task on my hands. Intelligent, and obviously desperately concerned, he was not to be fobbed off with medical platitudes. I knew I had to win his confidence and trust, and I like to think I managed to do so, even though his future prospects seemed far from rosy at our first consultation. After a very rapid preliminary examination I also knew that the likelihood of a cure for him was extremely remote. What I could offer him was symptom control of the huge mass that was destroying him from within, and the possibility of palliation by radiotherapy of the secondary tumour spread.

The massive operation to remove the primary was technically successful and Jeremy made a spectacular recovery. I was truly delighted with his progress and felt justified in my cautious optimism that, if the radiotherapy was equally successful, our combined efforts would give him some more years rather than months of useful life. I still had no illusions of a complete cure, but cancer is unpredictable, and after all there had been reports in the medical literature of spontaneous regression of secondary tumour deposits after successful removal of the primary cancer. I should have felt much less self-congratulatory had I known at the time that the response to radiotherapy was to be poor, and that this forceful giant of a man would ultimately be reduced to the role of a totally dependent paraplegic.

Those were the good days and Jeremy departed from my little surgical cosmos full of hope and determination, or so I believed, leaving me with the satisfaction of a job well done. I was not to see him again for many months, but the steady flow of reports on his progress that crossed my desk were not encouraging.

So often at this stage, when patients are being cared for by the multi-disciplinary approach, they disappear into the nebulous world of 'terminal care' and you hear nothing until the ultimate short note from the family doctor confirming that your surgical success has come to an untimely end.

I was very pleased, and indeed felt honoured, when Jeremy decided to renew our acquaintance and asked for my help on some problems with his terminal management. Even as a hard-bitten medic with twenty-five years' surgical experience, I was shocked when he arrived for assessment. By now he was bed-ridden and his body was shattered, but his mind was as alert as ever and he lost no time in attacking my surgical machismo image. He was very involved in taping his Diary and invited me to help him plot the last entries, detailing how he would make his final exit. None of the scenarios appealed to me, but we opted for progressive renal failure due to infection and his quietly lapsing into a coma. We discussed many things, not least whether I had made the appropriate decision in attempting to prolong his life in the first place. I never felt, however, that he was resentful, but rather that he was trying to persuade me to be more objective. We discussed a decision I had taken, which had not been too well received by some of my colleagues, not to operate on a local celebrity who had a similar tumour. I wondered how much Jeremy had influenced me in that decision.

Our last meeting was especially poignant. The interrelated role-playing was coming to an end; we both knew we had lost the technical battle. We consoled each other rather like players in a losing team after a hard game. I mentioned his courage and that I had learned a lot from him. He complimented me on my surgical skills and the concern I had shown. I left, much moved, wondering what good had come of it all.

The importance of the narrative that follows lies in the wholly convincing way it articulates what many patients must feel but cannot adequately express. It is especially pertinent at the present time, when terminal care and the hospice movement are attracting more and more attention, and attitudes to death and dying are changing. How much better to have a dignified and satisfactory death, with adequate time for grieving with one's loved ones, than an unduly protracted existence as a result of well-intentioned but ineffectual medical interference.

Medical attitudes to malignant disease have also changed dramatically in recent years. Surgical demonstrations of anatomical knowledge and technical expertise are largely irrelevant in dealing with most forms of cancer. The concept of the 'fearless surgeon' has always struck me as rather odd, since surgery is significantly more dangerous for the patient than for the person who performs the operation. The modern surgeon, realizing his limitations, is more genuinely concerned with treating the patient as a whole rather than concentrating on his disease.

Finally, the patient. Each individual and his circumstances are unique. More widespread communication and knowledge have resulted in a better informed public with possibly more limited expectations of the medical profession. Many patients now wish to be involved in the decision-making process which will determine their fate, others do not. Jeremy was one of the former, and I value and appreciate his testimony as it is conveyed in this book. Both relatives of patients and medical advisers may well find after reading it that their assumptions about the terminally ill have changed.

'Donald MacKieff', ChM, FRCS
Consultant Urologist

ACKNOWLEDGEMENTS

I should like to thank Madeleine, Colin and Richard Warburg for their unstinting support while I was writing the Diary, and during the search for a publisher. I am especially grateful to Madeleine for her comments on, and discussions about, the various drafts I made, and for sending extracts to friends for their views.

My thanks also to Gillian Geering, Joy Cotter and the many others, too numerous to name, who willingly read, and constructively commented on, the Diary extracts they were shown.

I should like to thank 'Donald MacKieff', who helped Jeremy Warburg beyond the call of duty; 'Liz', the Community nurses and 'Mary', who helped make it possible for Jeremy to live at home; 'Sister Kinder', who put humanity before union rules; and 'Peter Worthing', who helped control Jeremy's physical pain.

Finally, I am indebted to the National Health Service for the invaluable help it gave, vital for keeping a seriously ill patient at home. The care of a sympathetic GP and Community nurses is already understood by most people. What perhaps is sometimes not appreciated is that without a service like the National Health it is not always possible to die, in dignity and peace, at home, surrounded by those one loves. This unmatched Service also gives near-relatives and friends the privilege to be involved in a process that affects us all. Private health care is designed for short-term hospital treatment. It does not, and seems unlikely to, take on the role played by the NHS in terminal care in the home.

It should be noted that the names of most individuals in this narrative, with the exception of members of the family, are fictitious.

T.L.W.

PROLOGUE

Jeremy Warburg was diagnosed as having cancer in the summer of 1985. He was not entirely surprised, having sensed his vulnerability to the disease more than twenty years before.

Jeremy had written several successful books and numerous learned articles in the field of English Language, but the writing of fiction was always his main interest. He therefore felt the need to spend more time writing creatively. This prompted him, some twenty years ago, to make the difficult decision to relinquish his tenured post in the English Department at University College, London. An enjoyable year as a Visiting Professor at Earlham College, Indiana, followed. Nevertheless, although he was offered a professorship which would have allowed him time for creative work, Jeremy resolved to forgo academic life entirely in order to write fiction. To this end he and his wife sold their house near London and bought a somewhat dilapidated mid-Victorian vicarage in the West Country.

Jeremy (Jifda), his wife Tessa (Teil, Bean), their daughter Madeleine (Mad, Minnow) and their identical twin sons Colin (Col, Cockle) and Richard (Tick, the Tock) were wonderfully happy living in the beautiful Somerset countryside, which was even more idyllic before the coming of the motorways. The close-knit family lived frugally and almost self-sufficiently, restoring the old house, renovating the garden, planting an orchard and growing their own vegetables organically. Jeremy felt peace within. He completed several novels and some experimental prose.

In due course the children left for University. Tessa started a knitwear design business. Jeremy, although he had fulfilled a creative need through writing novels, failed to find a publisher. Remembering that his father, Fredric Warburg, had enormously increased the success of the firm of Secker and Warburg by courageously publishing Orwell's *Animal Farm*, rejected previously by other publishers, Jeremy decided to form his own imprint. He called the new venture The Thorn Press, persuaded Tessa to be the general manager, and set about finding titles that would sell. Specialized non-fiction would have to fund the fiction list he was keen to foster. He started with Tessa's *Earning and Saving with a Knitting Machine*. Reviewed in many magazines, it sold well. Two knitting books later, Jeremy spotted the potential of the *Heritage of Knitting* titles. *Knitted Lace Edgings* was published to quite remarkable success, establishing a series which continues to sell unabated. Consequently, two of Jeremy's novels were published under the Thorn Press imprint. One, *A Woman's World*, was well reviewed, and rapidly sold out of its rather small printing. All looked set fair for a flourishing new career for Jeremy – as publisher and self-publisher.

A curious lassitude now took hold of Jeremy. An odd lethargy, an ever-increasing detachment from social contact, became apparent in him. Enthusiasms for new projects failed to translate themselves into action. Jeremy felt a debilitating ache, then a persistent and nagging pain, in his back and chest. Doctors were consulted, but insisted they could find no physical cause. Eventually Jeremy announced something was seriously amiss. An X-ray was taken and considerable 'bony deterioration', the sign of a cancer secondary, was found on a rib.

An appointment was arranged with a surgeon. He ordered further X-rays and a bone scan to try to find the cancer primary. A large tumour was pin-pointed in his left kidney. An operation was advised, and almost immediately, and successfully, performed. Realizing that medical intervention might not be enough to prolong Jeremy's life, Jeremy and Tessa adopted a macrobiotic cancer-prevention diet from Japan. The bone secondary was treated with radiotherapy.

It proved almost impossible to establish a prognosis. Estimates ranged from an unlikely, but conceivable, ten years to a somewhat panicky three weeks. At this the family, now scattered, was hastily called together. Madeleine, based in London, was running a video software company. Colin, in Southampton, had started his own computer software business and was now married to

Anna, a recently qualified doctor. Richard had emigrated to the United States as a scientific researcher and married Ruthi, a physician's assistant in Boston. All hastened to Somerset for what might have been the last time they could be together.

The immediate crisis passed. The family dispersed.

Jeremy, made increasingly desperate by encroaching pain, spent the next three months undergoing intermittent radio-therapy treatment. At first the promise was that this would shrink the tumour and alleviate the pain. Later he was told that radiotherapy was almost certain to arrest the growth, preventing it from pressing on the spinal nerves and causing paralysis. Eventually he and Tessa realized they were not being told the truth. Optimistic assurances, followed by evasions, then a curi-ous unwillingness on the part of Jeremy's medical advisers to discuss the matter at all, caused them feelings of anxiety, lone-liness and isolation. Bewildered, they withdrew from medical contact as much as possible. By December it was clear that, pious pronouncements notwithstanding, Jeremy would be dead quite soon. He and Tessa now understood they had to estimate the time left for themselves. They decided to trust their own instincts about any further treatment.

Ruthi was pregnant, a scan showing a boy, a grandson-to-be for Jeremy and Tessa, due to be born the following March. A family reunion was organized. They met, as often as their differ-ent commitments would allow, during the Christmas week of 1985.

The family habitually kept in touch through audio cassettes. Jeremy now saw their significance and the idea of taping a Diary came to him. In it he would observe, unexpurgated, just how it feels to know one has only a short, indefinite time to live. He would candidly relate medical attitudes to his plight. He longed to smooth the path of others in his predicament.

By March even recording became difficult for him. Jeremy, appreciating that he could not write the Diary up himself, en-trusted the task to Tessa. Nevertheless, he did his utmost to convey his true and unadulterated feelings to his last breath. The text which follows is closely based on that material.

The Diary starts on Christmas Eve, Jeremy's and Tessa's wedding anniversary. It continues through the following six months until the day Jeremy dies. Happenings, present and past, are told through the sick man's perception of the world. The early entries are long and detailed, factual and rational. A change becomes apparent. Courageous determination to face up to the situation without self-pity is interspersed with confusion, resentment and even hostility. Jeremy's mind, though functioning to the last, is sometimes clouded by morphine, at other times sharpened by pain. Good-humoured acceptance changes to uncharacteristic irritability, ambivalence and occasional anger. His body crumbles, tortuously and embarrassingly. Nevertheless, much enjoyment of life remains to him.

We cannot conquer all disease. Many of us will face protracted dying as victims, relatives or friends. What we can do is make these last months, weeks or even days of life count as the precious time they are. We can choose not to build a wall of false hope that cuts us off from meaningful relationships, we can choose not to prevaricate in the face of death, and we can choose to treat those who are about to die as the complete human beings they still are.

If the thoughts and feelings in the Diary, so poignantly expressed, so courageously laid bare, so eagerly bequeathed, can succeed in this important sense, the diarist's fervent wish to help his fellow sufferers will have been fulfilled.

December

Our thirty-second wedding anniversary. Teil and I have been married rather more than half our lives. Unlikely either of us considered the implications of serious illness on that long-ago day. I remember very well mouthing the 'in sickness and in health' bit, but I doubt if we gave much heed to that well-worn phrase. Certainly I gave no thought to cancer, or the slow, tortuous course that that disease could take.

Madison, Wisconsin. The Dairy State, the lovely lakes, fairy-tale sunsets. We were studying for our American MAs.

'You been to America before?' the dumpy little registrar quizzed me, looking up at me through hedgerow eyebrows, his Middle Western twang resonating through his sinuses.

'Yes. Once.'

'What dates?' he barked now, the eyebrows meeting to make one enormous hedge. I saw Teil look at me intently.

'Well, first in September 1952.' He wrote it down. 'Then back to England in September 1953, and I've just returned, December 1953.' Puzzling, this curiosity regarding dates which were, in any case, red-inked on to my passport.

'He asked whether you've been *married* before,' I remember Teil exploding, '*not* whether you've been to America before!'

My cancer was diagnosed six months ago. I must have had it for many years before it was 'discovered'. This anniversary, I'm pretty sure, will be our last.

'And the ring for the groom?' Hedgerow turned to Teil.

'There isn't one,' she admitted hesitantly.

UnAmerican. Letting down her compatriots! He turned away from her, his eyebrows parting in disgust, and snorted.

'Till death us do part,' we intoned obediently. And fervently. Both of us children of divorced parents, we were determined on a lasting union. It seems a particularly cruel irony that a marriage as profoundly happy as our own will end by my death at only fifty-seven. My father died aged eighty-two. My mother is eighty-four and going strong. I could surely have expected to live for another twenty years or more! There's so much to live for: to celebrate the birth of our first grandchild, books to write and publish. It's not to be. We're already sure that I'll be dead within months. We'll never celebrate our anniversary again.

'I can feel this odd stiffness in my back. As though something's clawing at my spine,' I explained to Teil on a walk just over two weeks ago. Willow-fringed roads glistening, slippery with rain. I take my stick when we go walking now, but I still felt more than usually insecure.

'You'd better ring Chapman before he's off for Christmas,' Teil urged me, alarmed. 'He said he's ninety-five per cent certain he can stop the tumour spreading.'

'What for? He'll only say come in for further useless treatment. After the holiday, of course. Can't possibly disrupt his festivities!' Put not your trust in the smooth promises of radiotherapy consultants. No doubt the threatened 'unmitigated disaster' if I didn't undergo radiotherapy was happening anyway. The tumour's on the march, advancing towards my spine.

'Will it be safe to leave the X-ray till after the holiday?' I'd already checked with the consultant at my last appointment.

'Perfectly all right.'

'There's no risk?' I was quite prepared to come in earlier.

'Well, I'm not God.' I never thought he was. Interesting he made the connection. Don't think his 'ninety-five per cent certain' includes my case. Adding the possibility of paralysis to an already terrible illness. 'I see you've got the latest Walkman.' Showing some interest at last. 'Is it good?' That's what he really wanted to discuss. Anything rather than my disease.

'What's the point? He won't come to the phone or return my call,' I'd prophesied to Teil, disconsolate. But I steeled myself to ring him.

How right I was in judging his reactions! I left a message with his secretary about the state of play. He hasn't been in touch. Just left a note with her, should I be so importunate as to ring back. No hurry about the X-ray.

I feel a little better now. More mobile. 'Let's go round the garden.' I don my boots, the duvet coat that Richard gave me, grasp my walking-stick. 'We can pick some winter heathers. White for luck! Let's take some autumn cherry for the lovely scent. And that pervasive winter honeysuckle.'

Teil cuts the sprigs for us. We'll decorate our dining-table, set for two. 'Are you up to evensong, d'you think?'

'Perhaps it might be better to wait till midnight mass.' I enjoy evensong at Wells. Cathedral School choir, Madrigals. Carols for Christmas Eve. Can't manage it today.

'See how you feel after dinner.'

Festive macrobiotic fare. Tiny pieces of fresh scallops, done in a stir fry. Teil's special malted *crème*, by now a favourite of mine. Sparkling Perrier water. Neither of us minds the privations of the cancer-prevention diet. We mind the cancer, the curtailment of my life.

'Let's go round the orchard and look at next year's fruit buds.'

Apples, pears, plums and cherries in full bearing. A medlar, a fruiting quince, a mulberry bush. All planted by us when we came. Will I be here to eat the fruit? I totter precariously across the hummocky paddock grasses, Teil steadying my left arm, the stick in my right hand. My steps are faltering. Turkey oak branches I had to stoop under are above me now. The light is fading, but Glastonbury Tor, protruding high above the flat acres of grassland round it, St Michael's tower perched on top, stands silhouetted black against the glowing embers of the dying day. I've left directions in my will. I want my ashes scattered to the four winds from the top of the Tor. I wish my remains to stay in this area with its echoing past, to mingle their own vibes with others already there. Many have died before me here, some of them in agony.

Arrows of cloud, gull grey above the darkening green horizons of the Somerset Levels, point the slate roof of our Victorian vicarage. 'A square house,' the local joiner called it, admiringly, replacing sash-cords in well-worn windows.

'You're going to live *here*? In this red-brick monstrosity? Away from everyone?'

Relatives thought us mad. We saw the look of pity in strangers' eyes. Victoriana wasn't fashionable then. We bought our 'square house' for a song. Thick-walled, solid, dependable. Firm launching-pad for our three children.

The finish of a peaceful day. We stay at home, hold hands, listen to King's College choir herald the birth of Jesus. I try not to think of the non-years ahead of me, the lonely years ahead of Teil. What have I done that this should happen to me now? I do not know.

CHRISTMAS DAY

I worried all night about the weather. It's over a hundred and fifty miles from us to Madeleine's London maisonette.

'I'll drive,' Teil says, trying to save my strength. 'You'll need all the energy you can muster.'

'I'll do my bit, while I still can. I'll drive first.' I double check locking the front door. 'Don't rush me. We'll be there before one.' Macrobiotic Christmas lunch at Mad's. Teil's bringing basic grains, Mad will supply the fish and vegetables.

'*Right* lane for London, honey. Get into it *now*.' All those confusing junctions on the motorways. 'Why don't we stop at the next service station?' Maybe Teil's right. 'Just a short break.' We've always shared the driving.

I rather think I dozed along the way. The drone of the trusty Volvo on the motorway put me to sleep.

'You've made good time, then.' Here already! Just after twelve.

'Hello, Minnow. Merry Christmas!' Merry? Just a phrase I mouth. I never find Christmas a source of merriment or joy.

'Merry Christmas, Jifda.' She's looking somewhat peaky. Starts to cough. Because she smokes. Reminds me of my mother, hacking through my childhood. 'It's because of singing at midnight mass. I couldn't let the choir down. It's made my cold worse. How're you feeling?'

'Not bad at all.' I ache, but what's the point of saying so? 'Have you brought the support pillow?'

'All under control.' She carts my paraphernalia into her home. Offered to let me use the double bed we gave her. Dear daughter, she tries so hard to make me comfortable. Think it better if we go to the hotel. A room each, so Teil can get some rest. I'll only toss and turn.

'And the sheepskin?' Can't sit without that at my back.

'Already in the living-room,' Mad says, solicitous. 'Mind out! I'll lock the cats in my room.' Ruthi's allergic to cats, so she and Richard will be joining us at the hotel tomorrow. I'm exhausted now and very hungry. 'I'll put the corn on. We can start with that.' I relish corn on the cob. The cellar is stacked with goodies Mad's bought for the occasion.

'Marvellous things you've bought, Minnow. Look at that, honey! Mange-touts, corn, artichokes. *And* kiwi fruit and melons. *Exotica macrobiotica. Two* huge pineapples! All set for the game tomorrow, then.' Quite true. Mad's bought enough to feed an army.

'Turbot today. If you do the rice, I'll make the sauce.' She looks at Teil uncertainly. 'And a salad for us. Is that all right?'

'Of course. I'll put the rice on.'

'Richard says he wants to eat exactly what Jifda eats. I told him I simply can't arrange that. I don't know how to cook macrobiotically.'

'I'll explain,' Teil soothes her. Dearest Tock. Offered me one of his kidneys if both of mine turned out cancerous.

'Have you put up a Christmas tree?'

A Christmas tree? I haven't even registered it's Christmas. Just the last time I'll be in London. Last time I'll see my aged aunts, who will outlive me. Last time I'll see my ailing mother, who will nevertheless outlive me. Last time we'll be together with my brother and his family. Last time I'll see Richard as 'myself'. Next time he's over from the States I'll be dying. Or dead.

'Why don't you have a nap, honey? In Mad's room, while we go and see to the hotel? I'll get your sheepskin for you.'

'Right. Off you go, then.'

I doze off immediately. The front door banging wakes me up.

'All checked in. Mad was very clever. She got you a double-bedded room, no extra charge. I'm in a single on another floor, but there's a phone connection.'

'What will we do about dandelion coffee tomorrow?'

'I thought we'd ask for boiling water in the restaurant when Richard and Ruthi join us for breakfast.' Good thinking. They'll be arriving early from Heathrow. 'Mad's fetching them and bringing them right over. We can all breakfast together.'

We try watching *All Creatures Great and Small*, one of my favourites. I simply can't cope and glance at Teil.

'Thanks for the turbot lunch, Mad. It was splendid. Fabulous sauce.'

'Was it really all right?'

'Delicious. We'd better go.'

'Must you? Already?' She looks upset. 'I thought you'd stay till eight at least.'

'The journey hasn't helped. I'd better get Jifda settled in.'

''Night, Minnow. Lovely lunch.' Sweet, my daughter. She's lovingly doing all she can. I'm too tired to express my appreciation, or my feelings, I love my daughter dearly.

The hotel room's adequate – large, somewhat cool and rather drab. The phone rings as we enter it. Who knows we're here? My mother? Surely Mad hasn't. . . .

'Oh hello, Mad.' Teil's picked up the receiver already. 'Don't worry. We've got a second sheepskin here. Of course don't bother to come round! You're not feeling well anyway. He'll be fine.'

[*22*]

My last Christmas. No better, and no worse, than most. Golden moments when the children were small. But even those were marred for me. My mother there, and it was spoilt. When she was not, I felt the guilt. Now she prefers it on her own. And I'm too ill to care.

BOXING DAY

'Hello, honey. It's nearly eight. You up yet?'
'Of course I'm up. Eaten the porridge from the Thermos.'
'How was it?'
'Bit cool, actually. But edible enough.'
'I meant the night. Perhaps we can find something for you in the restaurant. I'll fetch you now, shall I?'

Down to the dining-room, waiting for Mad to bring the Tock and what I named his Frock, until an unknown florist improved on that.

'What lovely lilies.' Huge bunch of my favourite flowers, almost filling the small room at the Durstone, where my cancerous kidney was removed. 'Who are they from?'

'The card says Tock and Flock! Very appropriate, now that Ruthi's pregnant.'

We sit at a table at the far end of the room, in hopes of privacy. Magnificent self-service counter, groaning with 'poison' from a macrobiotic point of view. I ask for boiling water for my dandelion coffee granules and delicately sip a little apple juice diluted with Highland Spring. Suddenly I notice Teil isn't helping herself to breakfast but at the far end, greeting our threesome.

So moved I get up to meet them. Grasp a chair-back to steady me, and then walk, as quickly as I can, towards them. I embrace my second son, younger by an hour than his brother. Strange. Apart from Mad and the two of us, no one could tell them apart. Until they married.

'They're such different personalities,' Ruthi marvelled when introduced to Colin. 'How can people mix them up?'

They're both like me – physically, too. Not as tall, but more

[*23*]

handsome. There are different aspects of my personality in the two. Richard's the extrovert, strong and powerful. He doesn't suffer fools gladly. Sensitive underneath. Colin's the quiet one, the one who's lovingly persuasive, the one who talks me round. He's tough when needs be, a pillar for me to lean on. Deep down the twins are very similar; two sides of the same coin.

'Richard idolizes his father,' Ruthi confided to Mad on the telephone. 'He's taking Jifda's illness very hard.'

I empathize with him. He's far away, can't help me physically, the way Col and Mad do. The strong emotions we share are channelled, at remove, through the transatlantic telephone. I miss the Tock. Miss his obvious concern. Miss seeing myself in him: young, energetic, strong. I ache to see my stalwart son. He'll carry on a spark of life for me, himself and through his unborn son.

'The scan shows it's a boy. Would Jifda like it if we call the baby Jeremy?' Ruthi asks Teil.

'I think he'd be enchanted. Touched. Really delighted. Yes.'

It's against Jewish tradition to name a child after a living relative. So good of Ruthi to overcome her natural reluctance. No need to worry; I'm as good as dead.

'We're due at the aunts' at ten. For a morning "do".' I haven't told anyone but my children about my disease. No wish to be the spectre at the feast.

'Ruthi will need a rest. I'll cook the lunch.' Teil's going to give the aunts a miss in case she gives the game away.

'Nephew Jeremy! You do look well. Lost a bit of weight?'

'Just keeping fit.' I'm wearing one of Teil's Fair Isle creations. It keeps me warm and covers up my thinness.

'And Richard! What a treat. Come and sit by me. I'll show you the family photographs.' She turns to me. 'Jeremy, a piece of Battenberg. Your favourite, I know.'

I pick up the familiar, chequered sponge, two lurid pink squares against two in bright yellow. The richly sugared marzipan is attached with a bright crimson jam of indiscernible fruitage. I fumble with my napkin, trying, somehow, to spirit the cake away.

'Look at that clock!' Richard points to an inoffensive timepiece and, attention drawn from me, gulps down my piece of cake.

'Finished already, Jeremy? We're such a greedy lot!' Aunt Joan heaves herself happily towards the trolley, endangering her equilibrium with the effort.

'No, really, I've just had breakfast. . . .' A chocolate-covered éclair, oozing with cream, lands on my plate.

'There,' she puffs happily. 'Jeremy always liked the cream ones best!' A little recollection. 'Is Tessa well?' Teil's absence hasn't gone unnoticed.

'She's cooking lunch. We're off to the Davids after that. No time, you see.'

She's unconvinced, but lets the matter drop.

'Have you seen Richard's photos, Aunt Peg?' Mad moves her body to obstruct the view while Richard whips the creamy mass into his paper napkin and then his pocket. I can see it bulge.

'More coffee, anyone? They do such lovely cakes at Marks and Sparks.' Aunt Joan, exhausted now from cake-tray duties, sinks mercifully back into her easy chair, clutching a strawberry meringue.

It's pouring with rain, the Volvo's windows misted up. Teil drives, uncertainly following Madeleine's directions.

My brother David welcomes us outside his house. Pity it's taken him almost sixty years to find a brotherly affinity with me. Too late; not that he knows that. He knows I've got back trouble.

'Hello, everybody. Come in, do.' Elizabeth. Warm, and welcoming us to her home. Thane, the budding publisher, sits himself next to me to discuss the world of books. Katie, still at school, smiles charmingly across the room. Tall, striking Karin is just back from Australia. Penni, lively as ever, introduces Paul. I couldn't make the wedding. Too near my operation. Made it to this get-together.

'Here we are, Jeremy. Brown scones and butter, baked specially for you.' Kind Elizabeth. 'That's all right, isn't it?' I pick the raisins out uneasily, smiling my thanks. Butter is a forbidden fat.

'Thane! I haven't seen you for ages.' Madeleine, alert across the long room, perches herself on the floor between me and my nephew. Her cupped hand is clamped against her waist, just by me. Seeing the receptacle, I thankfully deposit the raisins in it.

'Let's get down to the important part of the evening. What shall we stake? 10p each, as usual?' David is badly out of touch.

'10p! A pound's more like it.' Teil'll trigger another heart attack if she's not careful!

I temporize. 'How about 50p?' I think David can live with that.

'Who's going to count the pineapple leaves?'

'We'll need two.'

'I vote for Jeremy.' Penni is one of my fans.

'Seconded!' Katie smiles engagingly at me.

'And Karin,' Madeleine puts in. 'Go on. In unison.' We write down our secret guesses for the combined number of leaves in the two pineapple tops on a piece of paper. The person guessing nearest to the actual number wins the pot.

'No cheating, now! Count every single little leaf!' I've finished. Karin's leaf core has quite a few tiny ones. Very deceptive.

'That's gone past my score.' David is chagrined; he loves to win. 'Right. Twice eighty-nine plus seventeen makes a hundred and ninety-five. Anyone near that?'

'I put down one hundred and ninety-six. Does that count?'

'Jolly good. Of course it does! You've won. Ruthi's the winner by two lengths!' David holds up the paper to confirm. 'The nearest to her is a hundred and seventy-six.'

'Upstart! Elizabeth and I have never won.' Teil grins at Ruthi. The latest Mrs Warburg's won. I'm glad. I really take to Ruthi.

FRIDAY, 27TH DECEMBER

'Hi! How's everybody?' Ruthi in full sail, her smiling face hiding her understanding of my disease. She's a physician's assistant in the orthopaedic department of a major Boston hospital.

'I've ordered a cooked breakfast for you, Ruthi. Macrobiotic lunch today!' Teil will cook lunch while the rest of us visit my mother. The last time I shall see her. Something I've contemplated many times. Hardly expected to achieve it in this way. My back stiffens ominously. I feel the claws take further hold.

'I'll just go up to my room . . .'

'There's one down here, Jifda. Just outside the dining-room. Shall I go with you?' My son anticipates my needs.

'You *are* going it, Ruthi. You look big enough for twins!'

As I expected. Distracted, preoccupied even, with Ruthi's pregnancy, my mother scarcely glances at me. She knows I have severe back trouble. I wrote to her, to cover my absence at Penni's wedding. True, but not the truth. She doesn't even ask me how I am.

'You wouldn't think, would you, that Jerry is my baby?' Sweet smile, arch look. 'So tall and strong.' Hooded eyes flick swiftly round the room. 'You wouldn't think he'd been inside me!' The familiar choking in my throat. 'I *knew* he was something special the minute he was born. They all said so!' The 'they' who ruled my childhood, who sent me to public school, who criticize me still. 'He never visits me.'

I foresee her at my funeral, a dear old lady in her eighties. 'He's gone. My favourite. My baby!' Pathetic look, demure. Brimming eyes. 'I loved him so. Dearer than life.'

I've often longed for a time without my mother in this world. Hoped for a few years. Now even weeks or days seem unlikely. I'll predecease her as my brother Hew has done, as David shows signs of doing. I've left instructions in my will: no funeral.

'Still busy with your science?' She turns to Richard, then almost at once turns back to Ruthi.

'Actually, I've joined a law firm . . .'

'I had my three at home,' she interrupts. She's interested only in Ruthi's pregnancy. 'I expect you'll have yours in a hospital?'

'I'll go to hospital for the birth, yes. But I'll go home almost immediately. We have a special system . . .'

'It was different in my day. They made us stay in bed for two

[27]

weeks.' The radiant look. 'I've never felt as alive as when I was carrying.'

We start the long trip back to Somerset. I sit beside Richard, too ill to drive. Just one more time at home with him, that's all I've got. Madeleine and Colin can still be with me, each on their own. To help Teil out, perhaps, so she can have time off from my disease. Then I can be alone with each of them. I shan't be able to do that with Richard. I'll have to make the best of what I've got, enjoy the company of my second son while I still can. I must conquer the pain and see something of my son, my sweet son. Have him to myself for a short time. I shan't see him again. Not while I can enjoy it.

Teil takes over from Richard ten miles out of London. Jet-lagged, poor lad. The young couple sleep, exhausted, in the back. I doze beside Teil. When I wake up, we're passing Bristol.

'I'll do the rest.' I want to contribute, still want to be part of life, not just an onlooker. Want to protect my wife from too much work. Can't shield her from the grief to come, or from the pain of seeing me die. I'm powerless to help her in the future. I see the strain in her face, now. I can still lessen it a little.

SATURDAY, 28TH DECEMBER

Early to bed last night for everyone. All of us tired out. I'm eating my breakfast groats at eight, apprehensive that Richard might sleep late.

'Hi, Jifda. Did you sleep well?'

'Hello, Ruthi. Yes, thank you. What about you?' I always lie about my nights now. 'Hello, Tock.' He's up! 'You rested enough?'

'Help yourself to toast and cereal, Ruthi. No need for you to eat a macrobiotic breakfast.' Teil's concerned to provide food Ruthi likes.

'I'll eat what Jifda eats.' Dear Richard.

But I savour my groat porridge now. I simply don't mind the diet. It's not important.

'Would you like to come shopping, Ruthi?' Teil has the whole place stocked. She just wants to give me a chance to be alone with Richard.

'Sure, I'll walk back later. You go ahead when you're done.'

'I think we ought to check the road's not flooded.' It's unusual for Teil to fuss.

We walk out to check the Tarmac. A lovely, brilliant day. The moors around our house are more deluged than we've seen them in all the time we've been here, flooded and frozen solid by last night's dipping temperatures. The sun glitters on sheets of ice stretching like fairground mirrors, uneven surfaces reflecting images askew. Gulls hoping for a feast of worms are slipping, flapping over the frozen grassland, shrieking their territories. A stately heron glides slowly past, cushioned on air, circling hungrily above the iced-up 'rhynes' draining the fields. Frost flakes turned into drops shimmer like crystal pendants on willow chandeliers. Cattle, their breath forming little puffs of cloud, herd densely on the topmost stretches of their lowland pastures. Idyllic rural setting. My heart is full. I live in an enchanted place.

'This is the bit that's always flooded when it's bad. It seems reasonably clear.' Our flood barometer!

''Bye now. Back in a while!' Ruthi waves as Teil steers the elderly Volvo round icy patches on the road.

We tramp, my son and I, over the fields and roads we trekked when he was young. He offers his strong young body for support, as I had furnished mine to him so many years ago. I'm flagging after only two short miles, and those at snail's pace. He isn't even in his stride as yet. I can see, between bare branches criss-crossing the moors, the orange of the Volvo nosing back.

'Lift, gentlemen?'

'Ruthi's being lazy!' Richard laughs, helping me ease myself into the car. 'What about all this exercise you say you need?'

'The roads over the moors are under water in at least three different places,' Teil tells us. 'Partly iced over. Very dangerous.

I've never seen floods in those spots before. The Volvo managed, but I wouldn't like to see Ruthi walking through that ice.' I don't think Teil had trouble persuading Ruthi to ride back.

After lunch I take a badly needed rest.

'Shall we go out again?' Tock asks me. I'll have my son to myself again! It's hard to resist the pleasure.

'Is that wise, honey?' Teil worries.

'Anything I shouldn't do?' I'd asked Donald MacKeiff – MacKnife! At the check-up after the operation.

'You do exactly what you like,' he'd reassured me.

'Climb a mountain, for instance?'

'Certainly.' Not that the Levels are full of mountains to be climbed, but he said nothing to suggest I need be all that careful. In any case, I feel like real living, not just some shadowy existence under the Sword of Cancer.

The stiffness which began in London is increasing. Coproximol brings some relief. I find it best to half lie on one of the sofas in the living-room. Teil sits by my feet at the other end. For years I haven't been able to manage anyone else beside me. It made me uncomfortable. I hadn't the slightest inkling that these were the first signs of the crab's cruel claws.

'Great TV set.' An impulse buy, because our entertainment is now home based. The young couple sit, leaning lovingly against each other on the other sofa.

A peaceful, gentle, almost blissful evening. Grateful that I still am. If I could wish for anything, well, yes, I'd ask for more. But I don't yearn for more. Sitting in the warmth of their affection, I'm replete.

SUNDAY, 29TH DECEMBER

'Hello, Dad. Glad to see you.' Colin's cheery greeting, and warm embrace. His keen blue eyes look at me searchingly.

'Hello, Jifda.' Anna is full of the joys of Guernsey. Her dark brown hair is elegantly coifed. 'We've brought you a book to show you where to eat.' She's fond of eating out.

'Was it crowded?' Teil and I are toying with the idea of a short break there. We feel it's near enough, and safe enough, for me to go there.

'We virtually had the place to ourselves.'

'Was that the side door?'

It's Mad arriving. The family's complete, my whole immediate family. It's hard to arrange now Richard's based in Boston.

'Hello, everybody. Did you have a good time in Guernsey, Col?' Mad comes in and kisses me. 'What did you think of it, Anna?'

'Right! Time for the champagne!' Teil's determined cheerfulness makes her voice sound unnaturally high. Champagne? What can we drink to? Good health? Not mine!

'To Jifda!' Madeleine says enthusiastically, raising her glass, and neatly solves the problem.

I'm sitting in my rocker, heading the large oval of the dining-table, propped on all sides with cushions, my sheepskin in place. The festivities begin. I feel a sudden collapse in my spine – not precisely physical, just the rapid acceleration of my disease. My fragile back incapable of carrying the burden of ordinary life. An unremitting ache begins to grip me.

'This cashew ring is really good, Teil. Can I pass you some, Jifda?' Ruthi's found something macrobiotic she can stomach!

'Not just yet, thank you.' I cannot eat, cannot hear. I can hardly keep up the appearance of a normal answer. I see Ruthi gaze at me; her eyes veil over. *She* knows. She won't tell Richard. I can rely on that. Anna looks in my direction, glances beyond me, carefully avoiding contact. She's seen it all before, though she denies that cancer, even at the stage that mine's at, necessarily kills.

Teil's specially prepared macrobiotic feast becomes a nightmare of eternity. I can no longer cope. 'Sorry. Excuse me for a little. I'm just going to have a rest.'

I escape upstairs. The ache has turned into a piercing pain, shooting along my spine. Coproximol. Aspirin. Codeine. Nothing works. I ease myself into a new position, each tiny movement carefully thought out.

'Shall I ask Anna if she can prescribe something stronger?' It must be getting bad if Teil considers asking a young girl in her second houseman year to help us.

'No.'

'Perhaps Ruthi could suggest a better way to support your spine.'

'It's got beyond that.'

Colin and Anna leave, transporting Anna to her hospital duties. The last reunion of my complete immediate family, and I'm glad to see them go! It's past my strength to enjoy company. I'm glad to have fewer people to dissemble with. I sit on the sofa which supported me in such an ecstatic state the night before. I'm uncomfortable. Richard sits down beside me. My son, whom I love as much as I'm capable of loving, is causing me more pain. Can't manage his sitting there.

'Tock, I wonder if you'd. . . .' I catch Teil's eye and signal her to stop. Know she's going to ask him to change places.

'Yes? What did you want me to do?'

'Er . . . could you turn up the volume on the TV?'

'The remote control's in your hand, Teil!' He laughs. My children do not know the agony I'm in.

'Early night,' I sibilate, gritting my teeth to steady me. 'I can manage.' I wave Teil down. Once by the stairs I haul myself up by the banisters, to lie on my mattress turned to nails.

MONDAY, 30TH DECEMBER

A dreadful night, literally and metaphorically. To say my back aches would be ridiculous. A searing, agonizing stab in that part of my spine, I judge, nearest the secondary on my rib. So as not to exacerbate the torment I inch, or half inch, myself into slightly less gruelling positions. Hours later I realize that sitting is an improvement on lying.

I creep down to the empty living-room, bouncing pillows down the stairs before me. I find some comfort in a large club chair, padded around with cushions topped with pillows, sheep-skin lined. My fitful sleep is interspersed with a dread I have never experienced before. It dawns on me that I'm dying, and any hopes of living a handful of years are receding in the face of excruciating pain. Not only dying, but I shall die in unremitting agony.

It isn't death I fear, since I don't know what death means. What I am sure of is the living, know nothing about what happens after death. Is there an afterlife? I'm pretty sure there is, though I can't guess what it consists of.

First crack of light under the shutters. I've never welcomed day so much. Hear Teil coming down the stairs. Grateful she's an early-morning person.

'Hello, Bean. I'm in here.'

The footsteps stop, restart. The door opens.

'You're up early! Bad night?' Her voice is strained. She knows what's going on. There's nothing she can do except stand by me.

'No, not bad. Horrific. Diabolical, in fact.' It's not what she wants to hear. But I need her sympathy. I long to communicate my torment to another human being.

'More pain?' She comes over and puts her arms around my shoulders, lips on my hair.

'If that's the word for it. One's more inclined to call it agony.' If I'm expecting words of comfort, I don't get them. Instead she's rather quiet. Slight sniff. She goes off to open the enormous shutters. Soft, dull grey outside the bay. Tiny streaks of yellow. A new day dawning.

'It's time you had more effective pain-killers. Clearly, neither Coproximol, nor the ten milligrams MST Liz prescribed, is ad-equate. I'm not sure that the MST is the right type of morphine.' I know she and Liz have talked at length about my taking mor-phine. Liz Walsh–Comfitt is an excellent GP, but . . . I *don't* want to increase the dose of morphine. Don't want to become an addict. What if I do recover? The diet might still work. I might have a spontaneous regression! There might even be a miracle. What do *they* know about it? 'Liz stressed that even if you do become physically addicted to morphine, it's not addiction in the ordinary sense. You're taking morphine to kill pain, not feelings. She assures me that she could wean you off morphine easily.'

I'm not reassured. The beginning of the end. Not ready for that. My whole being rejects it. Teil, I'm pretty sure, thinks addiction's neither here nor there. Don't agree. I'm already on 10 mg of morphine as it is. Now even that's not enough. I'm horrified by that.

'Just take more of the MST.' She's pressing me.

'No, I'll stick it out.' I couldn't see her face against the light. See the tears now. Waste of time.

'I'll make some breakfast.' Voice gruff, but a grimace of a smile.

This time we have it on our own. None of the children stir. I'm glad. Haven't the strength for them.

'I'll get it.' Phone shrilling. That Colin to say when he's coming back? Surely not business during Christmas week? 'You're in Bournemouth for the morning?' I hear Teil say. 'Of course come over later. How about a meal? Come as early as you can.' Come over? I don't want anyone to visit.

'Is Colin coming back today?'

'No. It's the Andersons. Earlier than they thought.' Our American knitting book distributors. They lunched us in New Jersey on our last trip. Enjoyable. I'd be keen on a meeting, normally.

'Jeremy! Lovely to see you. Sorry to hear about your back. I know what it's like. I slipped a disc a year ago.' Like hell you know what it's like, Bill.

'Glad to hear you're enjoying England.' Stiff, idiotic thing to say. They're so busy talking about themselves, they don't notice.

'We've brought the plans of our new store. We're thrilled.

Marvellous architect. Have you seen the latest issue of our new magazine? A real glossy. Full colour, top designers, top artists. The works!'

'And they print in England! One up on the Italians!'

On and on. Trivia of their business. Drivel about knitting. Searching questions about the damned diet. I sit, rocking, infuriated. I hardly speak. No one cares. I signal frantically to Teil. Time they went! Now. Want them gone! I see her register, but she's not acting.

'You must be tired after your day. Richard, you'll guide them to the guest-house, won't you?'

'Of course. Just follow the orange torpedo!'

'Really, you don't have to bother. It's early yet. We'll find our way.'

'Better have a guide. The moors get misty and confusing after dark.'

They're gone at last. I appropriate the chair I found so comforting last night. Sit by myself. No one to make me feel uneasy or anxious. Madeleine, attentive, fetches another sheepskin. Ruthi suggests a rolled towel in the small of my back. It makes no difference. They try. They try to help. There's nothing they can do.

NEW YEAR'S EVE

Last page of the 'English Countryside' calendar. Crisp, winter sun shining on stiff, frosty grass. Hunting-pink coats, dotted like Flanders poppies in a field. I crumple the page and throw it in the bin. Got it in one! 1985 is finished, done.

'Did Gissel send those thingamies this year? You know, the shapes for melting down to play the lead game?' I call her Gristle to myself, adapting Gisela to a more English form. She's not a bad old stick. Talks too much. Sends little lead figures from Vienna every year. And Sachertorte. 'Is there a horseshoe?' Teil's still in the kitchen. 'You cooking for the week? They're leaving tomorrow!'

'Macrobiotic food takes a lot of preparation. I'm trying to make it festive, as I said. Gissel sent six lead moulds. Just enough, as Anna can't be here. One horseshoe. Or you can have a magic mushroom, a sucking pig, a . . .'

'Keep the horseshoe for me. For luck. Did Mad get the new spoon?'

'Yes, from Woolworth's. A ladle with a long wooden handle. Much safer than the tin one Gissel sent.'

I'm a bit nervous, this year, of pouring hot lead into cold water to predict the future – not because I might spill the melted horseshoe and burn myself! It's just that I remember another New Year's Eve. That time with George when we were dons at University. I could have sworn he was never going to marry.

'Madonna and child, George! You're going to get married and have a baby!' Teil immediately pronounced about the shape George's melted fish took on. Giggling, and drinking in 1956 with a good Pouilly-Fuissé. (I prefer *pétillant* to the overrated bubble.) And she was right. Within weeks George had met, and asked out, Cynthia. They were married in late summer, and she got pregnant right away. What shape will my melted horseshoe cast into tonight, to foretell what 1986 has in store? A coffin? A wreath, perhaps? Or an urn to hold the ashes? That would be logical. I'm going to be cremated after all.

Teil was unusually quiet about the shape her own cast took last year. Not too communicative about the casts in general, though she's usually quick enough with the interpretations! Then, after we saw MacKnife, she finally said what she thought she'd cast – the same shape as the year before her father died. Put Gissel down for it. She was, after all, coming up for eighty.

'Do stop pacing, honey.' Teil hates my pacing in the kitchen. 'Shall we skip the lead game this year?'

'No, certainly not. It's what we do on New Year's Eve even if it is a crazy continental import! It's our tradition.'

'I know, but . . .'

'We'll play the game.' I'll show my children how to die, as I've shown them how to live. With dignity. Without cringing.

How can I last till midnight? Nothing on TV. We sit through some awful film because it involves Americans. For Ruthi's sake.

Time to go upstairs and change. My tuxedo was a present from my grandmother for my twenty-first. Savile Row, no less. 'Last you for life, sir,' the suave tailor assured me. 'Plenty to let out.' Never had it done.

Knew I'd fit into it again tonight. But, no sooner had I got the whole outfit on, than I suddenly found myself in tears. Not, I think, self-pity. Just the pity of it. I have two more major novels planned. Always wanted to write, always been sure I can. Written several novels. None was published. Non-fiction, of course, in the bag. Successful. And wanted. Even pressed for. My fiction won't be recognized till after my death, I know. And now – wan, pale and evidently very ill – I know the time is near for dying. My tears are for my unwritten work. Teil will look after what's already written, as though it were her own.

Comb in hand in front of the mirror, I arrange my hair. It's still copious, fading only at the sides. Beard has rather more grey than before. Large, mist-blue eyes look back at me, still tearful. I brush the tears aside and start downstairs.

It's almost midnight at last. At last! Crazy to wish the time away, there's so little of it left. But I want to forget all this festivity just the same and return to normal. Just Teil and me, just as we used to be when we were first married.

Suddenly cameras are clicking. I feel like a film star stepping down the wide staircase! Clapping of hands, cheers of approval.

'You do look smart!'

'I've never seen you in that suit!'

'When did you get that wine-coloured bow-tie?' There's enough black about already. I went to the shops with them this afternoon, surreptitiously sloped off to buy it while they were busy chattering.

'Jifda, you do look slim!'

'Fits you a treat.'

'Shirt's a bit crumpled. I don't know where the iron's kept.' I've never been much good at domestic chores.

'It won't show in the photographs.' Practical, as always, her new dress highlighted by an Irish crochet collar, Teil stands beside me and puts her arm around my waist. A very presentable pair, I think.

'Come on now, smile!' Richard flashes some photographs. Last pictures? Hardly. . . . 'And another one.'

Time to play the lead game.

'Right, now.' I clear my throat. 'We'll go in order of age, starting with the youngest. Richard, that's you.'

The others take turns to melt their figurines, placing them into the ladle perched on a heated cooker ring. They cast their fates. Liquid lead hissing into cold water solidifies the metal instantly.

'A swan! Look at that! Arched neck, and half-furled wings. You've cast a swan, Teil.'

Swan-song? The end of our marriage, of our life together?

Now it's my turn. I try to flick to avoid the squat, rounded shape of an urn. Succeed. Because, when I pick the figure out of the water, it's an unmistakable reaper with his scythe.

'The Tree of Life, Jifda!' Ruthi turns it upside-down, sweet girl. But I know it's no such thing, and I can see Teil knows it, too. The grim reaper, dancing his dance of death.

January

I've made it into the New Year! There was a day, last March, when I didn't think I had a hope. Not that my cancer had been diagnosed.

'I can't find anything. Nothing to worry about. Just *anno Domini*. Bit of arthritis possibly. I get it myself quite often.'

There's not a single complaint I've taken to Tom Quigley which he hasn't had himself. Only one thing, so far, has produced a medical reaction. Blood in my urine fifteen years ago. Papilloma in the bladder. He acted then.

'I don't think the pain I'm describing could be arthritis. Or if it is, I pity all arthritics.'

'It *is* uncomfortable.'

I wasn't talking about discomfort but something entirely different. Sensed I hadn't long to live, even then. Made sure *The Complete Man* was revised sufficiently to stand. My *chef-d'œuvre*.

Even Tom Quigley finally agreed something needed investigating and scheduled an X-ray. He rang me: 'Ah, Jeremy. That X-ray. It shows a certain amount of bony deterioration.'

So, right all along. Seriously ill. Always knew I'd die of cancer.

'Shall I come round to see you?'

'In the morning.'

'I can come right away . . .'

'That's all right. The morning will do.' For him, perhaps. For us it meant a whole night to be endured.

'I couldn't have been more surprised,' he told us the next day. Bone cancer – a secondary. He made no bones about it! By then it was July. An almost immediate appointment with MacKieff. Bone scan, X-rays. A tumour on the kidney, that secondary on the rib. No further secondaries; perhaps a hot spot or two.

'The kidney's got to go. No question.' Donald MacKieff was adamant at our second interview, after the tests.

'What's the prognosis?'

'People always expect doctors to know these things.'

'I'm talking about the statistical probability.'

'Four or five years, perhaps.'

'And the best?'

'Ten years.'

Teil challenged him. 'You're saying you can't cure cancer. It always returns.'

'Yes.' No prevarication or over-optimism there.

'And what's the shortest time?' I asked. Was he hesitating? Hard to tell.

'Two years.' Not what my instincts led me to believe. However, I was glad to think in those terms. 'Matter of fact,' he continued, 'a colleague of mine had precisely the same problem. It was all over in three months.'

'A urologist? And he had no inkling?' Teil asked, astonished.

'No idea at all. A tragedy. Same sort of chap as you, really,' he turned to me. 'I think I can handle you!' He was referring to the friendly repartee we'd gone in for from our second meeting. We both enjoy it.

'Suppose I don't have the kidney out?' I didn't quite feel up to bantering about that.

'That kidney's got to go.'

I agreed to the operation. Whether I'd have agreed so readily if I'd known the pain I'd go through during the week that followed it, I'm not clear. I'd just as soon have died then and there. And if I'd understood the size of the secondary, and its significance, I might well have refused.

MacKieff dismissed the lesion. 'They'll just shine a light through it.'

'You can deal with the secondary?' Teil asked.

'Not my pigeon. My radiotherapy colleagues see to that.'

They no longer offer any treatment for kidney cancer in Ruthi's hospital in Boston. Anna says I was helped by the removal of what she calls a highly toxic mass. She insists it would have caused more trouble even than I've had. The toxins would have spread all round my body.

I now know that kidney cancer's almost always fatal, that the average length of life after diagnosis is a year to eighteen months. But the crucial point, which I wasn't told before, was that the so-called regression of bone secondaries, which is said to occur only with kidney cancer, assuming the cancerous kidney is removed, is based on *one single* entry in the medical books. One entry! That's equivalent to little more than hearsay, to an old wives' tale, anecdotal at best, something the medical profession would laugh away if a patient mentioned it! I'd have preferred to know that at the outset, so I could make an informed decision about the operation.

'I'll discuss it with my wife, and then decide about radiotherapy.'

'In other words *you'll* decide,' Gemma Lazenby said, confronting me at the first consultation a few days after the operation.

'I always consider carefully what my wife says,' I retorted, incensed, 'but I make my own decisions.'

'You want to be told the truth, I gather.'

'Yes, definitely.' Perhaps she tried. Incapable of telling me face to face.

'Relatives don't always realize how intractable this disease can be,' Lazenby explained to Teil.

'You mean my husband may die very soon?' Teil was talking to Lazenby on the telephone after a local GP suddenly announced I'd be dead within three weeks.

'You may look back on all this as though it was a nightmare.'

'How long? Weeks, or months?' Teil demanded to know.

'Within the year, I'm afraid. It hangs about in the bones quite a long time in some cases.'

In our view, this is the only really accurate prognosis we've had.

So, is it worth making New Year's resolutions? Half-resolutions for half the year? Because, when one gets down to it, that's how long I think I've got. Should I resolve to live as long as possible? Resolve on a dignified death. Resolve to order my own funeral. Resolve to stay in charge!

THURSDAY, 2ND JANUARY

Managed one whole day of 1986! Maybe everyone's quite wrong. Maybe I'm not dying at all. I don't *feel* as though I'm dying. My legs are perfectly all right. Just tiredness, that stumbling yesterday. I stayed in bed late this morning simply to recover from all the festivities.

'It's Liz, honey.'

It's giving Liz the wrong impression rather, lying up here. Irritating. Seems she's taken over from Tom Quigley and is now my GP. Very nice woman. Sympathetic. Spends time with one. Doesn't rush.

'I'd up the dose to thirty,' she's saying.

'As much as that?'

'Well, actually, I realized I'd rather underdone it before – ten milligrams is simply a booster dose. Thirty is the smallest clinical dose! I thought you'd let me know soon enough if you needed more.'

'I'll think about it.' I'm not going to be rushed into taking more morphine. Teil's spending an incredibly long time showing Liz out. A chat, presumably.

'I really think you ought to get rid of the pain if you can,' Teil keeps urging me. She's rather insistent.

Finally I acquiesce. Those two women do go on.

We're alone again, back where we started from, Teil and I. Why should things have changed just because some bone scan says so? And there's a bit of pain? 'I'm sure Jifda won't let a few cancer cells get the better of him!' Anna said last July. I don't think I shall. Want to live. Have books to write!

Extraordinary thing. Chapman is on the phone.

'I tried to ring you before Christmas. The line was engaged.' He could have tried again, presumably.

'Shall I come in for an X-ray next week?'

'We could have an X-ray every day! I think March will be time enough.'

Always that put-down. March? *March?* What's that supposed to mean? Last time I asked for an X-ray, when Gemma Lazenby was still in charge, she acted as though I were some tiresome idiot. Next thing I knew, I had this little billet-doux, which arrived on my birthday: '. . . further treatment is indicated'. Chapman could be just as wrong. Should I insist, while I have the chance? Ask more questions? I found myself tongue-tied, 'Well, I'm not God,' he said. I flinch at the memory. And 'We could have an X-ray every day' is hardly encouraging. Isn't it bad enough to have the ghastly disease without these consultants putting one down? They think I'm difficult because I dare to say anything at all. I ask one or two questions – not many, I'm too terrified, too exhausted, in too much pain. Even so, their very looks make me wince. Must they be so inhumane? Say things calculated to make me cringe?

'Oh, not till March.' That's all Teil has to say. Odd. Usually she rails against the doctors.

'Why didn't he say that last time? Why cause me more anxiety, and then make me feel small? After all, it was he who suggested having an X-ray in January.'

'Presumably he can't face up to his uselessness. Or death, perhaps. Who's got time for *their* hang-ups?'

Not like MacKnife. He's compassionate. Spends time with me. Allows me to talk. Know he's busy, but I don't take up that much time. And he's got more than I have! A friendly word or two is all I want. Is that really asking too much?

I remember radiotherapy. A science-fiction world. The nightmare of those endless corridors. Attendants in white trousers and short white tunics, unisex automatons walking silently on rubber soles. And huge orange letters blazing DANGER – DO NOT ENTER outside closed, monolithic treatment-room doors, which opened like enormous jaws. Ushered in for my turn and told to get on to a steel table. No help was offered. Doors swung shut after the attendants scuttled out. Alone on a hard, narrow table in the centre of a bare white cell. Nothing but glinting metal, apart from my cringing, cancer-riddled body. Whirring machines, cyclopsing on the cross marked on my back.

'I'll just tattoo your back,' the nurse said briskly.

'Tattoo? You mean mark indelibly?' So sure I'll die they actually tattoo my back without asking permission?

'Yes, with a pen.' She's impatient. 'It won't hurt.'

'It won't come off?'

'It'll fade after a few baths.' She's irritated now. No idea what I'm about.

The deadly rays penetrated my body. 'Keep very still,' they repeated constantly, parrot-like. Surprised they didn't play a cassette instead. The cold metal bit. Nausea gripped my throat.

Lazenby was never around to explain what was happening. Chapman occasionally turned up. Pathetically I tried to win some interest from him. Sport, music? Dare I try asking him about the progress of my disease? Slip it in as unobtrusively as I can. 'Yes, yes. Nothing to worry about. Delius is also a favourite of mine.' They know not what they do. All that's behind me for the moment. At any rate till March. Chapman's the consultant. Presumably he knows what he's about.

'Why don't we go into town?' Teil is saying. 'Try lunch at the vegetarian restaurant?'

'You know I can't eat their stuff.' Vegetarian, but not macrobiotic. Not by a long way. They revel in vegetables of the nightshade family: potatoes, tomatoes, aubergines. Poison to me. I can't have milk products, or anything made with flour. They don't serve plain brown rice.

'Well, just for the outing, then.'

She won't let me drive the car back. Ridiculous. Had a little trouble with the gate when we went out, scraped the paintwork slightly. Nothing to get excited about. Pretty scratched already. The car is nine years old, after all.

An outing to deposit the rather meagre Christmas period receipts.

'Why can't I drive?' Teil's nipped into the driving seat while I'm locking up.

'I don't think we're insured for you to drive.'

'Whatever do you mean?'

'It's the increased dosage of pain-killers. You've taken thirty milligrams of slow-release morphine now, as well as Coproximol and a tranquillizer.'

'Coproximol's nothing more than a glorified aspirin!'

'Maybe, but we simply can't afford to have the car out of action. What would we do without a car?' She's being absurd. True it's now difficult for me to judge distances precisely. Gauged them within an inch or two before. Tend to drive over the odd hummock at the roadside now. Nothing significant.

'I feel much more secure handling the wheel than being a passenger.'

'I'm sorry, honey. Try sitting in the back and holding on to the head-rests.'

It doesn't work. Have to get her to stop while I get into the front. I hug the door handle and the opened glove compartment. 'You'll have to stop lurching. These moor roads are a disgrace, they're so bumpy.'

'Sorry, honey. I'm only doing twenty.'

One can't go much slower, I suppose.

'*You* don't look as though you've had much of a break,' Mrs P greets me, as soon as I walk into the building society.

I parry her as best I can. 'All this festive food and late-night parties.' Sharp eyes look at me reflectively. Do I really look so ill? Thought I was camouflaging my thinness rather well with the duvet coat. Evidently it doesn't fool Mrs P. I try to divert her: 'Crocheted any of the collars yet?'

'I'm still reading,' she says defensively.

My knees are beginning to feel weak. I make for the chair by the table on which they keep the *Daily Telegraph*. Covers up the leg-buckling nicely. Teil arrives and looks at me, sitting down.

'Just checking the news.' I don't want even Teil to know just how wobbly my knees feel.

She smiles at Mrs P and the other ladies, then turns determinedly to me. 'Well, if you've looked at everything you need to. . . .'

Marching orders. I lever myself up carefully, bend over the table as though I'm still reading, covering up my need to hold on to something. Manage to straighten up, and hold the door for Teil. Walk through myself, fairly steadily. Teil grabs my arm as soon as we're outside, steers me towards the car-park and the car.

SATURDAY, 4TH JANUARY

Something's wrong with the messages my brain's sending to my legs. My intention may be to stand up – as I've done perfectly successfully for some fifty-six years now – but find my left leg simply sits there, not moving a muscle. I move it with my hands and it responds, after a fashion.

'My left leg seems to be leading a life of its own.'

'What d'you mean, exactly?'

'It has a distressing habit of giving way under me. Makes me fall over . . .'

'Fall over?' Teil's getting worked up. Shouldn't have mentioned it. No point. Keep mum in future. Manage to steady myself against the door. 'Shall I ring Chapman?'

'Definitely not. Whatever for? He's been rung. He finally rang back. He has absolutely nothing to contribute.' He'll summon me for some tests or other. Good for his records maybe, but no good to me, I'm clear. Waste of time and energy. 'It'll pass. The stiffness has got better. So has the pain.'

'That's because of the larger dose of MST.'

'Forget it. Sorry I mentioned it. Let's go to Curry's. Buy the video recorder you think we should get.'

'Can you manage the car?'

'Provided you drive at roughly the pace of a running cow!' Serve the farmers right if they're caught behind us for once. We're always caught behind their wretched herds. The roads are too narrow for passing cows. Fairly undeveloped road sense – Somerset cows, anyway.

'I'll get the parking sticker,' Teil says, jumping out of the car before I've unbuckled my seat-belt. Feel an even greater pang than the first time I had to let her carry the shopping. Couldn't carry an ordinary shopping bag. Dumbfounded that this could happen to me, a six-foot-four, able-bodied man in his prime allowing a female shrimp of five foot four to carry the load. Thought I'd pulled a muscle. Now know I'm seriously ill. Can't drive, can't carry anything heavier than a newspaper. I can't, apparently, even be trusted to get a parking sticker. Where will it end? What shall I be able to do? I insist on fixing the sticker to the windscreen.

We examine several video recorders. I feel my legs beginning to give way under me. My legs? Will my legs go – after Chapman insisted he was 95 per cent certain he could stop that?

Teil peremptorily acquires the salesman's chair for me and discusses equipment with him. I listen as in a dream. Things are happening yet not happening. I don't feel part of the events going on around me. My eyes light on flickering TV images. They look as real as the world around me.

'Just a couple of things I need from the health shop,' Teil is saying. 'Can you manage, or shall I take you to the car?'

'I'm perfectly all right. Just all this sitting about while you talk for hours.'

We pass a place that sells shopping trolleys. 'I'd better get one of these,' Teil says. Flat, non-commital tone.

'Good idea.'

Another blow. A cold, hard calculation by my wife. I can no longer carry the shopping for her. A trolley, on wheels, instead.

SUNDAY, 5TH JANUARY

An ordinary Sunday. I pray. A normal, uneventful Sunday. We treat ourselves to *The Observer* and *The Sunday Times*, amble about the garden, soak up the January sun. Am I really as ill as everybody says? Doesn't feel like it at the moment.

Teil went to get the papers. Didn't go to mass. Strange. I'd have guessed this harrowing experience would have the opposite effect.

I used to be an agnostic. Was unable to marry Teil 'in the Church' because, in 1953, the powers that be insisted on my signing a document agreeing to my children, if any, being brought up as Catholics. 'I shan't put anything in the way of that,' I conceded, 'provided of course I don't take moral exception to any particular practices.' The Catholic Church, after all, doesn't have an entirely unblemished record. In the final analysis I'd have to exercise the duties of fatherhood as I thought fit. Signing the document would put me under a moral obligation I could not honourably break. I preferred not to sign.

Ten years on and the Dutch theologians made their presence felt. An expert in matrimonial matters pronounced my verbal undertaking adequate. So, ten years after our American registry marriage, we were married in the Church! Some years after that I became a theist, following a quite sudden revelation that God is. Not exactly faith. Just, I know He is. No inclination to become a Catholic, though.

Bathtime. An almost daily ritual we enjoy. Teil has her bath, I keep her company, then I have mine and she sits on the chair to chat.

Teil's already gone upstairs. I'm about to follow her. I get to the staircase. Fall rather heavily. Teil's in the tub already, so I manœuvre myself up unaided. She gets out and helps me into the bath. I wallow in the relaxation of warm water. My body still looks reasonably well. The fourteen-inch scar across my abdomen is scarcely visible. We chatter as we've done for years. Has our life really changed dramatically? Hard to believe.

'Can you get out?' Illusion shattered. I can no longer use my legs to heave my torso out of the bath. Cunning is called for. My strong wrists will help. 'We may have to use a certain finesse.' Teil looks at my body, thin but still long, and relatively heavy. Some 150 pounds. No way she can lift it. She helps me put my legs over the side of the bathtub. 'Don't try to move yet. I'll bring the chair over.' She aligns the chair with the bath rim, using her body to anchor it. I clutch a bath-grip with one hand, a tap with another, and haul myself up, sitting on the edge. The hardest part's achieved. I grasp the chair-back and embrace Teil's neck, easing my buttocks on to the chair. Mission accomplished. 'I'll get the towel.'

How much longer will I be able to risk having a bath?

'I'll ring Chapman in the morning,' Teil announces. She doesn't ask, simply states.

I say nothing. Just silently acquiesce.

MONDAY, 6TH JANUARY

Black Monday. Almost all of it bad news. I'm sitting in my living-room chair in reasonable comfort, undeniably nervous. My legs are definitely misbehaving. Going . . . going . . . not quite gone. What else must I endure?

'Liz says she'll be here soon,' Teil announces from just inside the door. She has an irritating habit of putting her head round the door to say something and then rushing off. Gone before I can reply. Back in a few minutes, though.

'I've just rung Chapman. Amazing! I was put straight through to him.'

'What did he say? Bring him up to see me?'

'Not quite. He'll have to talk to a doctor who's examined you before he can say anything about paralysis.'

'So? What does he suggest?'

'He could get a neuro-surgeon to examine you and give you tests. There *might* be a chance of an operation to remove some of the tissue, or lesion, pressing on the nerves which control the legs.'

'*Another* operation?'

'And just as useless, no doubt.' Teil isn't inclined to have much faith in the outcome of such surgery. 'Anyway, we agreed Liz should ring him when she's examined you. He sounded sympathetic for once. Said his secretary will bleep him for us.'

'So he *can* be contacted!'

Legs definitely going. Not sure I'm taking it in. Taking it in cerebrally. I reject it on any other plane. Examine my legs. They look as they've always looked. Not outstanding, aesthetically speaking. Too thin. Gangly pegs with very large feet and crooked toes. One of the cartilages in my right knee slips out quite easily. It takes days to manipulate it back. In spite of these deficiencies, I'm rather keen on my legs. Want to use them. Keep them working.

Liz arrives. Breathless, as usual. Rushed off her feet. Cornerstone of the practice, we reckon. 'The legs are actually not working?'

'Not as bad as that. They work sometimes. I'll show you.'

I get up and walk across the floor, like a toddler proudly displaying a new ability. An old skill I'm desperate to retain. It upsets Liz.

'Don't worry. That's very good. I'll just try a few simple tests. Close your eyes and see if you can feel what I'm doing.' I feel her delicately touch my big toe. She actually bends one of them back and forth – I'm not quite certain which one. 'Can you feel that?'

'I can feel something.'

'Am I bending this toe towards you or away from you?'

So she's been bending both of them? 'Away, I think.'

'Push your knee against my hand. Hard as you can.' I push, surprised to find her hand resisting easily. She's only a woman, after all. . . . 'Now see if you can push my hand with your foot.' Same thing. Am I holding back? Too gentlemanly, in effect, to kick her over? Or is she simply a very strong woman? 'I think the damage is pretty minimal,' she says, leaving to use the phone in Teil's office. . . . 'Dr Chapman feels you should go in for a few tests,' she reports when she returns.

'At the Radiotherapy Centre, you mean?' That ghastly place!

'Well, the Infirmary. A neuro-surgeon would actually do the tests.'

'But, surely . . .' – Teil is worried about further surgical intervention – 'even if he found that he *might* be able to do something to stop the paralysis, an operation at this stage would be appallingly painful, wouldn't it?'

She doesn't deny it. 'There is that.'

'D'you think I should go?' I ask Liz. I see her juggling with the problem.

'On balance, I suppose so. Yes.'

I'm petrified of going to the hospital, absolutely clear that if I go I'll never come back. Alive, that is. All the same, I make no protest. Liz evidently thinks I should go. I'm too overwhelmed with the paralysis to say anything further to her myself. I just sit there, saying nothing.

We've no real notion what to do.

'Lazenby said the reason the kidney was removed *before* the radiotherapy was because operations are tricky after such treatment. Something about the blood not clotting properly. *Now* they're talking about an operation at the actual site? Quite honestly, it sounds a load of rubbish to me.'

'You're always prejudiced against the medical profession.'

'Not always. No doubt they do everything they can. My job's to make sure that that's better than doing nothing.'

I don't want to go to hospital again and I make this clear. Teil prepares to do battle on my behalf. Retires to her office. I, exhausted, go to sleep.

'Hello, honey. I've brought you a cup of dandelion coffee.'

'Lovely. Thanks.' I've just woken up. Three already. Must have slept for two hours.

'Lots to tell you.' Can I even listen? Wouldn't it be easier just to do what Liz suggests? I can trust her. Anything rather than think. . . . 'I rang BACUP first. A charming nurse maintained that in over twenty years of dealing with cancer patients she'd never seen a single case of paralysis due to cancer. 'Fraid we have to forget that, though. After all, we know better!'

'So what did she propose?'

'A "Pain Clinic". She suggested I contact a Dr March at the Basingstoke Hospital. I'll have to find the number.'

'You must be getting exhausted.' There's no way I could do this for myself.

'It's nothing. There's so little I can do. And we've got to try to get it right. A London hospice next.'

'Good work.' Make sure, this time, we know the score.

'The doctor there agreed we were absolutely right to be extremely wary. He advises us to contact our local hospice, which I did. One of their nurses will come and see you, provided our GP contacts them first. Some GPs refuse to work with them. Hospices will only work within the present framework of a patient's care.'

'I'm sure Liz will co-operate with them.'

'They didn't have much to say about having tests, except that they couldn't see how these preliminaries could do any harm. Unfortunately I can, only too well!' And so can I. Could do me in with their ruddy tests. 'I'll tell Liz how things stand. I gathered she thought you were keen to have more checks. Something positive for you to hang on to, perhaps. You didn't say anything this morning.'

'I know, I simply couldn't.' I haven't the spirit or the energy to argue, let alone insist, on the management of my case. I'd just go along with whatever they parcel out.

Liz, it turns out, agrees with Teil. The hospital rings to say a bed's available in Chapman's unit. Chapman's? What about all this palaver to do with neuro-surgeons? Just a question of Chapman looking me over! So bloody what? Had plenty of opportunity for that before.

'Ruthi! How nice of you to ring.' Teil's picked up the phone. 'Just thought I'd see how things are going.'

'You must be psychic.' Teil explains the situation. Ruthi's orthopaedic department sees a fair number of kidney cancer patients. We'd welcome her opinion. She gives it, immediately, unhesitatingly.

'Forget it. We're all coming round to the feeling that you don't do *anything* about kidney cancer. Just forget it.'

An American opinion to add to the others. The decision, of course, has to be mine. Well, ours.

TUESDAY, 7TH JANUARY

Should there be all this fuss if I'm dying anyway? Am I taking up valuable resources, better left for people who have a chance of surviving longer? The answer, perhaps, lies in Chapman's latest prognosis: 'Your husband will die because of cancer, eventually. But he won't die *of* cancer. He'll die of some infection, like pneumonia, or a renal problem.' Some such jolly thing. Nothing life-threatening as yet. I have, I presume, the right to several months more.

Do I want to live like this? Without the use of my legs? With severe pains in my spine? Anyway, *could* I commit suicide even if I wanted to? I'm not very practical!

'Of course you *can* commit suicide,' Teil tells me briskly. 'We know quite well it's not a question of pills. Exit reports talk of plastic bags over the head. No one can actually stop you.' Her face looks strained. We've often discussed this, long before any question of illness. Always said she'd never help me commit suicide. Never act in such a way as to prevent me, either. The crunch has come. Her voice sounds quavery. 'I'm not advocating it, of course. Nothing of the kind. I'd be horrified. It would mean you think nothing I do makes any difference. I'd hate it if you committed suicide.' She smooths the pillows behind my head.

[53]

That's something. In spite of all the work, the horror, the uncertainty, she still wants me. I feel warmth flowing through my body.

I could, of course, overdo the Coproximol. It would be simple to take twenty, or fifty, or whatever! Easy to hoard them. Don't feel any urge to do so.

My reveries are interrupted by Teil.

'I just caught Liz. She'll contact the hospice. I knew she would.'

'Oh yes.' I'd forgotten about that. Well, pushed it to the back of my mind. Not enthusiastic. Yet another person trying to persuade me to take more morphine. I'll be a raging addict at this rate. Can't really understand why Teil's so keen. It's my affair, after all, how much pain I choose to put up with. Front-door bell . . .

'I've brought a walker for you, Mr Warburg!'

Nurse Kalmett comes in, carrying a metal stand. I'm supposed slowly, laboriously, to shift myself about with this contraption, like a doddery old man.

Liz thinks very highly of Nurse Kalmett. 'I've got a really good nurse who works with me,' she told me. 'Best if you meet her before you really need her.' So I would definitely need her services?

'And what's that other thing?'

'A commode. Just in case things get worse.' She starts lugging it in. I've no intention of investigating that!

'That could stay outside for the moment. Isn't the walker a bit short?'

'It can be made taller,' Teil says. 'Mostly used by little old ladies, I suppose,' she adds, not very tactfully. I'm not even an old man – an old woman now.

'I'll be on holiday for a week,' Nurse Kalmett tells me. A neat, trim figure in her navy blue uniform. Has dark, slightly greying hair, cut short. Appraising eyes. Pleasant, quiet, evidently capable. Not a great smiler. 'I expect things will work out all right till then.'

I can no longer answer the phone.

'The domiciliary hospice nurse can come at three. All right?' Teil asks.

I've no pressing engagements!

Peter Worthing arrives promptly. Thinning brown hair, glasses on pudgy nose. Round face, early middle age. Dapper, genial, fluent talker. Easy manner, informal dress, no uniform. Brief-case. Takes out a large pad and pencil. 'Can we start with the history of your disease?' Somewhat unexpected, but I oblige. Amazed I can do it so precisely and, for me, so concisely. Only possible, in my view, because I've kept a diary! He shows no surprise, however. I take it most sick people give their diseases much thought. 'We don't really cover this area. It's quite a few miles out of my way. But we do have another patient near here. Brenda.' We've been at it for a good hour now. When are we going to get to the point? 'So what are you taking for the pain at the moment?'

At last!

'Thirty milligrams of morphine when the pain gets really bad. But I try to make do with ten milligrams most of the time.' Proud of the fact that I don't need to take too much.

'Anything else?'

'Coproximol, as and when needed. And some Diazepam.'

'Yes, I see. By morphine I presume you mean MST, the slow-release tablets?'

'Yes. I *was* prescribed some liquid morphine at one time. Dr Walsh-Comfitt says MST tablets are much more convenient. She says the liquid deteriorates fairly quickly anyway.'

'Yes. Quite.' He's dismissive. Not good enough. 'In fact the MST is relatively new. We've been using it for a year at the hospice. It's not yet well understood by the GPs, though it's an enormous advance on Diamorphine. That has to be taken at four-hourly intervals, right through the twenty-four hours.'

'Four-hourly?'

'For proper pain control. Let me explain about pain. Once you let it get the upper hand, it's hard to control. What you need to do is to really hit it over the head with relatively large amounts of pain-killers. You can always cut the dose down later.'

'I see.'

'Think about it in graphic form,' he continues, drawing a diagram. 'Think of pain as a sort of series of waves. Now imagine a straight line *above* the largest wave. Let that represent the pain-killer. As long as the pain-killer line is above the waves of pain, you have pain control. Otherwise you don't.'

'That might mean taking a lot of pain-killers.' Just as I thought. He's trying to get me addicted.

'Not really. In your case, for example, you've been on ten milligrams of slow release. That's only a booster dose, you know.' He looks up from his notes.

'So what's a dose?'

'I'd say you can get away with thirty milligrams twice daily for the moment, *provided* you take it in the right way.'

Sounds somewhat ominous, that 'at the moment'.

'You have to take MST in the proper way. Fix two times of day for that. The tablets release the drug over a period of twelve hours. If you keep precisely to the times, you'll control your pain. Otherwise you're simply confusing everything. The slow release takes place, and is overlapped by more slow release, and you simply have a muddle.'

'Thirty milligrams twice a day?' I'm dismayed by the amount.

'Yes, a drop in the ocean. Brenda's on two hundred at present.' He thinks that's derisive! 'There *is* another problem, though. There are two types of pain. Soft-tissue pain and bone pain. MST is very good against soft-tissue pain, but it does nothing much for the bone pain. We use Frobin against that, but there are many other brands if that one doesn't suit you. You just take it once a day.'

A light is dawning. *That*'s why I can't really control the pain. Not getting the right pain-killer! I'm still adamant I don't want to take too much morphine, whatever all these people say.

'And the Diazepam?'

'That's a good idea. Keeps you from getting too stirred up.'

Particularly true of me, I'd say.

Perhaps I should have taken one or two Diazepam before our bathtime.

An exhausting day. Teil's having a bath. We think it unwise for me even to try. But, while she's in the tub, I think, why not? Possibly the last occasion I'll be upstairs. Last chance to see my writing-room, where I've spent so many hours at work. Last time I'll see my bedroom. Last opportunity to have a bath with Teil.

I can no longer walk without the walker. In fact, my legs have gone. Within two days of ringing Chapman. Too late for operations, anyhow. He had his chance last autumn. All I can do is wriggle myself forward on my bottom. That's how I reach the stairs. Fine Victorian staircase. Wide treads, mahogany banisters nicely curved. My hands clasped round them, I lever my rear, tread by tread, humping myself up, then into the bathroom. Teil's still in the tub. Not, to my disappointment, pleased to see me.

Actually feel inclined to write to the *Guinness Book of Records* about my feat. Perhaps not quite their sort of thing. Possibly I can manage without. But, now I'm here, I might as well have a bath. Teil gets out and reluctantly brings the chair alongside the tub once more. Together we manipulate me into it.

I luxuriate in our long bathtub, filled high with hot water. Will I ever have a bath again? Teil's angry. Appalled at my foolhardiness. We extricate me as before. She can't bear to see me propel myself downstairs. Just shoves a cushion at me – to land on, coming down. I add my towel and bump my bottom down, step by step, landing alternately on towel and cushion. Takes twenty minutes. I'm rather pleased with my performance, proud of my achievement.

I pay for it in pain, of course. It's hardly helpful to jar my spine, already riddled with cancer. Take Coproximol and glory in my prowess, in spite of Teil's disapproving air.

'Guess what? Dr March rang!'

'Who?' Not *another* doctor. I'm beginning to think I'd really rather do without the medical profession altogether.

'You remember, the "Pain Clinic" man. It's absolutely incredible. A complete stranger, and he takes the trouble to ring.'

'That is rather impressive.'

'I think it's marvellous. I'm so glad we didn't just let you go off to the Infirmary. Dr March *is* a neuro-surgeon. He thinks it very prudent of us to consider the possibility of neuro-surgery with the utmost caution.'

'In other words, Chapman talked to a neuro-surgeon and knew perfectly well nothing could be done.'

'Who knows? I get the impression that many of them will do anything rather than come straight out with unpalatable facts.'

'Misplaced kindness?'

'Rot. They can't come to terms with death – or think we can't, and they'll have to deal with that. What we can't cope with is not being told the facts!'

'Did March say anything else?'

'He thinks we can't do better than take hospice advice on pain control. After yesterday I can only second that.'

'Nothing further for us to do?'

'No. He did mention how sorry he was to hear of our predicament. Said it was one of the most unfortunate situations one can find oneself in.'

'Did he?' Outlook's bleak of course. But as bad as that? Not sure what he means.

'You just stay here,' Teil says, almost triumphantly. 'We'll live the best way we can contrive. Liz and the Community nurses will support us, I'm sure. And I know our children will.' Colin is already scheduled for this weekend.

In many ways I'm lucky. Met some sterling people in the last few months, perhaps some of the finest human beings I've ever come across. MacKieff. Liz. Several nurses. And now March.

Can't work much. Bit of a problem. Used to writing. Attending to Thorn Press business. Chatting to knitting editors. Fortunate Thorn knitting books are doing well. Where would we be without that?

I sleep in the living-room chair now. Teil's off early. Sleep fitfully, now that I hardly move. Couple of hours here and there. Read between whiles.

'Hello, Bean! What are you doing up at this time? I thought it was only about two! Is the clock wrong?'

'No, I just couldn't sleep and thought you might be awake.'

'Lovely!'

And why not? Our whole world's turned topsy-turvy. So why not night into day?

FRIDAY, 10TH JANUARY

Colin's off to Bridgwater, clinching an important business deal. Contract worth thousands.

Gratifying all my three children are well established. I shouldn't like to leave this world feeling they aren't set up. The late twenties are an important time. Ambitions, careers, recent marriages, the next generation. All to be sorted out. Now the added burden of a dying father on their plates. I'm overwhelmed by their devotion, the obvious reaching out to me of every one of them. Each in an individual way, each a delight. I couldn't ask for more.

Because of yesterday's little escapade Teil thinks I should use the downstairs bathroom.

'Might be as well if Colin helps you.'

'No need to involve him. I can manage perfectly well.' He's never seen me naked, never seen my scar.

'He won't mind at all. He says he'll be glad to help.' She's not the one who'll feel embarrassed.

'I coped easily last time. It's just that you don't like the un-

[*59*]

conventional methods!' I wish she wouldn't involve the children when it's obviously not necessary. Don't like being dependent on them. Undignified.

'No trouble, Dad. I'll be glad to give you a hand. I'm here the whole weekend, anyway.' Colin is backing her up, too. You'd think I'd lost my mind as well as the use of my legs.

'You'll have to wait for me to get myself there.' It takes a bit of doing, dragging myself down that long corridor.

'I'll push you on the rocker, Dad.'

It's increasingly difficult for me to use the walker. I suppose they're right to dissuade me from humping myself about. I knew there'd be trouble. Score marks all along the linoed floor. 'I'll get you back on the castered footstool' is all Colin has to say about it.

'Here we go, Dad. Grab hold of my neck and I'll lift you out. Slowly, now. No hurry. I can take your weight.'

'Succour unto thy father in his infirmity,' it says in the Old Testament. It's taken almost two hours of succouring already. The amount of effort required is colossal. We must find some other method of cleansing me. Can't ask Colin to drive seventy-five miles every time I need a bath!

'We could put a bed in the dining-room for you,' Teil's saying as Colin casters me along.

'I want to be in the chair in the living-room. That works very well. What's wrong with it?'

'You can't just live permanently in that chair.'

'Why not? I'm comfortable in that.' The nurses will just have to blanket bath me, or whatever. I find the living-room quite agreeable – TV and music centre at hand. Shutters keep out the light. Plenty of room. What's the problem?

SATURDAY, 11TH JANUARY

Reasonable night. In my chair. Can't extricate myself now. Entirely dependent on Teil. To open shutters, fetch and carry.

Use the bottle on my own. One advantage of being a man! Can't empty it. Humiliating. Mortifying. What's going to happen about a bowel movement?

Thirsty. Can't get a drink. Only six in the morning.

'Hello, honey. I thought you might like something to drink.'

'You must have heard my thoughts. I'm just longing for some apple juice! I simply can't get out of this thing any more.'

'But you're not toppling out yet, as Liz said you might?'

'I don't think that's going to happen.'

'Good. I think we should make more permanent arrangements, as Colin's here to help me.'

'Meaning?' She's trying to get me upstairs again!

'If you're staying downstairs, and I agree that's best, we should get some of your belongings around you. We could set up the dining-room as your room, perhaps. It's much easier to keep warm than the living-room, and nearer the kitchen. The french windows will give us the chance to air it readily. And you can see more from there.'

'Then I wouldn't be in the living-room. The heart of the house.'

'There's only the two of us, honey. It's cosier, in many ways. Colin and I can fix it up. If you don't like the set-up, we can always bring you back here.'

Fair enough.

Colin's ready to push me into the dining-room. Quite nicely adapted. My chair backs on to the far wall, facing french windows. Long john table on my left, stacked with radio, cassette recorder, family photographs, business files. Bedside cabinet on my right. Holds vitamins, medicines, clothes, bottle of Highland Spring, tin of oatmeal cakes, writing materials. They've brought down my pot plants. Dining-table in the far corner on the right. Remote-controlled TV angled at the left. Video recorder underneath. Standard lamp behind me. Anglepoise and portable phone beside me. Not bad. Oh yes, couple of chairs for Teil and visitors. Might work out.

'The cushions aren't quite right yet.' People are so impatient.

The slightest deviation from my norm and it's really uncomfortable.

'Sorry, Dad. This better?'

'I thought you'd like this little table in the room, with all your published books held in by Madeleine's book-ends.' Teil brings my life's work in.

'That looks nice.'

'We've bought you a washing-bowl, and one of those quilted jackets. Much better than a dressing gown.' I've always wanted one of those. It's big enough, amazingly. 'I thought, while Colin's here, we ought to set a bed up for you. Just to try it out. You *might* find it more comfortable.'

I knew it! 'I keep telling you, I like the chair!'

'You haven't tried the other. How will the nurses manage?'

'That's their problem.'

'Could we just try it? We'll put it all back if you don't like it.' They wear one down so. OK, let 'em try. Reserve the right to ask 'em to change it all back again. Out of that room like bats out of hell. Hear Colin thump the bed down.

'There we go, Dad. How's that?'

'The pillows aren't right.' Where did all these pillows come from?

'Let's try a foam block behind you.'

'That's slightly better.' I don't like it. Nothing to hold on to. Feel vaguely exposed, somehow.

'It's fairly disagreeable.' I knew it wouldn't work.

'We'll put the chair cushions behind you. Maybe that's the answer.'

'It's better. But it isn't right, I keep telling you!' Usually she's right. This time she's definitely wrong.

'Probably having your legs bent helps, I realize. But you may get used to it. It could be better in the end.'

'I might have to wake you in the middle of the night,' I warn.

'We're quite prepared for that. Look, this is how you use the phone's intercom.'

It's quite a good device. Noisy enough to wake the dead.

I knew it couldn't work. One o'clock and I'm very uncomfortable. Shift position as best I can. Fiddle with pillows. Move my bottom. Manhandle legs to different angles. Turn on some music. Try to think of higher things. Discomfort turns to pain. Pain threatens to turn into agony. Five. Six. No sign of Teil. I can't cope. Turn on the intercom. Code is one blast for come when you can, three for urgent action, continuous for emergency. Can't turn it off!

Teil and Col are here in seconds. They see I'm not dying, so turn the bleeper off. Set about returning me to my chair.

'That's wonderful. It's such a relief!' I'm aggrieved. I knew she'd made a mistake. 'Told you it wouldn't work.'

'Sorry, honey. What about the nursing?'

'What nursing?'

'Well, you know . . . cleaning and so on.' Is she trying to convey something in particular? 'You're all hemmed in.' She's still plotting. I'm not going to budge this time.

'I'm comfortable in this chair. I don't want to move.'

'No one's going to force you,' she says, to calm me.

Lovely looking day. Streaks of pale pink across the sky. Heehaw of mute swans, flying paired, across the light horizon. They mate for life. Sun's rays begin to sparkle on the glass. A cup of steaming dandelion coffee. A dish of wholesome groats. Another day of life.

''Bye, Dad. See you in a fortnight.'

Col's leaving. His strong and willing arms no longer there to support me. His calm acceptance of my infirmities no longer there to encourage me. He and Mad are alternating weekends. Teil says she needs the help. Unlike her. Is the strain getting too much? What happens to me if she runs out of puff?

'Isn't it rather a long time since you've peed?'

'Is it? I don't know. I haven't thought about it.' And I don't want to!

'I don't think I've emptied the bottle since this morning. I'd better ring the Duty Doctor.'

'Not urgent, is it? Can't it wait till the morning?' Is she starting to fuss?

'I'll ask them.'

She's off before I can stop her.

'Something's got to be done.'

'You don't mean go to hospital?' I'd never get back. Know I wouldn't.

'They can catheterize you here. But female nurses aren't allowed to do it for male patients. It has to be carried out by a male nurse, or a doctor. Either gender!'

Phone again. Must be urgent.

'Tom'll be here in half an hour.'

It's raining now, and very dark.

Tom Quigley's been my GP now for over twenty years. He's never had to visit me. Tricky to find us in the dark. But he manages, rapidly followed by a Community nurse – large, hefty, jolly lady. Hearty. Smiles a lot. Mrs Sturbow. She puts her arm round Teil. 'You're very brave,' she whispers. I don't follow that.

'You're the expert,' Tom is saying, turning to the nurse. 'Just remind me what to do.' He's not too well himself. Can't really handle an illness such as mine. Good of him to come out.

'The equipment's improved a lot.' The nurse expertly cuts open a sterile pack and hands the contents to Tom. Long plastic tube inserted. Almost immediately, liquid spurts out into a plastic bowl. Blissful. I hadn't realized my abdomen's so swollen, badly impeding movement. At least two pints. Maybe more.

'When do I take it out?' They've emptied the bowl and fixed a plastic bag to the end of the tube. Pinned the bag to the side of the chair.

'Take it out?' Tom asks, as though he hasn't noticed the tube's still there.

'The catheter. When do I take it out?'

'I think we'll leave it there. For the time being,' Tom mumbles, carefully turning away from me. As usual. So I can't see his face.

This is a permanent feature? A fact of cancerous life? I'm incontinent in that area? My God, what next. . . ?

I'm literally pinned to the chair. Couldn't move even if my legs allowed it. I don't really mind. Perfectly content to sit here. Not in pain. Provided I stay in the chair! Everything I need at my side.

Community nurses arrive. Jean Sturbow. Nurse Locksley is new. Youngish. Good legs. Vivacious. Friendly chatterer. Obviously efficient. She's come to evacuate my bowels, because I haven't had a bowel movement. Anyway I can't get to a commode, can't heave myself on to a bedpan. Prophylactic against accidents, presumably. Odd feeling. Doesn't hurt, but being moved about does.

'Rather a large amount of stool,' Nurse Sturbow confides to Teil. 'Your husband seems to eat a lot.'

'It's the high fibre diet, more than the quantity.' Teil explains the effects of the macrobiotic diet. 'Perhaps we can modify that now.' To some extent, possibly. I'm keen to continue. The diet is, after all, supposed to help my body conquer cancer.

Liz arrives, perturbed by my being in the chair. Obsessed, like Teil. Sticking to it. Congenial. Important to me. What's painful is the irritation round my left eye. And the red, itchy bumps on my forehead. Skin cancer?

Liz diagnoses the trouble instantly. 'That's shingles.'

'Shingles? I thought that was round the waist.'

'Yes. But I've seen it affecting one side of the face before. We have to watch out for the eye. Shingles can affect that seriously enough to require surgery.'

'You mean he might have to go to hospital?'

'I think we've caught it early enough. The sooner we can start applying Zovirax ointment, the better. Every four hours, throughout the night if possible.'

'Any diseases you can think of that I *haven't* got?' I jest.

Liz smiles vaguely, uneasily. Looks somewhat embarrassed. I must try not to upset her. She's not the bantering type.

Peter Worthing arrives. More visitors in one day than we usually have in a month! Glad to see him, though. Try to find out if I could go to the hospice. For a weekend, perhaps. Give Teil a break before the illness breaks her!

'Yes, certainly. That's what we offer terminal patients.' What's he mean, terminal? I'm not terminal, of course. 'Stays of up to two weeks.' Peter Worthing is quite agreeable to the idea. 'Most people don't die in a hospice, you know. They come in for a short time.' Exactly!

'Can I be in my chair?'

'I don't see why not.' There! He doesn't envisage any problems.

'I would think that nursing him in a chair might be difficult.' Teil is harping on again.

'Not necessarily. Just a preconceived notion, really, isn't it?'

At least I've got one ally. 'I could go up in the ambulance,' I put in, warming to the idea. 'My chair could be brought up in the Volvo.' I've thought it all out. Not unrealistic at all. Colin can help Teil.

She doesn't show any great enthusiasm. 'You do have single rooms?' she's asking now.

'I'm afraid we haven't. Three men in one room, three ladies in another. Curtains, of course, for privacy.'

Deflating. I'm used to being alone most of the day. Can't share a room now. I'll have to find some other way to give Teil an escape.

She takes ages to show Worthing out. 'He suggests you put the MST dose up to sixty,' she reports.

'Sixty! Why not go up in tens? I thought that's what that dose is for.'

'Worthing says don't mess about with such small doses – sixty milligrams twice a day is still nothing to be perturbed about.'

Not for them, perhaps. It is for me. I'll be completely addicted in no time at all. Have to keep a very close eye, myself. All these people, all of them, are bent on shoving the stuff down me. Trying to keep me quiet? Does have a pacifying effect. Want to stay alert. Still have work to do. Tape the Diary!

TUESDAY, 14TH JANUARY

4 a.m. start. Teil expertly squirts ointment into my eye. Getting the knack of it. 'Excellent! Half an inch of a thin white worm in your eye.'

'Sounds delightful.'

'You do have rather the air of a pirate about you. Reddish patches, scabs forming, half-closed eye. The asymmetric look!'

'Very rakish. Let's have the mirror so I don't miss all the fun.'

We're thinking of taking up new careers as pill and potion dispensers. Doc around the clock services, perhaps.

Nurse Kalmett is back today. 'Dr Walsh-Comfitt asked me to check the eye.' She examines it carefully. 'You're doing very well.' High praise. 'Can you fill me in on what's happened? I hear there's been all kinds of excitement.' I remember now. She's the head nurse. In charge. . . .

It takes me about an hour to relate events, just like the Worthing affair.

'How are you getting on with the creaming?'

Mrs Sturbow kindly provided Conotrane salve on Sunday night. Very important to lubricate my back. And all the joints. Avoids sores developing. My long arms are very useful. Double-jointed, too, as it happens. Can put my right arm behind my head, and cup my hand under the left side of my chin. Same with the left arm. The children used to adore this grotesque and faintly apelike apparition. Nurse Kalmett is rather more restrained at the display. Smiles faintly, and somewhat discouragingly. Possibly sees the point. I must try it out on Mesdames Sturbow and Locksley. Suspect they'll find it entertaining. Nice to contribute something to their day.

[67]

WEDNESDAY, 15TH JANUARY

I feel lively, even spry. Time to do some business. I'm up to it. Want to leave Teil as well placed as possible. I'm obliged to wait for rest of world to get to work, however. Editors don't normally start till ten or even later. Exercise patience.

The mobile phone is my lifeline to the outside world. No one can tell I'm ill. I can promote *Knitted Lace Doilies* just as I did the others.

Just one call and I'm exhausted. All for today. Will I be here for publication?

THURSDAY, 16TH JANUARY

Nurses left a hoist and wheelchair on their last visit, so I can have a bath. Wonderful! Good old NHS. They tried the hoist out on Teil, to general merriment. It seemed to work well.

'I'm much smaller than you are. And even now, I'm about thirty pounds lighter.'

Teil has grave reservations about the hoist. Can be quite stubborn. Obviously it works. I saw it myself. Nurses had a go at the Health Centre, too – with Nurse Locksley. She's bigger than Teil.

Troupe of nurses arrives. The great hoist trial is about to begin. I feel quite excited. Lovely to have a bath!

'Sorry, Mr Warburg. We seem to've got it the wrong way round.' The nylon harness bites into my back. It's too small for me and the wrong way round. 'No, don't move!'

I try to help by leaning forward. Topple out of chair on to floor. Weight of inert legs, presumably. No actual pain. No feelings below the waist, after all.

I suddenly realize they've brought the bed back into the room.

'The extra morphine will take care of the pain, Mr Warburg. You'll be much more comfortable in the bed.' They don't ask. Just act.

'I'd really rather not. It won't work. . . .' I try to remonstrate. They don't even hear me. Too busy setting up the bed and getting me on to it. No question of baths. Complete nonsense, obviously.

They evacuate my bowels. Disembowel me, as I call it, to general consternation. The whole business has taken about an hour and a half. Exhausted me. And them.

FRIDAY, 17TH JANUARY

Nurse Sturbow has somewhat injudiciously ordered a hospital bed. It takes three sturdy men to lift it. Teil's had it delivered to the office, though Ayliffe hardly needs it cluttering up the place.

Womanpower summit decides against exchanging my bed for the ungainly monster. It's too old-fashioned and uncomfortable, though it has a built-in monkey-pole. The name for this, possibly useful, piece of equipment has no appeal for me whatsoever. Helps a partially paralysed patient to raise the parts his brain cannot reach. Failing that remedy, a free-standing monkey-pole can be supplied, to be set behind my own bed.

'I'd like you to have a ripple mattress, Mr Warburg.' Nurse Kalmett is in my room, surveying the arrangements for my needs. I've already tried such a grooved, air-inflated plastic mattress. A noisy motor controls the airflow, sending waves through the contraption. It made things worse, not better. Theoretically it exercises the patient's body, preventing ulcers. My enthusiasm is distinctly muted. 'We have to try to avoid bedsores.'

No one asks my opinion. The installation date is next week.

'We can always get rid of it if you don't like it, honey. I'll just turn the motor off and let it deflate.'

Teil's still on my side most of the time.

Minnow arrives, bearing audio cassettes of the entertaining *Yes, Minister*. Also Alec Guinness reading Eliot's *The Waste Land*. I think Guinness's reading aloud sounds a little mad. Perhaps just affected. May just be my subjective impression. I prefer a more matter-of-fact approach.

SATURDAY, 18TH JANUARY

Second night on the bed. I have to admit: very good sleep. Six hours straight. Much, much better than of late. Perhaps because I can lie, rather than sit, through the night. I'm still able to be upright during the day. Capable of discussing strategy for next few months.

'We hardly need to keep rigidly to the macrobiotic diet. The tumour's obviously increased.' It should help Teil if we cut down on the diet. 'But I don't want to give it up entirely. I feel it still *might* stop the cancer from spreading to organs. Even if I'm paralysed, I *am* still alive. And that's something to be thankful for.'

'Of course. We could just switch to a whole-food diet. A little more fish, a little less fibre.'

'Exactly. It will cut down the work-load for you.'

'The early snowdrops are just budding. The large single ones by the golden elder hedge.' Mad's done the garden round and brought some flowers to show me.

'Lovely. Rather late this year.'

'Yes. No sign of the doubles, yet. The pussy willows are glinting silver, though. And the hellebores are flowering. I've brought some heliotrope to scent the room.'

I tour the garden in my mind. Alpines in the stone wall. The glade. The primrose path. All my design. Mad's telling me about the things we've grown and which I can no longer see. It hurts.

SUNDAY, 19TH JANUARY

Teil and Mad both ready to go to mass. Teil's wearing the frock I bought her recently. She looks very well in it. Still has a good figure. Says she's delighted to have a present from me. Glad I managed this last dress.

'D'you think she needs to come?' I turn my shingly eye towards Teil. It's hard for me to judge. I prefer not to bother, but don't want problems with my eye. Dark by now, and raining hard. Always on a Sunday!

Sheila Dorian is young. Recently qualified, I'd guess. Appears to take on relief duties for the practice. Tall, gangly, somewhat nervous. 'Yes. That's quite good. The scabbing is quite right.'

'I'm sorry if you came out for nothing.'

'Not at all. I much prefer to have seen you, anyway. Sorry I didn't make it yesterday.'

It seems there's not a single day without the need for some medical assistance.

MONDAY, 20TH JANUARY

Teil has popped off to see her parish priest. She'd like to have some sort of public ceremony after my death. Prefers a mass for religious reasons. Locals we know can come to it, if they wish. I simply don't care myself. I'm surprised to hear she expects to manage such an occasion. I shan't put any obstacles in her way if that's what she wants.

'I've rung Father Noncet, honey. He can see me this morning.' New man. Last one left only a month ago. A mass can be said for anyone, Teil insists. Not a requiem mass, of course. Just a mass for my intention with *The Lord's My Shepherd*, *To Be a Pilgrim* and *Jerusalem*.

I've given Teil a letter to show the priest, stating I'm a theist. Just in case the idea of an agnostic, or an atheist, would appear altogether too unkosher – if I may use that term! Any Jewish connotation, after all, is simply genetic.

She's been gone a long time. Problems, presumably.

'How did it go?' I'll agree to a mass only if the priest is well disposed.

'All right in the end, I think. He took a bit of persuading, though.'

I'm not at all surprised. Expected it. 'I don't want a mass unless he's perfectly content to say it.' No way I'm going to try to muscle in on religious ground because of my illness.

'I was a bit surprised he was so reluctant. It never occurred to me that he would be. You were right about the little piece you wrote about being a theist!' There! 'Anyway, he eventually agreed to say a mass, provided he can come and meet you first.'

'That's not unreasonable.' I'd do the same in his shoes. I'm quite interested to hear what he has to contribute.

'I said you'd be very happy to see him. I just asked him to give us a ring first.'

'What about the hymns?'

'He's perfectly happy with your choice.'

It sounds a pleasing occasion, from an aesthetic point of view. Provided I'm found acceptable. I'd quite like to be there. Shall be, perhaps, in the circumstances. Not quite in the flesh. In spirit. I've no objection to – not at all unkeen – on a mass being said for me. Hope it will bring solace to Teil and the children. I'm not averse to people saying prayers for me. Can't do any harm and, who knows, it might do some good!

I don't want fuss after my death. Mad has also asked if she can have a mass said, in London. She knows her parish priest quite well. No objections were raised in that quarter, though Monseigneur Petrarch hasn't met me. Happy to do it, apparently. My London relatives will have a chance to go to that.

Interesting response to my illness. This priest's had cancer himself. Mad asked why all the pain and ghastliness. He answered that the way to think about it is that I must be nearer to God than I realize. Does he mean nearer to death? I find it quite comforting. As Mad does.

Teil has just been in touch with Chapman, to get his estimate of how long I'll live.

'I expected this all along, of course.'

He *what*? He told us, together, he was 95 per cent sure he could avoid the paralysis, but actually *knew* that it would happen? In fact he turned the figures precisely upside-down? To make no bones about it, he lied? Not the only one, either! Others, nearer home, also knew, apparently. Ruthi. Wasted my time, my energy, my money and, above all, my spirit. Maybe even ruined the diet's power to help me. Encouraging me to have treatment which was obviously useless. Clearly I could have had a pleasanter, less painful, time before paralysis. I could have made proper arrangements. I was denied all this because *other people* insist I can't handle the truth. Candidly, that never caused me trouble.

'Your husband will live for a very long time yet, I'm afraid.'

'How long? Are we talking about months or years?'

'Well, not, I think, years. Perhaps till Christmas.'

'He can live as long as that?'

'I'm afraid so. There's nothing life-threatening.'

Teil recounts his words verbatim. Basis of our relationship. We don't wish to prevaricate. Chapman's frank sympathy for the length of time it will take me to die seems curious, but is at least honest. I don't see it quite like that. I'm glad to be alive. Glad to be able to lie here in reasonable comfort. A restricted form of life, but it's still life. I enjoy it, in spite of everything.

'D'you think Chapman's right?' I ask Teil, somewhat dubiously.

'Frankly, I don't.' She looks to see if I can take it. 'I can't see any point in lying to you. I think Lazenby was right all along. I judge July, August. I think that we should work to that time-scale.'

'I tend to agree with you.' Never thought I'd make another birthday – 14th October. Don't think I'll get to that. Possibly September. Not later. Can sense it won't be later. I give myself a little longer than Teil does. 'Perhaps September.'

'Right.'

'You could go away for a bit. Mad can take over.'

'She's offered, yes. I think we might have to think of a nursing home for a short time. At some stage.'

'I see.' I don't want that. Anathema to me. Can stay cheerful while I'm at home. Anything else is simply too terrible to contemplate. 'What about a living-in nurse?'

'I've talked to Liz. She doesn't think it's on.'

'Why not? I thought that's what they do.'

'I checked with two agencies. They'll do eight hours a day, five days a week. So it would need someone like Mad to be here as well.'

'Oh.'

'And a nurse would expect meals to be provided.'

'Terrific.'

'Anyway, the Community nurses deal with the nursing. That isn't the problem, as I see it.'

WEDNESDAY, 22ND JANUARY

Life outside goes on, of course. I don't notice much. Feel cocooned in my room, away from rest of house. From everything! This room is my world. Might just as well be no other. Telephone connection. Boston the same as London. Not entirely real.

Slightly different today. The outside world actually impinges, through noise and, astonishingly, sight. Blast of a hunting-horn, and hounds swarming all over the terrace outside the french windows. They nose up, barking excitedly, having scented me. Glad the windows are shut tight!

I've often watched the local hunt, amazed. Nothing like the images on films or TV. Two men in scarlet coats – the rest, a motley crew of some eight other riders, and the foxhounds, followed by a motorcade of Land-Rovers, cars and pick-ups. I don't know whether I'm for or against blood sports. Feel akin to the fox. Doomed to die soon, but don't know when. At least the fox can run, has a fighting chance. Strange phenomenon of people *driving* to follow the hunt. What are they there for? What do they hope to see? Hounds clawing at the fox, tearing it to death? Like the cancer cells clawing at me?

Maybe that's why I don't want people to know about my disease. They'd come to stare at me.

THURSDAY, 23RD JANUARY

Liz now comes every Thursday. Just as well. Need all kinds of prescriptions. The pill against bone pain has done nothing for me.

'We could try Oruvail. Thirty-ninth on my list of forty.'

'Right, Oruvail to the rescue.' Hope it does the trick. Unpleasant burning sensation in my bones. Can do without that.

Teil's planning to ask Liz how long she thinks I've got. The more opinions we can get, the better we can judge for ourselves. 'It simply isn't possible to say,' she insists. 'There's nothing to stop him going on for quite a long time.'

Months it definitely is, then.

Alec Turnpike's prognosis last September was two to three weeks. A week later the radiotherapy consultant rang, 'just to clear up a few points'.

'Yes?' Teil was astonished to hear from her.

'The GP sounded a little agitated when he got in touch with me last week. I hope he didn't give you the impression your husband is about to die.'

'Yes, he did. He said Jeremy will be dead within three weeks at most.'

'People are inclined to equate pain with dying.' Well, *people*, yes. But doctors?

'Actually, the GP said we should alert our son in the States. Tell him to come over within two weeks.'

'Oh, dear. I thought there might be a misunderstanding.'

Perhaps we should have been overwhelmed with delight. What we were overwhelmed with was anger. At being given quite incorrect information. At the consultant ringing a week too late. At having to relay false news to our children. At Richard and Ruthi – the Rs – rushing over then, so ruining our plans for my last birthday celebration.

Teil's bought three sheepskins. One to place behind my back, on top of the complicated pillow arrangement. A second under me. A third under my legs, pulled up between them so they won't touch. Otherwise pressure sores develop. Managing a non-moving body takes some skill.

'The feet need to be upright.' Nurse Kalmett directs the new nurse she brought with her. It's ripple mattress installation day. Requires only two nurses, much to my surprise.

'Do I really need that? I thought sheepskins would do the trick.'

'I'm sure they're very good, but I'm still worried about sores developing. They're very difficult to get rid of once they appear.'

Suppose I have to try the wretched thing.

The new nurse is Terry Armiter. Late thirties, I'd say. Ready smile. Calm air. I like the look of her. She's sympathetic without being fussy. Definitely amiably disposed.

'That's right, Mr Warburg. Just going to unroll half the mattress on this side. Then, if we can have you leaning over the other way, I'll come round and unroll the other side.'

Sounds pleasant, too. Relaxing voice. Explains what she's doing. Only difficult part is their easing me over the roll.

The ripple mattress is rapidly set up. Din starts. Not quite as bad as the one I tried before, but definitely noisy.

'Maybe Colin can think of some way of cutting down the racket,' Teil says. 'He'll be along later.'

I hope so. How can I sleep through this constant buzz? Rather like a bluebottle, but without the chance of swatting it.

'Let's try boxing it up.' Colin places the motor between two cushions in a cardboard box. Closes the whole thing with Sello-tape. The buzz becomes a wheeze. At times a whirr.

SATURDAY, 25TH JANUARY

Colin triumphantly holds up the 'Bluebell' pastel. I've always liked it. My grandmother's. Told me she'd leave it to me. She died while I was in Wisconsin. My mother denies her mother specifically left it to me. Lately, though, she's said I can have it if I like. Didn't.

I asked Col to fetch the picture from her after all. Told her he'd got his car; convenient for him to pick the picture up for me. Simple as that. She didn't suspect a thing. Or, if she did, didn't mention it. It's not like her. I assume she suspects nothing of my illness. Preoccupied with her own death. She makes what mileage she can out of being eighty-four. Question of her executor, for instance.

'Of course it must be Daidie.' Wistful half-smile. A stick, no doubt, to beat me with. I'm not her eldest. David is. 'It must be the first-born son.'

Naturally.

'A certain amount of pressure is being put on me to inform people other than my immediate family about my illness. I can't see the point. All this nonsense about shock if I die. Presumably they mean *when*, not *if*.

SUNDAY, 26TH JANUARY

Quite a good discussion on how to organize our lives to the best advantage. Modify the diet, as already agreed. No need for Worthing to come each week. Can get advice on the telephone. Refuse kind visits offered by locals. Even cut the children to every other weekend. However kind, however helpful, it adds extra strain. Neither of us can handle it.

'I'm bound to say that for once I agree with the feminists.'
Teil's livid with the nurses' suggestion that she should 'forget all
this stuff'. She's referring to her running The Thorn Press and
writing her latest knitting book. 'What, precisely, do they think
we live on? And even if we could manage for a few months,
what, exactly, am I supposed to do after you're dead? Throw
myself on the funeral pyre?'

'I don't suppose they mean it like that.' It's quite worrying. It'll
be disastrous if she can't do some of her own work.

'Because I'm a woman, I'm supposed to drop everything. It
wouldn't have crossed anyone's mind to suggest that you forget
your job.'

'Something in that. Working from home doesn't help either.'

'I have, anyway, dropped quite a few things. And I'm not
writing the macrobiotic cookbook.'

'I rather wish we were doing that.'

'Sorry. I just haven't the energy to do that as well as the
knitting book.'

Hordes of people invade the house because of me. Nevertheless, looking after me mostly devolves on Teil. Except for actual
nursing. I'd be obliged if the nurses stuck to that. What makes
them think they can counsel us on the way we order our lives? If
the advice so far is anything to go by, we're better off without it.

MONDAY, 27TH JANUARY

It has been propounded that we need extra help, by Nurses
Sturway and Locksley in particular. Nurse Kalmett, too. All
these people think it a good idea if Teil has more assistance. We
are both very uncertain about it. As yesterday's discussion
showed, we want less, not more, people involved.

The proposal is that a Marie Curie nurse comes for two whole
days a week, and some nights. The Marie Curie Institute provides nurses, free, for cancer patients. Up to £1,000, Liz says.

This sum, naturally, means nothing unless one knows how much a nurse costs. As we're constantly being told I'll live for months, it's hardly going to go that far, is it?

Teil's getting exasperated. Actually wants them all to bugger off and leave us to it. 'I'm not interested in nurses coming for complete days. What are they supposed to do? I'm perfectly happy to look after you, most of the time. I'd go berserk if I had to put up with a nurse here all day. I haven't a clue what it's all about. So I can cook for her, I suppose! Or talk to her! I don't want to know. We live here because we like being isolated. So it's unusual. So bloody what.'

'Exactly what I think. I'm glad we're still agreed.'

'As for the nights, I haven't an inkling what they're on about. Have some nurse sit in your room with you? You'd go nuts.'

'She could sit in the living-room. I certainly don't want her here.'

'We don't need a nurse cluttering up our living-room, listening to TV under me. I couldn't sleep!'

'Forget about it, then. They can't force you.'

'If they *must* go in for this Marie Curie business, perhaps someone could come and help you cream yourself. You find that a bit tiring, don't you?'

'Yes. I can't entirely manage it.'

'And washing your top. You could have some help with that?'

'I'd appreciate that.'

'Right. Two hours at most. I'll suggest they get someone to come and see to those things for you. As long as she comes in through the french windows, and I'm not involved, I can go along with it.'

TUESDAY, 28TH JANUARY

I ask Teil to bring me our copy of *What to Do when Someone Dies*. I see the nurses look at it askance, as though it isn't a proper book to have about the place. Seems only sensible to me.

I've thought about funeral arrangements at some length. What

I'd like. What would be practicable. Soon as I grasped I'd not just got cancer, but secondaries as well. That was last July, before the operation. I made a new will, wrote down my ideas for my funeral. Well, my preferred lack of a funeral.

I've had a good six months since to ponder. I've no desire to change my preferences as to what should happen to my body after my death. Quite clear on that. See no reason why I shouldn't arrange it all. Hardly the sort of thing Teil will wish to research immediately after my demise, expected or not. The children will undoubtedly rally round and help, but they too might have other things occupying their minds. As for cremation, I'd like to know where I stand and with whom. Otherwise I strongly suspect they do one down, mess one about. All this may appear somewhat bizarre, even a little gruesome or morbid, but as far as I'm concerned it's none of these. Simply a question of unearthing information, deciding on the best firm for the purpose, and letting Teil have the benefit of my researches.

The Yellow Pages. Show three funeral directors near us. We're geographically well placed for any of them. Start with Mullard.

'Morning. Could you let me have the cost of a cremation, please. I'm arranging a funeral for a relative.'

'Certainly, sir. It really all depends. We shall need a few details. The address. The type of coffin. Whether . . .'

'I just want the simplest, least expensive type of cremation available. The cheapest coffin, no frills, no funeral service, no lying in state, no cars.' Nothing, in fact, except to be burned rather than buried, complying with whatever laws apply.

'That would come to roughly £450, sir, provided the deceased is within a ten-mile radius of us.' That's absolutely staggering! The death grant is £30.

'What about a burial, then? Is that cheaper?' Might as well find out while I have the opportunity!

'That would be £200, sir. Most people prefer to have a little more than the bare coffin, though. Now if it was me, sir, I'd prefer my coffin lined. A much better presentation.' Well, I'm certainly not him. It's of absolutely no concern to me. 'And a shroud always enhances the appearance, sir. If it was one of my relatives, I'd much prefer to see a shroud.' Not entirely clear what it's to do with him, or why I should care what he'd want for his relatives. I'm not one, after all! Conceivably Richard, say, who hasn't been able to come before and now wants to pay his last respects, or whatever, would need something to soften the blow of seeing my dead body. Might find it more acceptable, possibly, if the coffin's lined. Corpse wrapped up in a bit of a shroud, perhaps.

'I see. Well, thank you very much.'

I'm somewhat shaken – not by the subject-matter, simply by the amount of money involved. How can people afford it? I ring the second firm, rejoicing in the name of Graves – very appropriate.

'I'm sorry, sir. This is not something we can discuss on the telephone.'

'Why ever not? I'm only asking you for a rough estimate . . .'

'It simply isn't a matter which can be discussed in this way, sir. I would be glad to call round, if you wish, sir. Where has the bereavement taken place?'

I'm having none of that! 'I've just talked to a competitor of yours. Apparently there was no difficulty for him.'

'I can't comment on that, sir. I can't help you over the telephone.'

So be it. I shan't be creamated by Graves. I'll have to settle for someone with, perhaps, a less distinguished name.

Elated by these remarkable discoveries, I ring the third firm. Furness: not bad, not inappropriate, and possibly quite good, even exciting. A furnace is, after all, what I require. A lady answers for the firm.

'I'm making inquiries about the cremation of my aunt's body.'

'You'd like us to call round, sir?'

'Not at present. I'd simply like you to tell me the cheapest, simplest form of cremation I can arrange.' A mean, uncaring nephew!

'If we can establish a few details first. Do you wish the body to remain in the house, sir?'

I do. Want it to remain in the house for a day or two. So Teil can have a little time with me. Adjust, so to speak, to my dead body rather than my live one. She's told me she'd like this. And in case Richard won't have been able to fly over in time to say goodbye. He might like to see me at home – dead or alive.

'Yes, I do. The cheapest coffin will do. No frills, nothing more.'

'Of course, sir. There's no problem about the body staying in the house normally. However, one or two points – if the deceased has died of cancer, say, or some other disease requiring the administration of a number of drugs.'

'How can that matter?' To an extent, of course, I've been taking drugs. This could well apply to me.

'Decomposition sets in fairly rapidly. It might be necessary for the body to be taken to our Chapel of Rest within a day or two.'

'I see. Well, that should be enough. The body can be taken from the house and cremated right away.'

'Cremation itself can only take place after the formalities have been completed. The death certificate signed by the attending doctor – in fact, two doctors. The death registered. That type of thing.'

'Why should that take more than a day or two?'

'I'm afraid it often does.' Possibly one has to take into account the cost of being taken to a Chapel of Rest. Presumably the body would in some way be embalmed to counteract the effects of the drugs before being ensconsed there. No specific mention of that, however.

'The difference between an accompanied, and an unaccompanied, cremation is roughly £30,' the helpful lady from Furness continued. 'And that applies to the service, too.'

'At the crematorium?'

Slight pause.

'I'm afraid the cost of being taken to the crematorium has to be added.' Naturally. Taken there as well as burned. A fact of death! 'And the remains can be put into several different types of container. We would suggest a metal one, for permanence.'

'I'm not interested in that.'

'In that case, sir, a simple plastic box.'

That will suit me nicely. That's all that will be needed for scattering my ashes from the top of the Tor. That's what I have in mind, by those of my children who are present and up to the task. I presume at least one of them will be. So the container's neither here nor there.

WEDNESDAY, 29TH JANUARY

A Marie Curie nurse has now been added to the nursing gang. Mary Houlder, a fairly plump lady in her sixties. Arrived this morning. Seems somewhat slow, but very pleasant and willing. Helps Nurse Kalmett change my lower sheet. A fairly painful process from my point of view and not particularly easy for them.

The new nurse stays on after Nurse Kalmett. I wonder a little bit why? Assume she's gathering information for the Marie Curie Institute. I find myself telling her about my illness.

'Would you like a sherry?'

'That's very kind.' She sits herself in the armchair and sips sherry. Finish my history as rapidly as I can. 'Is there anything you'd like to say to me?' I ask. Still can't figure out what's going on. What's she doing here, exactly?

'Not really. But I'm a good listener!'

I'm shattered. Finally grasp she's the one coming daily – well, five days a week. She's supposed to wash and cream me. I've absolutely no wish to chat to her, amiable as she is, let alone on a daily basis. I've neither time nor energy for such things.

'She simply sat drinking sherry and listening to you?' Teil's distinctly irritated. 'Is that what you want?'

'Absolutely not. I just didn't know how to stop it.'

'She said something about your being rather talkative.' Teil's been telling me for some time now that I'm positively garrulous. I never used to be. Teil thinks it's the morphine. Can't say I've noticed anything myself. 'I'll sort it out tomorrow.'

Teil will have to explain the situation. I'm obviously too cowardly, or too polite, or too public-school brainwashed. Something of the sort. Worn out anyway from yesterday.

THURSDAY, 30TH JANUARY

'I've had a little chat with Mrs Houlder,' Teil's reporting after that amiable lady has left. 'Given her a list of things she might try to work through with you. She appears to be content with what I suggest.'

Maybe now I can do some work when the nurses leave, instead of tiring myself out attempting to entertain Mary, as she's asked me to call her.

'She helped me cream myself this morning.'

'Good. I put down creaming, washing, leg movements. Perhaps tidy away the washing things.'

'I don't know what this protruberance in my belly is. Rather difficult to live with.'

Liz prods the bulge. 'I think it's simply loss of muscle tone. Because you're no longer mobile.'

We had a very interesting discussion about the contrast between the Western and the oriental approach to medicine. Liz reads around her subject, is not blind to alternative therapies. A GP to be respected, and there aren't too many of those. I'm lucky to be in her charge.

'Perhaps it would be helpful to have some physiotherapy. It will have to be private. The NHS doesn't run to home physio visits.'

'That sounds a good idea.' I'd really like to learn to be as mobile as possible.

Instead of showing Liz straight out, Teil goes off for another chat. Discusses the possibility of, at some stage, arranging a nursing home for me. Teil feels she's got to have a break, now, while I'm reasonably stable.

'Liz says there's a good nursing home three miles away.

They're building a private wing – single rooms. It's due to open in mid-March. That would be excellent. I could visit you easily. Two weeks should do it. Give me a chance of second wind.'

'Mid-March? Somerset time, presumably. Could mean mid-April.'

'That might be too late. I'll give them a ring.'

FRIDAY, 31ST JANUARY

'Sister Carrington sounds very capable. Knows all about cases such as yours. Says they can easily manage at The Elms.'

'When are they opening?'

'That's the snag. They hope the end of March.'

'Hope? Sounds like April or later to me. Can they do the disembowelling?'

'No problem at all, apparently. There is one difficulty. They only take people for a month at a time. Financial reasons.'

'A month?'

'I know, it's too long. I suggested they let us hire the room for the minimum time, then you can come and go as you please. They agreed.'

'Surely that will cost the earth?'

'At least it will give me a chance to recharge my batteries.'

I know she's drained. The trauma of my impending death. Looking after me. Coping with all the professionals who come because of me. Can see I've got to let her have a rest, otherwise she won't be able to last the course. However tiresome for me, I have to go.

February

I've considered carefully. The time has come to divide my sets of, mostly, nineteenth-century novels among my children, and nephews and nieces. I don't know them very well. Would have liked to. I like children, as it happens. Delighted to have had chance of getting to know my nephew-nieces. I warned my brothers against my mother. No use. Her insinuations prevented their fostering relationships with me. David has understood recently. Too late.

'Hi, Minnow. Lovely to see you.' Bright and cheerful. Nice.

'Hello, Jifda. Great book distribution day, isn't it?'

'I'd be very grateful if you'll help me. Shall we start right away?' The list is all sorted out. There's a good deal to get through.

'Could we wait till after lunch?' I suppose so. Disappointing.

'Let's go through the list, then.'

I'm leaving Teil my *Tristram Shandy*. Greatest book in English literature. Read it many times. Think she may like to have my copy.

'I'll just have a cup of coffee, Jifda. Then I'll be ready.' Just arrived from London. Needs a rest. I explain procedure to her in detail. She seems a bit tense. 'I don't want to be rude, Jifda, but could I just finish my coffee first? I'll be glad to go through it all in a few minutes.'

Why is she so edgy suddenly?

'I'm not exactly sure where each set is, Mad. Or how many books there are in each one, or what they are.'

[*86*]

'That's all right. I'll inventory them for you.'

'Kipling for you, I think. And the Masterpiece short stories. You'd enjoy the World Classics. The fairy-tale books will help with your work.'

'Thank you very much.'

'Dickens for Colin and Anna. Collectors' Editions of the Everyman series. Nearly a hundred books.' Eminently suitable for them, I feel. Not as classy as Mad's, but right.

'I'll just sort all that out.'

She disappears for some time. Runs in and out, assessing books, explaining discrepancies.

'Richard and Ruthi can have the special editions of *Peter Pan*, *Alice in Wonderland*, that sort of thing.' Only parents in my lifetime. 'And the Modern Library editions. They'll look well on their bookshelves, don't you think?'

'I'm sure they'll love them.'

'Fielding won't come amiss. The volume with Arthur Rackham's illustrations is quite valuable.'

'They're very lucky. I would have liked one or two of those. I do make children's programmes.'

I forgot about that. It's too late, now. 'Sorry about that, Minnow. I've already promised them.' Tiresome.

Disraeli and Prescott right for Diana. Defoe and the Classics set for Karin. Penni and Paul will, I imagine, enjoy Trollope.

'Could we stop here, for a bit, d'you think?'

'Stop? I haven't finished yet.' Thane seems to me a Thackeray man. Katie might well enjoy the set of novels in different coloured bindings. And John Hew can have George Meredith. Roughly twenty books each, which I hope they will enjoy.

'I'm getting a bit tired. Up and down the stairs, you know.'

'You haven't been moving books, have you?'

'No, not moving them. Just checking through them all.'

Teil doesn't want anyone to disturb anything in my rooms, as yet. Wants the status quo left until I'm actually gone. I understand. Appreciate it.

I find it enjoyable going through my books, even if at secondhand.

'I really have to stop now, Jifda. I'll do some more later.'

She looks quite strained. Inexplicable to me, but I settle for it. I've no choice. No time tomorrow, though.

She left me to have a doze. Then tea.

'Could we finish the books now, Mad?'

She is somewhat reluctant, but complies. A little tense, a little terse, a little difficult to get things done. I'd have liked to tie up a few more loose ends. Finish the main job. Find it satisfying. Apportionment accomplished. Like to think I've done my bit.

SUNDAY, 2ND FEBRUARY

I specifically invited Anna. Present her with a memento: agate amethyst necklace. Co-ordinates with soft mauves, wines and purples she favours.

I hear Colin's new car drive up. Endearingly he backs it up to french windows. I know nothing about cars. Right for him, I dare say. Attractive colour.

'Would you like to have your first course with me, Anna?' I find it overwhelming to be with more than one person.

'Yes, certainly.' Very polite, as always.

'I've got this for you.'

Her languid look turns almost immediately to interest. 'Thank you very much. Yes, it does look nice.'

She never goes over the top, but I gather she likes it. Gratifying. Want her to enjoy it.

'It's very difficult to get comfortable.' Must stop myself from talking about illness!

'Shall I adjust the pillows for you?' Resigned.

'No, no. It's nothing.' Change the subject. 'How's your new job?'

I try to take it in. Can't do much with it. Don't want her coming again, until I'm 'actively dying'. I've no right, really, to *assume* I'm going to die, passively or actively. I may not. I'm actively concerned to do my best at this visit. Good lunch. As pleasant company from me as I can muster. Only too aware my illness is a tedious bore for her. She sees to sick and dying in her job.

Candidly, I can't cope with visitors who aren't really close. Can't handle the extra strain. Know they're bored. Or curious. Can't feel what a close relative might feel. No time to build new relationships. All now depends on the past. Not much of that with Anna.

MONDAY, 3RD FEBRUARY

Early post. I enjoy opening it. Something I can do. People still send reasonable tribute. Reviews of *Irish Crochet Lace* going strong. Tot up the cheques.

Teil looks exhausted. Washing-machine's frozen up. No idea it's so cold. Warm in here. I don't realize what's going on outside the house. Only dimly aware of others' difficulties. Can't concentrate on them.

Teil's gone for an early night. I suddenly realize I'm somewhat smelly. Assume I'm leaking somewhat in the faecal area. It's happened before. Horrified. Isn't leaking. Actual bowel movement. Involuntary bowel movement. Incontinent!

I mop up as best I can. Mortified. No disembowelling these last three days. Recognize I'm incontinent from a faecal point of view. Maybe I should have realized it earlier. I'm catheterized, so obviously I'm incontinent from that point of view. Definitely established. Complete incontinence. I'd not really expected that. Everything's been somewhat quick and sudden. I'm extremely nervous about Teil's reaction.

'I'm sorry, pet. I'm afraid I've had to clean up.' I know she's already twigged because of the smell. See her making a great effort to control herself. Lips clamped shut. Clears up in silence. Seething. Infuriates me.

One is always reading, or hearing on TV, that serious illness brings people together. Particularly terminal illness. Teil and I, it's only right to state as a simple fact, have been extremely close for many years now. Share our home, our children, memories of young children, like many other married couples. But share much more. Interest in my creative work. Foster it to the best of our ability. Jointly run The Thorn Press. Soul mates. Illness can hardly bring us closer. I didn't expect it to affect the closeness, though. Nor has it done till now. As far as I can judge. Suddenly, we have a row. After years of hardly a cross word, we quarrel. Harsh, unpleasing, unloving things are said by both of us. The cancer is threatening to tear us apart.

Teil's trying hard to heal the rift. I cannot change so quickly. Don't respond. She tries time and again. I can't manage to answer her.

Fitful, shallow sleep. I'm wide awake at three, sorry for myself for the first time since my condition was diagnosed. In spite of the hour, I bleep Teil. Write a note first, in case of further blunders.

She comes. We talk. She's back to being sympathetic. Calm. Caring. About my physical state. Above all about my spiritual state. What does it profit a man to be out of pain if he suffers the loss of his love? Resolve to charge the dragons the next day — together.

TUESDAY, 4TH FEBRUARY

'I'll talk to Nurse Kalmett.'

'About a nursing home?' I know she's planning to ship me off. Inevitable. It's clear she's near breaking-point.

'Making sure they evacuate you every other day, at least.'

'D'you think that would do the trick?'

'That, and increasing the hardening-up ingredients in your diet. Go back to the much-maligned McVitie's Chocolate Home-wheat biscuits. You might enjoy that!'

'You mean the stuff that's supposed to kill me off.' I see her bite her lip to stop the tears. Pathetic, really. She tried so hard to help me dietwise. I'm sure it worked up to a point. Made me more equable. No sign of last night's mood when on the diet. Alleviated pain, as well. But didn't halt the tumour.

'We'll have to talk to Liz about your going off for a short time. I'm sorry. I just have to have time to recharge.'

I'll have to come to terms with going away, possibly permanently. Two weeks at the very least. Sooner rather than later, so Teil can recover and be in reasonable nick for the weeks or months that still remain to me. Otherwise I shan't have a wife to look after me. In which case I can forget about survival anyway. Quite apart from the unfairness on a wife who's always done everything she could to help and sustain me for so many years.

'She'll suggest the hospice, I take it.'

'No. That won't do. You have to have a room to yourself. We can't have that, whatever the cost.'

She still cares enough to risk her health. Still cares! Still loves me. She's willing to lay down her own health if needs be. I can't ask more. Feel calmer. A weight off my spine.

'We can make sure it doesn't happen again.' Nurse Kalmett listens to my tale of woe. 'There's a fair amount of stool even now.'

I can hardly credit it after last night. Must return to even more pre-macrobiotic foods.

A metal contraption, stand and upright, is slipped under my bed. Monkey-pole! Horizontal crossbar dangling a nylon tape, finishing in a hand-grip.

'You just grasp the bar with either hand, or both of them. Then you can lift your torso.'

I try. Possibilities for both good and bad. Yes, I can move more. But it increases pressure on my spine. Needs working on.

Two physio ladies, due at three, arrive at four.

'Held up getting a patient to hospital.' Chief physio lady. Hefty. In her fifties. Strong, straight grey hair in mannish cut. Trousers. Tunic over them. 'I do know how you feel. I was unable to walk myself at one time. The doctors said I would never walk again.' I feel a thrill of anticipation. Is there a chance she could get me mobile? 'I don't want to raise false hopes, of course. But we can always try.'

'Perhaps you'd just tell us the history of your disease.' It's getting monotonous, but I can hardly refuse. Second physio lady's less overpowering. Fairly hefty in her own right, all the same. 'Did no one show you how to breathe after your operation?' she now demands.

'Breathe? I thought I knew how to breathe!'

'Breathe properly, I mean.' Visions of improper breathing. Naked breath, perhaps? Tone of the brisk schoolmarm. No nonsense from you, my lad. 'You don't move properly, either. Did no one show you how to move?' The second physio continues her interrogation.

The breathing instructions are enormously helpful and encouraging. 'Every hour on the hour. That's my motto!' Somewhat unrealistic, in my view. Take care not to mention that, however.

'Now let's rearrange these pillows behind you.' Chief physio pushes me forward unceremoniously.

'Please be careful. That's rather painful.'

'You'll live.' Pillows rapidly, expertly adjusted. 'Lean back.' Staccato orders. 'How's that?' Certain amount of concern.

A quite dramatic difference. Really helpful. I hear Teil return from shopping. 'Could you show my wife?'

'Right. Here we are, Mrs Warburg. A little diagram for you.'

'Thank you. Yes, I think I can follow that.' I sense at once that Teil doesn't take to the chief physio's somewhat domineering manner.

The second physio is completely unimpressed by the ripple mattress, pulls it unceremoniously out from under me. 'No point in that contraption under sheepskins. Those are the things that count. That frightful plastic's worse than useless.'

I wonder, uneasily, what Nurse Kalmett will say.

The day starts pleasantly enough. Mary Houlder. Deliberate. Gentle. Motherly. Take to it. Enjoy unperturbed, tranquil approach. Why shouldn't someone mother me? I've always been keen on that.

I doze pleasantly throughout the day. Feel up to working on the Diary, just before dinner. Scheduled for six forty-five. Six-thirty. Knock.

'Yes?' Must I constantly be disturbed? Just because I can't move!

'May I come in?'

It's Teil. Well, who else?

'If you like.' I try to sound off-putting without being rude.

She comes in, smiling. Fifteen minutes early. Irritating. Don't want to know.

'Would you like a drink, honey? Gin and tonic, or a sherry?'

'I don't feel like a drink.'

'Right. Just the supper, then'. I infer she's gone off until the time agreed. Wrong. She turns up with supper within five minutes. I'm not ready. Working. Why do I have to accommodate to other people's schedules? I'm doing something not so unimportant myself! Supper early, on a whim. . . .

'We agreed to a quarter to. I haven't finished yet.'

She explodes. Snaps completely. Crashes the steaming, aroma-laden food in front of me. Quite, to me, inedible.

'I went to enormous trouble to make something really delicious. After all these months of macrobiotic eating.' The food coagulates into a cold, disgusting mass while Teil berates me. Voice harsh. Resentments I'd no idea she harbours. 'Slight misjudgement of time, that's all. Rather a different way of cooking.' Finally she winds down, removes cold food. Offers new food. I respond with mulish indifference, unable to speak. The shock of such a scene, at such a time in my life. Limp. Aching. How could Teil, of all people, respond to my petulance like this? Why does she explode rather than simply put the meal in front of me? How can she be so furious, so unexpectedly hostile?

I understand, or think I do, the strain she's under. The invasion of our privacy. Normally we enjoy solitude and quiet. Now there are multitudes. Nurses. Doctors. Marie Curies. Physio ladies. It's a very different world, worse than the direct demands. And all the time she knows I'm dying.

I emphathize. All that I can forgo. But I can't do without my wife's loving presence. The peace we used to share. The desultory chat about affairs of no great matter. The excitement about things that are. My work, and how she'll see to it. Her work, and what she plans to do. Without this soul food I cannot properly survive. I see the appalling situation clearly, perhaps for the first time. Realize I'm completely, entirely, dependent on Teil, to make this horrendous situation tolerable. I need my wife as I have never needed her before. How can I get her back? Will she desert me now?

Prospect so ghastly I cannot speak. I hear her attempts to end the row. Turn my head away. She tries many times, on and off. Returns after her bath. I'm too stunned. What can I, should I, do?

She removes all pills except the ones I actually use. Leaves the room.

She returns in the middle of the night. I can speak at last. Pour out my feelings. I feel better. A little better. But will this illness part us before death does?

THURSDAY, 6TH FEBRUARY

Lower order of nurses today. I feel irritable and not all that co-operative.

'Did you see *The Street* last night?' A young, curly-haired one speaks across my prone body. Looks away from me and at her colleague. 'Really good, I thought.'

'Smashing.' The second nurse, so young she could still be at school, tries to remove my shirt without my help. I resist. 'Could you just lift your arm up, Mr Warburg?'

I'm already at my limit. 'No. It aches too much.'

'We'll leave it for today, then.' She's relieved. It means there's less for her to do.

I'm uneasy about these young women's ability. They proceed as though I'm some inanimate object they have to clean. I insist they take some notice. 'Looks nice and bright out. Is it warmer?'

'Did you say something, Mr Warburg?'

They're too busy with each other. Offhand with me, disturbing their gossip!

Teil broaches the subject of a nursing home with Liz. 'The Elms isn't open yet?'

'No. End of March, at best. I think that's too far off.'

'What about the Durstone?'

'Will they take him there? I thought it's only available for short-term surgical cases.'

'We're thinking along assessment lines. We can get a week, I think.' She turns to me. 'I'll find out if one of the consultants will assess your case.'

'MacKnife – I mean Donald MacKieff – will almost certainly oblige.' I'm sure he'll champion me in any way he can.

'The timing will depend on the Matron. She's the one who's in charge. I'll give her a ring later today.'

'He's quite stable at the moment, isn't he?' Teil's worried about sending me off, my suddenly dying. 'Will you be able to check him thoroughly just before he goes? Just in case?'

'Of course. And you can always get him back, you know. Just arrange for the private ambulance and pick him up. No one can stop you! He'll be a voluntary patient, after all.'

'That's a relief. Yes, thank you.'

'And don't take your drugs. Only enough for the first few hours. They'll take them from you. Legally, they have to dispense these drugs each time.'

'Right. I think he should go from the sixty to ninety milligrams MST. The pain levels are increasing.'

Teil's on her hobby-horse again. I'll decide! 'Nurse Kalmett said not to tell anyone local I have cancer,' I interject. I see a chance to contribute something myself. At last. 'Otherwise we might get drug addicts raiding my room!'

Quite an exciting idea.

The new diet, I'm pleased to report, is doing what's required. No more problems about incontinence. This is the crux of the matter with Teil. No way she's going to have me at home if I'm incontinent. Must make sure I'm not. I don't care what I eat, or don't eat. That problem's got to be sorted out. Biggest one at present, as far as I'm concerned. Want to spend the rest of my life here. At home.

Liz rang to confirm. Durstone is definitely on. Also Mac-Knife's very willing to have me under his care. 'He seems to take to him,' she mentioned to Teil, somewhat mystified. 'Calls him a splendid chap, and that he'll be delighted to look after him.' Consultants don't normally involve themselves personally with patients. Keep their distance. Well, that's cheering. At least someone actually, positively, wants to know! Fancy that.

Father Noncet arrives without warning this afternoon, but it's not too inconvenient. I rather feel that, dying or not, I have the right to decide when people should, or should not, visit me. Actually, think I have less time, and so more right, to choose how to spend it. Anyway, he's turned up. Teil ushers him into the room. She hadn't much choice.

He's certainly not at all what I expected. He sits in the easy chair while Teil perches on a hard-backed one. Drinks the tea Teil's brewed. Accepts the chocolate biscuits I offer him.

'Thank you, yes. I do indulge occasionally. Very nice.' Takes a second one, settles back in the chair. 'Not too cold, considering it's February. Not bad at all.'

Is that what he's come for? To discuss the weather?

He launches into a monologue about his parish, his problems with the parish, the fact that he has never been a parish priest before. He was once a teacher at a Catholic school, apparently.

'Is there anything you'd like to ask me?' I finally manage to put in. The man was supposed to visit because he didn't feel he could allow a mass said for me unless he'd at least met me, discussed my attitude to God, or some such thing, presumably. There's been no hint of a discussion about God. Or religion. Or funerals. Or even a mass! In fact, no sign of a discussion, really. He simply ignores my question, drones on relentlessly with his tale of priestly difficulties.

I'm getting tired. Haven't been anything but bored. What's it matter to me whether this man agrees to say a mass for me or not? It might matter to Teil. The children perhaps. As far as I'm concerned it's neither here nor there. I want him to go. Don't want him coming back. I start fidgeting and look at Teil.

'Let me show you the garden, Father.'

'Ah, yes. Of course.' He gets the message and stands up. 'I'll come again,' he informs me. No question. Just a statement.

Oh no, you won't.

'I thought he'd be much iller,' Teil reports him saying as she was showing him the winter heathers. 'He looks astonishingly well.'

How d'you get more ill, I wonder? I'm relatively comfortable, I suppose, provided I take my massive doses of MST morning and evening. I don't cough or bring up sputum. Or hallucinate. Or lie back too exhausted to speak. Everything's discreetly hidden. My useless, static legs are covered with bedding. The catheter's invisible. Collection bag, filled with clouded urine, is on the side of the bed that can't be seen. First bedsore is under me. Swollen abdomen covered by duvet. My operation scar, of course, is discreetly concealed beneath my shirt. And my hopelessly cancerous spine is enveloped in pillows and swathed in sheepskin. Though I'm thin, I'm not yet emaciated. Show a reasonably normal face and upper torso to the world. No life-threatening episode in my disease as yet. But I'm bedridden, known to have a fatal illness. Excellent ground for sowing religious seed, I should have thought. No sign of it that I could discern.

Colin arrives from a business trip. I'm feeling somewhat snappish, what with other people doing deals, and useless priests, and Teil arranging to ship me off. I make the odd snide remark.

'I don't know when it's coming, Colin. Ask the oracle.' Not even allowed to order the china. Though it is, after all, my memento to Teil!

Why should I be pleasant all the time? Where's it got me? Got me this disease! Might as well say what I think while I still can! 'The grave's a lone and silent place.' No grave for me if I can help it. But silence, anyway. Whatever is done with my body.

SATURDAY, 8TH FEBRUARY

Rather worrying development. Urine in the bag looks very dark. I'm colour blind, can't tell some greens and reds apart. Still, I can see the urine's very dark, and not dark yellow. I suppose it's red. Blood.

I'm a bit apprehensive, in spite of the 120 gm MST. Nurse Locksley is jolly. I engage her in a little idle badinage. It helps the illusion of normality.

'How's the disembowelling coming along?'

Nurses find this expression worrying. Nurse Locksley is no exception. 'Really, Mr Warburg. The things you say!'

'The diet's up to your requirements now? You're satisfied?'

'The change has been a great help.'

She's not prattling as much as normal. Usually she's rather cheery. Babbles volubly about nothing in particular. Makes friendly noises. She noticed the urine, of course. Thinks I'm nearing the end? 'Had any more hilarious hoist trials?' I try out on her. Generally she's amused by that episode.

'Don't think me rude, Mr Warburg, but I've got to get on. We'd get through much more quickly if we didn't chat quite so much.'

First the remark dismays me. Then infuriates me. The nerve of it! She's one of the more garrulous of the nurses, normally burbles all the way through her duties. Teil says the morphine's made me somewhat loquacious. I asked Colin's candid opinion. He confirmed Teil's judgement. I hate the idea of boring people. Make conscious effort to talk less, and not about illness. Write a note to remind myself. Nearby, where I can see it.

Nurse Locksley rabbits on without the benefit of morphine! I'm the only one who's supposed to be seen but not heard.

'The urine looks a bit dark,' I blurt out, despite my resolutions. It's too much of a strain not to mention it.

'Yes,' Teil immediately agrees. 'I discussed it with Nurse Locksley.' She did? She said nothing to me about it. 'She looked at me as though I'm a simpleton. As though we should expect such things and accept them without question.'

'She doesn't think it's significant?'

'She appears to think I've only just realized you have a fatal disease, because of the blood in the urine!'

'What's that got to do with our trying to do something about it?'

'Damn all, as far as I'm concerned. She's obsessed with our not disturbing the doctors unnecessarily, as she sees it.' The week-end, of course.

'So what's the state of play?' I don't want to bleed to death when there's still life to be lived. Why should I?

'I've checked with Anna. It's safe to wait till Monday, when I can contact Liz.'

'It's not urgent?'

'No. Nothing to worry about, I'm told. Precisely how I was supposed to *know* that, I've no idea. My job's to see you live, as comfortably as I can arrange it, for as long as possible. Bearing in mind quality, rather than quantity, of life. You're still enjoying yourself, aren't you?'

'Yes, as a matter of fact I am.' I'm looking forward to my memento to Teil being delivered tomorrow. Villeroy-Boch 'Siena' pattern china. Fine-looking day today. Spring flowers to be seen. A release, however temporary, from too much aching and discomfort. Still look forward to the beautiful, the funny, the interesting, the fascinating, the wonderfully curious and the fair side of life. Well, why not? Why not another six months? Another year?

'Exactly what I thought. You shall have it. I'll make sure of that. I'll see to it the doctors look after you when needed. I'm completely indifferent to what Nurse Locksley thinks about bothering doctors. They've chosen that type of job. Occasionally it interferes with their weekends. Too bad.'

I still have my allies, my family. Teil and Colin looking out for me. Rooting for me. Want me around. The lunch tastes good.

SUNDAY, 9TH FEBRUARY

Skeleton staff. Skeleton! I enjoy Jean Sturway. Very cheerful. Brisk. Give and take of repartee.

'There we are, then. Everything satisfactory?'

'Yes, thank you. Still got a good deal to get through? Or are you able to get off on your own quite soon?'

'Quite soon, yes. Got through quite quickly, didn't we?' She's been talking to Rita Locksley.

'Very gratifying. I've got things to get on with as well, of course. So the sooner you and your colleagues can get through with me, the better off we shall be all round!' They imagine they're the only ones to have work to do!

Chief physio's due at two. I'd like to rest. Stay awake. Three. No sign of her.

'Seems to make a habit of being late,' Teil comments.

'She did help with the breathing. And arranging the pillows.'

'Jolly good. Hope she's as useful today. Then we'd better put her off till after Durstone, don't you think?'

'Probably. Let's see how we get on.'

Three-thirty. Still no sign of her. It's getting absurd! I see Teil's point.

Three-forty. Peremptory thump on the french windows. She marches in.

'So sorry to be a little late. Luncheon party. Just couldn't get my guests to understand.'

'I expected you at two.' I can't pretend her being an hour and forty minutes late is good enough. The Sunday appointment was her suggestion!

'Two? No, no. That's not right. Three.' I'm not going to argue. There's no point. I don't believe her, all the same. 'Right. Let's get on. What about those breathing exercises?'

'I've been doing them.' I'm on the defensive already. This woman's tiresome. 'I'll show you'. I'd better sound willing.

'Good! You *have* been doing well.' Seems genuine. Can't really tell. 'I'll show you what we need to do for the legs.' Series of instructions, somewhat complicated. Well meant, I don't doubt. Not as effective as the pillow juggling or the breathing. Peripheral. 'Can you remember all that?'

'Naturally. My mind is functioning perfectly well.' She's not the only one who can sound pert.

'Of course, Mr Warburg. I merely meant it's a lot to take in.' She's on the defensive herself. About time. 'Well, that's it for today. Shall we make a further appointment?'

'I'll get my wife,' I counter.

'My husband's off to the Durstone tomorrow week, Ms Ackroyd. I think it's best if I get in touch with you after he gets back.'

Teil makes smooth noises. I know she's simply putting her on hold. She feels chief physio's a disturbing influence.

Front doorbell. The china! Here in time for tea. I can hardly wait for Teil and Col to bring it in. I remember when we first saw it, how much we both liked it. It was too expensive then. Money has no meaning for me now. As long as Teil can manage. I want to give her the 'Siena' as a happy reminder of our marriage each time she eats.

'It's arrived, honey! We'll unpack it here, shall we?'

'Lovely.'

Colin staggers in with two large boxes. 'Here's the invoice, Mum.'

Teil's eyes narrow. The look of delight is replaced by a deep frown. 'They've put down the wrong price for the soup plates.'

I don't want to know about problems. Who cares about the price?

'Does it matter? Let's just enjoy it.' My memento to Teil. I don't want any hassle about it. See her register.

'Of course. I'll put this in the kitchen and sort it out later.' She turns to Colin, unwrapping the dinner plates. 'Let's set out three place settings for tea. And the creamer, the sugar pot and the teapot.'

Colin uncovers the teapot. I admire the shape, not just the pattern. The shapes are right.

'Isn't that lovely, pet?' Teil places the china on the tray in front of me. 'Come on, Colin. Pass the teacup.'

'There's a flaw in it. I'll just find another.' His sharp blue eyes appraise the cups. He passes up two more, then hands me one he considers perfect. 'This one will do.' Do? Will do? This isn't just some cheap earthenware set. It's proper china! 'Let me just see the saucer, Dad.'

I pass it back reluctantly. Don't want to know about defects. Can't see any myself.

'What's wrong with it, Col?' Teil has taken the rejected cup and examines it. 'I can't see anything.'

'Just feel the rim, Mum. Here, just look at these saucers. All nicked in the same place.'

'I see what you mean. Well, I feel what you mean! I can't see it, actually.'

'Once you know it's there, you can. I'll ring them up and deal with them for you, Mum.'

'I suppose so. In my office, then.'

A trail of discarded wrapping paper fills the room. Teil, looking somewhat disconsolate, brings one or two more pieces over to me.

'Why don't we just forget about the faults?'

'The trouble is, I can't, now I know. I don't want something imperfect from you.'

'Colin's just being over-fussy.'

'His eyes are too good! Well, you can hardly expect him not to say anything.'

It's spoilt. The whole occasion has been spoilt. Teil takes the china to the kitchen. They select flawless from flawed. I don't want it sorted out. Just want the china, complete, for Teil.

MONDAY, 10TH FEBRUARY

'I know what the physiotherapist maintains, but it's my back that may go, and then we'd be in quite a fix.' Teil does have these prejudices against some of the people who are trying to help me. 'I've worked out a perfectly satisfactory solution. All I have to do is lower the back-rest and remove a couple of pillows. You can lie back very easily. There's no need for all this business of pulling you down.'

'And how do I sit up?' It may work for lying down. I can't lie all day. I want some semblance of a normal life.

'We reverse the process. You heave yourself upright, using the monkey-pole to help you. I raise the back-rest and replace the pillows. Simple!'

'I suppose we'd better give it a try.' There's bound to be a snag. Teil's always saying there are things she can't do now.

'Actually, you'll be better off. It could help that tiny split on your sacrum.'

'You think that was caused by my being pulled down?'

'Partly, I've no doubt. Anyway, I can't pull you, so there's no choice. We can hardly get a nurse up just to help me ready you for the night!'

Exciting business development. New knitting magazine wants to use Teil's yarn gauge in their patterns.

'I have to work out manufacturing costs for the *Silver Gauge*. Then we can discuss policy together.'

I enjoy being involved with business activities. They're psychologically valuable to me. Give me a chance to take part in wordly affairs. In life! Some motivation to stay alive. I can still weigh up pros and cons for Teil.

I've done little recording for the Diary. Am somewhat depressed. Definitely fed up. Oppressed by the sheer extent and utter relentlessness of this disease. Evidently the cancer has no intention of giving up. Clearly I am, at least, considering the possibility. I find myself thinking that as long as I see the grandchild in, that's enough. For me. For Teil. Enough for everybody. Not suicide. Not my manner of doing things. I must just not try all *that* hard to sustain, let alone hang on to, life, the way so many people do. 'Ripeness is all' wrote the greatest writer of us all. Perhaps I'm ripe. At any rate for further pain. Not the dull ache that never seems far away. More pain. More actual pain.

I seem to cry quite often now. I've wept occasionally in the last six months, of course. Suffering. Frustration. But rarely. The last few days I've found myself crying easily. In all candour, I wonder why. It might seem obvious for one in my position. Confined to bed. To one room. Virtually immobilized. Some discomfort. Occasional pain. Still, I wonder why. Not self-pity, in my judgement – though that may not be the best for the purpose. I'm not worried about death. Or dying. Or pain. I think that's under control.

It isn't really sadness. I'm sad about leaving Teil. Sorry about my children. Particularly regret the grandchild. Represents continuity and so forth. But no, it isn't that.

I'm quite content for the most part. Enjoy myself. Often immensely. Often more than I've done before! Still, I cry over nothing. There's the difficulty of being held by Teil. I'm not easy to get at, lying between all these bits of furniture, surrounded by pillows and sheepskins. I cry over trivia, dropping a pencil. All right, it indicates helplessness. I could have picked it up myself with the pick-up stick. It didn't really happen because I'm so ill or diseased. It happened because I'm clumsy, or unlucky. There's no reason to cry. Is it a purely physiological phenomenon? At the stage my illness has reached? The terminal stage? I don't really know.

I'm hypersensitive, of course. Ridiculously concerned about the way I'm treated. How I'm talked to. Apparent behaviour of other people. Gets me irritable. Upset. That's what may lie behind all this tearfulness. I'm particularly sensitive to Teil's reactions. If she's short with me, or sharp, or brusque. A little impatient, perhaps, or takes too long to answer my bleep. Then the tears begin to flow. At least I falter a bit. Breathe hard. My voice breaks. I make a note to remind myself: don't expect Teil to be all that friendly before she's had a decent break. Hence, of course, the business of the Durstone.

Certainly I don't cry because I haven't done the things I wanted to. I wrote the books I wanted to, was satisfied with most of them. They weren't recognized sufficiently. Not my responsibility. And it's not because I haven't had a wonderful marriage for over thirty years. Or because I haven't been a caring, even an excellent, husband. Though that's for Teil to say. Or because I haven't been a good father. Perhaps for the children to say. Have no doubts myself. Perhaps I cry at the prospect of leaving Teil in the lurch, at the prematurity of my impending death.

Colin kindly put the two ancestor pictures in the long frames on either side of the 'Bluebell' pastel. They were relegated to a cupboard for many years. I like to see them now – Warburgs on the left, Raphaels on the right. I'll be an ancestor myself quite soon.

WEDNESDAY, 12TH FEBRUARY

Dawn. A new day. I seem to feel happier. A release, however temporary, from so much aching and discomfort. Relief from pain. Perhaps I'll feel cheerful again? As I have, so unusually for my normal self, for so much of the time since my illness.

I'm working hard on the Diary. Want to get a presentation off to a publisher before I leave for the Durstone. Chatto, I think. Carmen Callil. Think it's right for her. Exhausting. Will have to ask Teil to help prepare a synopsis and construct a letter. I hear her coming.

'What's on tonight? Anything good?' I always choose the TV programmes. Teil hasn't the time or energy. 'I just need something to unwind with!'

I don't feel like TV. Or video. Quite honestly, I just don't feel inclined. Too much jabber. Mostly mine, admittedly. Hardly the point. Know Teil's using the TV to shut me up.

'I don't really feel like watching TV.'

Teil's sitting in her easy chair, dressing-gowned. Relaxing. Can do that in the living-room. She looks surprised, somewhat perturbed.

'Shall I put on some music? Anything on the radio?'

Can't she bear to talk to me at all? I'm a bit fed up with the notion that I'm not to say anything. Not precisely 'Don't speak unless you're spoken to, little child', but her feelings are abundantly clear. Been checked out and confirmed by Colin. Everyone considers I gab too much. Benefit of morphine or whatever.

'Why don't you just go to the living-room and watch whatever you like?' I know she's got the old TV there. I feel somewhat fed up and dispirited. Possibly a bit tricky.

She departs for an hour or so. Comes back to see if I'd like company. I don't play ball.

'Why not go to bed? That's really what you want to do, isn't it?'

'You don't want my company?'

No need to take it so personally. Can't say I feel entirely unjustified in my attitude, expressed on the basis of her 'I'll only stay with you if you watch TV and don't talk' attitude. Possibly that's entirely unfair. May not be true. I strongly feel it is.

Something of a ding-dong. More on her side. I tend to stay,

perhaps surprisingly, quiet myself. Teil slanging away, then calming down. I defend myself with a type of shut-out mechanism. Might seem like sulking. Not so. I want her to leave me be. It's my room. Why not go?

She stays. Tries to coax me round, soothe the obviously extremely unsoothed breast. Attempts to bring down the level of tension. We're both in some sense to blame, presumably. Exactly why, I'm not sure. And in a sense both not to blame. She, poor woman, is grossly over-extended. I'm also over-extended, but in a somewhat different sense. Distinctly fed up with my situation, with what seems to me to be her irritable and resentful attitude to that. I'm quite well aware, of course, while she's hammering away, what she has to put up with. The demands of my disease. Entirely understood. Still, we're having a shindy, and a somewhat dangerous one at that. But she stays. Sticks it out. Tries to make it up with me. I don't respond. Not inclined to. It's not really personal hostility. I just feel numbed. Perhaps angry. I'm not entirely sure. Point is I'm no longer in this world. Not interested in what Auden, I believe, called 'Telegrams in Anger'. Can no more be bothered with anger than I can be bothered with patching it up. That explains it.

We eventually arrive at a sufficiently acquiescent frame of mind for Teil to go to bed. Not well disposed towards each other, but not badly either. Teil helps me into the lying position. I ponder the problems. Must cut down the droves of people visiting. How can she tolerate my talkabouts, as she calls them, if she has to jaw with all these others? I resolve to cut down the stream of helpers.

THURSDAY, 13TH FEBRUARY

Early start. Pleasant enough, considering the argy-bargy of the night before. Six. I put on light and open the hatch door, behind me on the left. Just about reach it. Open it wide. Signal I'm ready, and waiting, to be visited.

Teil appears within minutes. Breakfast together. Good discussion about trying to cut down covey of 'helpers'. Mary's day off. Golden opportunity to tackle Nurse Kalmett. I broach the subject immediately. 'I think, you know, that I can wash my top half myself.'

The set, almost resigned, expression on her face changes slightly. Flicker of interest. 'I think that's a good idea, Mr Warburg.' Thinks I should have done it all along? Then why push extra help on us! 'As long as you don't find it all too tiring.'

'I don't think so. And I can cream myself. And change my own shirt.'

'The more you can do for yourself, the better, of course.' She has a certain look of something akin to admiration. No, that's too strong. Of less resignation! 'Where's Mrs Warburg?'

'Hiding in her room.' I'm joking, but many a true word. . . . She's wondering whether the morphine's softened my brain!

I do the chores rather well. Doesn't tire me. Indeed, I revel in it. Feel quite elated. Teil and I both feel much better by lunchtime, from a psychological point of view. The load, each of our loads, has effectively been lightened. Last night's row has worked to the good, served a useful purpose, cleared the air. Eliminated excess people. Lunch is a pleasant meal. Friendly atmosphere. No doubt we shall overcome. I don't mean death, but the problems caused by dying.

I work on the Diary tapes. Try locating typing agencies in Yellow Pages. I must transcribe the tapes. Can't find one. There are none locally, I gather. Bleep Teil. She finds them under secretarial. I ring one.

'So you'd be able to get the work back to us within a week?'

'I can't promise. But usually we can.'

'And what about the cost? How much, for example, will it cost to transcribe one tape?'

'I really can't say before we've had one to go on.'

'And your service is completely confidential?'

Must check that out. Some very personal episodes on these tapes. The woman at the other end becomes very irritable. I can't

off-hand understand why. Our conversation deteriorates badly.
I'm a prospective customer, after all! Her attitude simply won't
do. I find myself being irritable back.

Colin, very charmingly, produced a sweet little portable computer last time he came, so I can write in bed. Teil can set it all up
for me, show me how to work it. I'll use that, perhaps. See about
it later. Tomorrow, maybe.

FRIDAY, 14TH FEBRUARY

Rather a sweet card in the post yesterday. Not signed or anything. 'I can't give you anything but love,' it says. Postmark's
Southampton. Colin, I take it. I'm a bit startled, and surprised.
Apparently he forgot to sign it. I know his memory's rather
poor, but I find it extraordinary that there's no personal message
and no signature!

The mystery has been solved. Teil tells me it's a Valentine and
therefore naturally not signed. I don't think she realizes I hadn't
grasped it. I think it's the first Valentine I've ever had, so I'm
particularly touched. I ask Teil to put this endearing and loving
card with Minnow's and the Rs' among the family photos alongside my bed.

Work hard today. Synopsis of the Diary. First draft of a long
letter. Post includes a reply from Century Hutchinson, improv-
ing somewhat on terms of the original contract for the macrobiotic cookbook. Not very much, as they concede. 'Hard times
for publishers,' they say. Even harder times for writers.
Especially this writer!

'What do you think?' I ask Teil. They're keen to have the book.
I'd like to feel I'm still contributing.

'I'll sleep on it.' She doesn't sound very pleased. She was eager
enough when she first approached them. I can't really see what's
changed.

'It would be nice to do the book.' Perhaps my last chance to complete a book. The Diary, after all, is bound to be finished by Teil.

'Of course it would. A very worthwhile project. But you're not able to eat a macrobiotic diet.'

'But you've invented flourless bread. And pastry. And biscuits. And you've got all those recipes we tested . . .'

'I know. I'll think about it.'

I'd relish doing the cookbook, look forward to sampling new recipes. Testing them. Even if the diet doesn't save me, it's helped. Cut down on pain. Given us hope. Might have done the trick, if it hadn't been for radiotherapy!

'They sound as though they'd like other material to consider.' That might interest her.

She dismisses it. 'Only when we've come to terms on this contract.' She'll have plenty of time to do more books, of course. It's different for me. We'll discuss the cookbook further, naturally. But I suspect we shan't accept the publisher's offer.

I must just mention my feelings about my work on the Diary. Doing it at such speed, and at such pressure, and with such fluency that, quite candidly, and I hope without blasphemy, I see it as, somehow, God's work. I don't want to sound pompous. Certainly, I don't want to sound blasphemous! It really does feel like that.

SATURDAY, 15TH FEBRUARY

I simply must not work so hard, even though I'm on to an excellent project. One can't always arrange these things. It isn't always you who writes the book; the book occasionally writes you. Don't feel I have much control over the set-up. Must put presentation into a form suitable for a publisher. Colin's computer!

'I'll set up the portable for you now, shall I?' Teil busies herself expertly. Excited. I prattle a little. 'I've got to read the instructions, honey. Could we just have a bit of hush?' Rather impatient of her. Churlish to grudge me my only contact with the world at large.

'Have you checked that the St John's ambulance is coming at the right time?'

She looks up. Seems unaware I'm leaving Monday. 'St John's? Oh, you mean Ambucare. Yes, all taken care of. They sound excellent.'

'Did you ask about the springing on their vehicle?'

'There's no need to worry, honey. They have the very latest type of ambulance. All mod cons. I told you. I made thorough inquiries.'

I'm still nervous about going. But I must go. Know that. For my sake as much as Teil's. Still apprehensive. Know perfectly well it's a pleasant enough hospital, as such places go. Still, it's difficult to take before it actually happens. I'll get by when it comes to it. Maybe even enjoy it.

I can't use the computer. Write by hand. Not displeased with the result. Need more time to finish. Arrange supper for seven. Corn, broad beans and rice, custard and blackcurrant tart. Served on our new china.

Teil's offered to put the synopsis and letter on her computer. Prints it out for me. She can't manage extracts at this stage. I understand that, try to dub tape to send. Use new twin-deck cassette recorder Teil's bought me for the purpose. Think I can manage. She'll have to check. Somewhat confusing, all these new bits of machinery.

Suddenly I feel very anxious about Teil's health. My demanding too much of her. Requiring demonstrations of love. I dread the approaching parting. Angry about it. Resentful. Reminds me of being sent off to a boarding-school, aged eight. Can't stand a suitcase in a room.

'Right. I'll put it outside the door. Just off for a few minutes to get some air.'

Out of the blue, or into the yellow of the room perhaps, there is another squabble. Sparked off by its getting through to me that I can't go out. It then occurs to me that I can't go into the garden, can't walk round, as we used to do. Bitter I cannot see the glade we planted. Tour the orchard. Walk up and down the terraces. All forbidden to me. A prisoner. No means of escape that I can see. Take it out on Teil in sulky immaturity.

'Maybe I can organize a wheelchair when you get back.'

'Who's going to get me in and out of it?'

'I'm not quite sure. . . .'

I've been in this room for some weeks now. Never moved from the bed. Just lying here. I examine the furnishings, stare at what I can see through the french windows. So busy getting used to this, preparing for it, I haven't understood what's been happening. Not at the unconscious level anyhow. I'm shocked at the true position. Stuck here.

'You just can't be bothered. As long as you get out!'

'I don't think you quite understood what I was saying . . .'

'You mean I can't think straight any more?'

'I just meant. . . .' She hardly endears herself to me suggesting my mind's not functioning either. 'You're very tired. You take all these drugs. It must be difficult to understand . . .'

'My mind is functioning perfectly well. Go on, go out and get your air. I'll read the print-outs in the meantime.' I take the sheets she's brought for me. 'If, of course, you think I can still read.'

SUNDAY, 16TH FEBRUARY

I wake even earlier than yesterday, depressed about the row. I perceive that my apprehension, dread, even resentment, about going to the Durstone is simply a reflection of childhood memories. Feel very badly. And there's Teil! Three in the morning.

'I'm sorry, pet. I know it was my fault.'

'Never mind. I woke up because I suddenly remembered you haven't got the intercom.'

'I turned down having it.' She doesn't even realize it's my own fault.

'Did you? Well, it's not a good idea. She puts the phone beside me. 'How are the pillows?' Fluffs them up for me.

'The whole thing reminds me of boarding-school,' I explain eagerly. 'I suddenly grasped what it's all about.'

'It's only for a week. You might even find the break useful yourself. Gives you a chance to see some other people. And a change of scene. That's hard to arrange here.'

Amiable chat. We part, friends again. I sleep for several hours.

I hand corrections of synopsis and letter print-outs to Teil for her to read.

'I think we need to do a little work on these. They're both rather long, I feel.'

'I suppose they are. There's quite a bit to say.'

'Let me see if I can cut it all down a little. I won't be long. We can always go back to your version if you prefer it.'

Teil reduces length of new versions dramatically. I agree the changes.

'We still have to choose extracts. Funeral directors?' That might make an amusing episode to read. Doesn't all have to be gloom and doom. A little light jocularity won't come amiss.

'Yes, I think that's very funny.'

'We'd better dub it. Send them roughly half a tape.'

Teil can post it while I'm in the Durstone.

MONDAY, 17TH FEBRUARY

Nine hours' sleep! I feel very much better. Suspect key is presentation ready to send off. Whichever publisher it goes to. No more need to work during the night. Can simply concentrate on the Diary tapes during the day.

'I've made notes for all the things we need to pack.' Good system. Write down everything as I think of it. Teil crosses off each chore as it's done.

'I think everything's under control. I'm sending three sheepskins and I've sorted out enough pills for one day. I know perfectly well they might not stock MST at all, let alone in large quantities.'

'Thought you said I wasn't on large quantities?' They all lie to me. Even Teil.

'You're not, as far as your type of illness is concerned. But you're not going to a hospice, which is used to such disease. You're going to a small, private hospital. They haven't necessarily even heard of MST. Worthing said so!'

She's right, of course. Best not to take any chances. Teil packs. I concentrate on remembering everything I might need.

'I'd like to take my books. And a Bible.' That's one advantage of writing. One's life's work is easily transportable.

'The ambulance is due soon. We'd better have lunch.'

It arrives while I'm still eating. I like to take my time. One of the things I can still enjoy.

'Don't worry, sir. We'll load your luggage and wait for you to finish.'

Two young, reasonably strong-looking men come in, carrying a tarpaulin stretcher. They insert it expertly under me, then lift me up, transfer me to the wheeled stretcher, and so into the ambulance. Quick, easy, comfortable. Teil adds my support pillow and a sheepskin to cover it. See the outside of our home again. Fleetingly. Doors close. I'm off.

Greetings as I'm wheeled down the Durstone corridor. Familiar faces. Helpfulness. Like last July. Settle in my room. Nurses follow chief physio's diagram for the pillows behind me. Hospital sheepskins turn out to be only one, and that an artificial one. The real McCoy's ensconced behind me. Ring Teil within half an hour. Forgotten watch. And earplugs. Need those. Young man in room next to me very noisy. Motor-cycle accident. Poor chap is badly hurt.

Supper at six. Look forward to the food this time. Grapefruit segments. Ham omelette. Lettuce. Mashed potatoes. Fruit salad and ice-cream. Rather enjoy it. Bit on the plastic side, but nicely served. They try hard to please.

Talk of suppositories instead of disembowelling. Turn that

down flat. Very tired now. Look forward to some leisure in the next few days. Must get some sleep in before MacKnife appears.

I wake up. Donald MacKieff's standing at the foot of the bed in a formal grey suit, navy tie. Makes him look trimmer than he is. Features still sharp. Beginnings of a paunch. Medium height. Hair just greying. Searching brown eyes. Every inch the successful consultant. I expected him in his green theatre gear. No late operations, apparently.

We get on splendidly, Christian names from the start. Bit of chat and banter. Questions and answers. Of considerable help. Raise the business of the catheter getting bunged up.

'I don't think the catheter's the problem. Here, let me show you. It's just a question of dislodging a little mucus forming at the top of the tube.'

An expert wiggle. I take note.

'How long d'you think I've got?' I put in now. Know he's often too optimistic. 'I really need to know, so that I can pace myself on the Diary.'

'I'd think about six months.' I can see that's a genuine estimate. Take off a couple of months, perhaps. About right. Check.

'That's realistic, is it? Not your usual optimism?' He did maintain I had two years at least.

'I think that's about right. It's quite impossible to be sure, you know. But that's my informed opinion.'

'So I can expect till roughly August?'

'I would say so, yes.' Interesting. Precisely Lazenby's prediction. So there's time for the book to be taken up. If it appeals.

'Perhaps you can give me an idea of the last episode, so that I can write the end before it happens, so to speak.'

'You mean the sort of thing that could happen?'

'Yes, I've no idea. No experience. Not like you.'

'Well, let's see. There are at least a dozen possibilities to choose from! Renal failure, I think. Some sort of infection due to the catheter. That might gradually kill off your character.'

Fiction, of course. Can't actually write my own end! Scenario according to MacKnife: the man becomes ill, then semicomatose, then comatose. Followed by death. Whatever actually happens in my case. Can arrange for the character to write the Diary until several days before his death. Then he would stop. I'd write an epilogue, using Teil's style, as though she were doing it. She can help with that. The Diary itself would be written in my style. Quite distinctly me. Very useful chat. Candid discussion. No holds barred.

'Just one thing, Jeremy.' Sombre tone now.

'Yes?' Has he decided I haven't got all that long, after all?

'Best not to bring up the matter of your dying, or the manner of your possible death, with the nurses.' He looks a little embarrassed.

'Of course not, Don. If that's what you wish.' Surely nurses are used to death?

'They find such a subject rather unsavoury. They like to think they're curing people. Death is a sort of failure on their part.' My death. Their failure. I mustn't talk about my death to the nurses because they can't handle such a subject. Black humour.

'Naturally I shan't bring it up if that's a problem. Silent as the grave!' He doesn't smile. 'But I still don't know precisely how people die. Could you just fill in a few details? You know, what exactly happens in the last few days, the last few hours. That sort of thing.'

'I'm sure you can use your imagination. You're a writer, after all.'

He's prepared to talk about broad strategy but is curiously reticent when it comes to actual cases. Well, there we are. Not too keen on discussing death himself, perhaps. Keener on discussing possible surgical intervention for relief of pressure on the nerves. Stop the decompression of the spine and restore some movement. He'll look into it with his colleagues.

Question is, would a neurological operation lengthen or shorten my life? It would hardly keep me alive, with half a dozen lesions now, all over the place. It might, after all, just fuck up the Diary. I might suddenly find I'd done badly with such an operation. Write less, not more. No way do I want that!

Lent Don my copy of *A Woman's World*, together with the *Cosmo* review. Told him that Warner Brothers are considering a film using the concept. He's interested, I think.

Some old, familiar faces. One rather elderly staff nurse, in charge of the night nursery department. She's always extraordinarily pleasant, which is a comfort to me. I take to her. She calls me 'young man'. I call her 'my lady'.

'What time is it?'

A nurse from Lancashire provides the time of night. I need to know because of the morphine. Hope Teil has sent my watch.

'My lady' comes in to say good morning. 'Still working on your book?'

'No rest for the writer!'

I'm a little achy, in spite of 120 mg MST. Hard bed, presumably, harder than the one at home. Cot sides make it easier for me to move. They've installed a monkey-pole. There's a proper cradle over my feet to keep the bedding off.

Telephone comes into action at nine. Ring Teil. Tell her Don's prognosis, and his ideas on decompression – or is it compression? – of the spine. There's a possibility of restoring bowel and bladder functions. She doesn't make much of it. Too tired, perhaps.

Eventful day. A bath! They have a solid plastic hoist here, a bucket seat that can be swivelled over a bathtub and then lowered down with me sitting inside it. Two nurses and a male attendant help me. I luxuriate in the water. Wash all over. Bliss! Very refreshing and psychologically helpful. Can't be done at home.

Haircut organized. Will save Teil trouble if I can get that done. Hard to get the semi-crewcut which makes me look my best. Just cutting will give Teil one less chore.

Lunch of consommé, lemon sole, chocolate ice-cream. Teil hasn't had to cook it. Tea one and half hours later, my particular tipple here being hot water and honey, washing down a scone and butter. I doze a good deal between meals, tired from the trip, from working on the presentation of the Diary. Pleasant to relax.

Clear I'll have to spend time in the new nursing home. I notice

the sheer number of staff involved in looking after me. Impossible, intolerable, that Teil should do all that. She could visit me at
The Elms for breakfast, lunch and for the evening. We could have
a reasonable time. The chores involved in looking after someone
as ill as I am are simply too much for one person to undertake.
Further deterioration would make it quite out of the question.

WEDNESDAY, 19TH FEBRUARY

Very stiff back. Mattress just too damned hard. Need a foam
mattress added, like at home.

I cream my back, take pills. Half an hour later I'm still very
sore. Pillow against my back. Still not the answer. I summon a
nurse. Her field, presumably.

'I'll do my best to get one, Mr Warburg.'

Two male attendants bring a foam mattress and help to slide it
under me. Heavenly.

A lady hairdresser appears, as promised, and proceeds to do
her best. Haven't seen myself in the mirror yet.

'All neat and tidy now.' A pretty, young-looking nurse with
smooth, taut skin. 'I'll see if I can find a mirror for you.'

She's as good as her word.

I put on a special daylight sleeping mask, a present from Mad.
It's convenient. Ask the nurse to wake me at half-past two so I can
record the Diary. Must get it done. Still enormously tired. God
knows why exactly. Getting this book on the road, perhaps.
Moving at quite a rate of knots for someone supposedly as ill as I
am. Well, why not? The more I work, the better from a psychological point of view. If I can get this book done within a couple
of months and last for six, why, I might see it published! Something to live for, to keep me going rather longer. So be it. The
Lord be praised.

Donald MacKieff comes at around four-thirty. He's not too
perturbed about the blood-filled blister that has suddenly
appeared on my heel.

'Nothing to worry about. Just keep it dry.'

'And what about this business of an operation?'

'I think that we're a little on the late side for that. Perhaps early January would have done it.' Too late. Well, I shall never know what would have been best.

'So, I shan't know whether I should have had it done until I see God.'

'True enough. Let me know what He says, will you? For future reference.'

'I'll do that little thing. Just listen out – I might have a whole heap of useful information for you.'

'Good. There's no need for concern, for the moment. You're doing very well.'

'I'm adopting a fictional approach, Col. MacKnife is helping me with the scenario for the last entries.'

'So it isn't what's going to happen to you? You might still recover?'

'Not really, Col. Too much cancer for that.'

'We needn't give up hope.'

'In the area of miracles, I'm afraid. Rare, and not necessarily desirable.'

Dear son. Wants to hang on to the notion of my survival for a little longer. I don't want to press the so-called facts too hard. Not invariably correct, anyway. Leave it at that.

Supper starts with fruit cocktail. Ham and pineapple. Meat kindly cut up for me. Followed by crème caramel, cheese and biscuits.

'We've come to see to your blister, Mr Warburg.' Cheery couple of nurses. 'Bit on the purple side.' Don didn't make much of this latest development to me. Made more of it to the nurses, evidently.

Teil rings. 'A blister? How could there be a blister? Haven't been walking, have you?'

'Nothing like that! Unless you count having a bath yesterday as walking on water! I'm not clear why it's happened. I don't think they know. Nothing to fret about, I'm sure of that.'

Take notes. Dictate a tape. Cream myself. Everything but sleep. Uncomfortable. Foam helps. Breakfast stirrings bring new faces, fruit juice, hot water and honey. Personal brown bread toasted. Paper – and morphine! – at nine. Chat with Teil.

Scottish nurse at ten – her name escapes me. She's come to see to my blister. Quite substantial. Somewhat disconcerting.

'Nothing to worry about, Mr Warburg. It'll heal in no time.'

Sister Erskine is in charge. She's briskly efficient, somewhat brusque, but reasonably pleasant. Not like 'my lady' though. I always prefer the plump, older types. 'I'm just drawing out the liquid. Then we'll need to leave it open to the air. That gives it a chance to heal. We'll have to position the cradle carefully.'

'I see.'

'I think we should arrange for you to lie on your left side, to help keep the pressure off your bottom. Avoids bedsores, you see.' No ripple mattress here. 'Then we'll come and turn you on to your other side. All right?'

I suppose so. The split on my sacrum has increased, apparently. Been dragged, rather than lifted, on this bed. Teil's right about the back-rest.

I lie on my side for an hour. Frankly, tumour starts hurting a good deal. Sit up for lunch. Record my latest tape. Nurse Meanley is to come shortly to lay me on my right side. My body position, now, is determined by the vagaries and whims of my backside. Such is hospital, and cancerous, life. I'm getting uncomfortable and buzz to be moved.

'I'm afraid I can't move you by myself, Mr Warburg.'

Try to shift myself over as best I can. I'm acutely uncomfortable. Buzz and convey this.

'Yes, I did hear you the first time. I'll be back with someone in five minutes.'

Somewhat hostile. Why? It's her job, isn't it? What can I do if they insist on putting me in painful positions? No sign of her. I buzz again after three quarters of an hour, try taking my mind off the pain by listening to the Diary. Good work, thank God, which should be fun, especially if I'm alive to enjoy publication.

'I'm extremely uncomfortable. I really would appreciate your helping me into a better position. I can't manage it myself.'

'I told you, Mr Warburg. I need some help.'

Leaves me for another hour.

Sister Banes, afternoon shift, finally appears. Nurse Meanley's gone off duty.

'Thank goodness you've come. This is really getting excruciatingly painful. I was told half an hour originally. It's two and a half hours now!'

'I'm so sorry. But you do understand, don't you? I wasn't on duty when all this was arranged. It's not my responsibility.' Resigned. Explains that she and her colleagues were very busy in the theatre.

I'm incensed, absolutely furious. To add unnecessary pain when I have so much already. To treat me badly in my state. I'll leave! Shan't stay where I'm not wanted.

'When will Mr MacKieff be in?'

Don will look after me, sort out this surly, grudging lot. Dictatorial incompetents. Bloody-minded charlatans. Self-important tyrants. Self-satisfied autocrats. OK, they're busy, overstretched. I'm a redundant patient in their eyes. But when one's dying of cancer, I suppose one's entitled not to be treated like a piece of shit, even inadvertently. Unless, of course, one's behaving like one. To the best of my knowledge I've got on well with the rest of the staff. If not, I'd like to be told, given reasons.

Not best pleased. I'm inclined, in fact, to stir up a bit of shit myself. Ask to be helped into a sitting position now, half an hour before supper. Food-serving rush then takes precedence over everything. I'll refuse to be turned in future, let my bottom get sore. Better than this portentous handling I've been subjected to. Makes one even more ill. Can hardly afford that myself.

Don comes at about seven. Genial. 'How are you?'

'Livid with rage.'

'Really? Why's that?'

'Well, very irritable.'

'I see. But why?'

'It's too late. I'm really too tired to go into it. It's all somewhat futile anyway. I'd rather write it up for the Diary than go over it with you now.'

He lets it go at that. Grasps I'm annoyed. Has a pretty shrewd idea why, I suspect. Probably knows all about it already.

'Right. D'you mind if I hang on to *A Woman's World* if I can't finish it by the time you leave? I'm rather hard pressed at work.'

He's made a start, obviously, and is interested enough to continue. OK as long as he sends it back within a week or so, with candid comments.

'Incidentally, I thought you might like to know I've taken note of what you said. I've decided not to operate on the patient I mentioned to you. The kidney cancer case.'

'Why?' I said, looking at him. 'Too tricky for you?'

He was half-way out of the room, but came back again like a whippet. 'You can't say things like that to a surgeon,' he said, amused, but slightly shocked.

'OK, I know,' I said. 'Just fun. But from what you told me, it did sound a waste of time. With a cancerous mass like that on his kidney, and a whole parcel of secondaries. Seems to me he's better off with your doing nothing. His best chance of living longer.' This is almost certainly true. Surgeons often want to *do* something, but it's by no means always right that they should. The cancer may have gone too far for that. Surgery may simply make it worse. Interferes with the body's immune system. Possible I should never have had the operation, myself. 'Did you ask him?'

'He refused to accept my diagnosis. Simply shut it out. As far as he's concerned, there isn't any problem.'

'You make it up, I know. All that rubbish about scans and X-rays!'

Wake up, shirt sodden with perspiration. Nurse produces a new one, helps me dry. I sleep on and off till breakfast.

I'm sure I can finish the Diary within two months of leaving here. Even if Don's on the optimistic side, I should get it in good shape for Teil by then. It will leave hardly anything for her to do. I'll fictionalize the end. Teil can do the epilogue. Give a little help with transcription, revision, editing . . . I can finish the job quite quickly. This may be the one that gets off the ground. Who knows?

Very cold out, but sunny. Teil confirms she'll visit me. I'm ridiculously pleased! Don't notice chores. The day increases in loveliness. Groom myself for my wife. Comb my hair. Use talc. Can hardly wait to see her.

She arrives at eleven-thirty and stays most of the day. Brings fresh food for me. Grapes, tangerines, bananas. Some more chocolate biscuits. A fresh brown loaf. More sheepskins. Tape from the Rs. I'm so pleased to see my wife, so delighted to have her company. You'd think I hadn't seen her for years! Enchanted to have her here. Quite absurd.

She leaves. They put me on my side again. I manage half an hour, but that's enough. 'Just put me back into a sitting position,' I insist. Ring Teil. Not because I'm afraid she hasn't returned safely. Just to reorientate myself. I was disorientated by her visit. Just one of those psychological quirks. She suggests I increase MST to rid myself of extra pain. Trouble is, will it rid me of the Diary as well? That would matter more to me than the pain.

SATURDAY, 22ND FEBRUARY

Wake up to find myself surrounded by hordes of nurses.

'What's wrong? Did I buzz you?'

'You fell asleep again, Mr Warburg, while you were drying yourself. We just took a peek, and there you were, half dressed.'

'I'm sorry about that.'

They cream my back, put my new shirt on, adjust my pillows, generally tend to me. I ache quite badly. Discuss increasing the MST. They agree with Teil.

Up the dose by 30 mg. Teil says don't mess about with 10 mg amounts. What are they for, then? Make a note to ring Peter Worthing. 'Drop in the ocean,' he'll say. Brenda's on 200 mg. Not much, even then. So, not to worry. But I do. Worry that I may get rid of the book with the pain. Quite frankly, if I have to choose, I'll choose the book. Better ring Teil tomorrow as well as Worthing. No point in my having pain as acute as this in the middle of the night. Just a drop in the ocean. Let's pray I can sleep until about six.

Just before six. Not too bad. Hot water and honey. Phone's not on till nine. Why do they start so late? And finish so early? I'd like a chat with Teil. Ring at nine. Find myself rather tearful and lugubrious. No idea why.

'Hello, Jifda.' It's Mad, telling me about her new job. I'd like to understand. Can't concentrate. TV instead of video. So glad she's pleased. I want the best for my children. Can no longer help them. Did my bit. Thank God I did my bit. Feel content about fatherhood. Not like Fred. Not like my father Fred. Wish I'd had a proper father.

'Delighted it's all working out so well, Minnow. Have a bottle of champagne on me. Ask Gill to join you. Drink a glass for me.'

Ring Teil, to reassure her about my tearfulness. 'It's nothing, pet. Just all this pain. Seeing you yesterday.'

'I've ordered the ambulance to bring you back. Monday at half-past eleven. You'll be back for lunch!'

'I look forward to that.' I just want to be with Teil, that's all. Just want to be with Teil.

Something occurs to me as I'm talking to Teil. I don't mention it to her, but it occurs to me. I elaborate on it in my own mind.

I'm no longer part of the ordinary world. I don't just mean cancer. It's partly the paralysis that cuts one off. To some extent.

I'm no longer part of normal, everyday activities, whatever the reason. Can't share in the rough and tumble, the give and take, of everyday life. I'm ultra-sensitive, easily upset by badinage, jocular ribbing, or maybe slight offence or rudeness. Relatively trivial matters. What used to be a joke takes on the air of an attack, a friendly insult turns into a deadly thrust. My family and friends have to reckon with this. I don't expect, or want, special behaviour, but need more than the usual measure of politeness, attention, concern.

Makes me a strain on others, as they are on me. Can't take any genuine part in ordinary talk or discussion. Politics, issues of the day, the ethical and moral concerns, the dilemmas of one's society − are not for me, any of them. The whole world seems absurd, inaccessible, pointless, futile, irrelevant, a barrier between one's wanting to be, and being, involved. The world doesn't make much sense, seems crass, and I'm withdrawn from it. Preparing to be gone. Gone to a different one. I have other concerns and considerations, other criteria and needs, other wishes and desires. I'm lonelier than before, particularly among my loved ones. Unwilling to offend them, unable to make significant contact with them. A matter for some sorrow, stretching even my sense of humour a shade too far.

My loved ones are, unconsciously at least, aware of, tolerant of, my difficulties. No friction between husband and wife, father and son, father and daughter. And for that, at least, God be thanked and praised.

SUNDAY, 23RD FEBRUARY

Can't manage the Sunday paper now. Too heavy, in more senses than one! Order a soft-boiled egg for breakfast. Absurd. Can't eat it. Ah, I know. It reminds me of our Sunday snack, our soft-boiled eggs on Sunday afternoons. No more.

'Hello, honey. How are things? Is the pain any better?'

'It's not too bad today. Did you have a good lunch?'

'Very pleasant. We missed you.'

Yes . . . well. 'The St James' people or whoever are coming at eleven-thirty tomorrow!'

'The ambulance? Yes. Everything's ready at this end. See you soon.'

Tomorrow. Home again tomorrow!

Spend the day watching TV. Can't concentrate on much. Odd. What I still like best is athletics. I still enjoy these people running round as fast as they can, jumping as high as they can, or the greatest length they can. Can't be bothered to analyse exactly why. Perhaps a form of compensation for my own physical disabilities.

Donald MacKieff arrives. 'I don't think we should change the catheter. It's working perfectly well. Never change anything that's working is my motto!' Hope he's right.

'What about this pot-belly? What's all that about?'

'Just loss of muscle tone, I think. They atrophy if they're not used. Don't worry about it.'

'The pain seems to have increased a good deal.'

He makes no real response to that. Nothing to be said, presumably.

'I'd get in touch with the hospice again. It's not really my department. I'm just a urologist, you know.'

I know. He's agreeable, compassionate. My voice falters a little. I even shed a tear or two. The pain is rather intense. It's not only that. I shan't see Don again. Doesn't take much to reckon that. He senses it, too. But – I like the man. I'll miss the badinage. Enjoy his company. Appreciate his ability to face my death and talk to me about it. As time draws in one is aware, increasingly aware, how few people are left one in this world. Kind man. Mentions how brave I've been. Right from the start, when he first diagnosed the cancer.

Always difficult to know whether one's being brave. Simply a matter of expediency, perhaps. One remains cheerful on the face of it. Possibly the best way of dealing with difficulties of this kind. Good of him to mention bravery. I believe he means it. Sees people trying to cope with cancer every day. I feel the honour he is doing me.

Don leaves for work in another hospital, to see to people who appear to me to be much worse off than I am.

MONDAY, 24TH FEBRUARY

Only five. Pain still with me. Aching still intense. Can't seem to get on top of it. Take more pills. Makes very little difference. A word or ten with Worthing indicated. See whether the backside and the foot can sensibly be traded off with the trunk.

Breakfast, and almost immediate nursing aid. Two girls I've never seen before. Part-timers, possibly. Asked to be disembowelled and packed early. Just as well. No sooner through than the ambulance arrives, a good hour early.

Nurses grossly mishandle me. 'No! Don't lift me. . . .' They lift me up and don't support my spine, to take off some piddling pair of pants. Pull me down the bed, creating havoc for my backside, I've no doubt. Excruciating pain. Try to wave goodbye as I'm wheeled down the corridor. No strength.

Last time I left in a wheelchair, thinking I had a chance of several years of life. Leaving presents, laughing. Not this time. In much greater pain than when I came. Not all good memories of the stay. No chance for presents. Won't be here again.

Sleep on the way home. Exhausted. Don't remember the trip. Glimpse my front door. A smiling, friendly Teil to welcome me. Arms open to receive me. The bed prepared. My room much as I left it. Lunch ready to be served on flawless china.

'I've set up a better system for you to contact me. I think the mobile phone might be too difficult for you to reach.'

'Yes?' Reach me? Why does she have to reach me?

'Actually a baby alarm. I've fixed the loudspeaker part above you, using the monkey-pole. It's switched on, and I can hear you through my end of it. It works through the mains. I can even hear you in the stable block.'

Teil's in charge again. I feel much safer.

Not a good start. Wake at two, in great pain. A good deal worse than I've had at any time since all this began. Must get in touch with Worthing. Quite a good man. Well, any port in a storm.

Other things might be involved. The way those last two nurses handled me. The artificial sheepskin they put behind me. May be easier to wash, but they do nothing for the cancerous back. That terribly hard bed. Just hope the next dose of MST will see the pain off.

Nurse Kalmett – a sight for sore eyes. 'They've made a terrible mess of your backside, haven't they? Only a small nick when you left. Quite a big slit now.'

'What about the blister?'

'I've no idea how you've got that.' Teil's arranged a makeshift cradle. 'We'll get it back to normal in no time. Don't worry.'

'I thought hospitals were supposed to know how to cope with all these things?'

'They always make a mess of bedsores.' Nurse Kalmett's resigned acceptance of the limited usefulness of hospitals is a surprise to us. 'I'll come back early this evening. Make sure that blister's on the mend.'

Good of her.

Liz arrives. 'We could start using the sixty milligram pills. Try taking three. You'll have less swallowing problems.'

Even I can see that the extra 30 mg won't make much difference.

I spend the afternoon asleep. Don't seem able to do anything else. Dimly aware of Teil coming in to see me. Her birthday. Not much of one. Know this arrangement can't last for very long. Makes me unhappy.

Teil makes a special supper. TV is depressing, so we turn it off. The atmosphere between Teil and me is good. Loving. Companionable. Soul mates. Just as before this awful illness. It's all that matters.

But all the time I sense this can't go on. I'll have to go again. But where? The Elms won't be ready till mid-April at the earliest. How can Teil cope for two more months? Finish the Diary and then depart. Using 'depart' in a somewhat euphemistic sense. Not suicide. Just that I shan't make an effort to hold on to the steering-wheel myself.

WEDNESDAY, 26TH FEBRUARY

The pain is terrible. Have to take more MST. Too much pain is counter-productive. In the end, doesn't help one's work. Distorts one's judgement. Better additional tiredness, weariness, than allowing negative feelings into one's writing – as happened, say, in the case of *1984*. Admirable the way Orwell wrote as he was dying. And wrote well. Still, in my view, any honest, percipient reader can hardly fail to notice he was slowly failing himself. The ideas remain – lovely, stimulating, original, truthful. But through the style one hears the auguries of death.

The writing, I find, is often permeated with dullness, with a loss of energy, a loss almost of will. So, what could undoubtedly have been a great book is only a fine one. That's not to be sniffed at. But it's not by any manner of means as good as *Animal Farm*. That's his great book, the one he wrote before illness overtook him.

It might well be said: this man's dying while he's doing his Diary. So why should he escape the charge of writing like a dying man? And that's the point, isn't it? The man is entirely aware of what is happening, is perfectly capable of writing about it in a fresh and, perhaps, enduring way. Because the subject-matter is all too familiar. And that's its strength. The Diary should convey accurately the thoughts, the feelings of a dying man, making it possible for the reader to empathize, to understand. Sympathize with the articulated gestation, labour and birth of the Diary. Blood, sweat and tears!

Doze most of the day. Through the evening. Through TV. Morphine's putting me to sleep. Notice there's something wrong with the urinary system. Of no great importance. Double the dose of MST of only a few days ago. If that doesn't knock things out a good deal, nothing else will.

THURSDAY, 27TH FEBRUARY

Another bad start. Woken by discomfort – pain, to put it bluntly. Cream myself, careful not to change position. Exacerbates the pain. Sleep fitfully till four. Pain starts in again. After all that MST!

Take Coproximol and Diazepam. Not much headway. Teil comes in at six, bearing breakfast. Not interested, but so glad to see her. Drawn curtains show a fine day outside.

Terry Armitage this morning. Gentle. Considerate. Talks to me and not over me. Terry and Madame Curie clean me and disembowel me.

'You're looking rather poorly,' Mary Houlder's saying as she slowly, gently washes me. Notices I'm knackered. 'Best not to work too hard, I would think. Try to take it easy.'

I take this philosophically. She means well. Can't grasp that what makes me tick is precisely what she thinks will make me untick. She's no idea what I'm about. However, our relationship is based on mutual respect. Well, why not? She may be un-comprehending about the sort of person I am, but she seems to care for me. Bound to say that's one of the best medicines I can now have.

Back again in the evening, soothing and solacing. Someone else tomorrow, to give them a turn. Turn? That matters more than me? Have to consider hiring Mary privately.

Very disturbed night. Wake frequently. Considerable pain, in spite of the whole box of tricks. Can't get the pain under control. Continues inexorably. Losing the battle for pain control. Can't afford that.

Must change my priorities. Death is nearer than I thought. Than MacKnife thought! He was optimistic, as usual. My affairs will need to be in order. Think they are. I've worked on that.

Crux of the matter is the Diary. I'll have to leave Teil in complete control. Leave it to her, as best I can. Preferably in a viable, editable condition, so she won't have too much of a time putting it together in a publishable form. Fortunate to have such a loving editor to leave it to. She'll do whatever still needs to be done. Hope God spares me to get the Diary in proper shape. Don't want to increase an already almost intolerable burden on Teil. Like to feel I've not only initiated, but completed, the book myself.

'No word from Chatto yet?' I ask Teil as she's bringing in the post.

'I'm afraid not.'

In spite of their tardiness, I think I've got a considerable book here. Very readable. An oddly fitting climax, if that's the word, to my long, and somewhat higgledy-piggledy, writing career.

New Marie Curie this morning. Young, fragile-looking thing. Slender build. High heels. What's she doing here? 'Could you just tell me what to do?' Long, slim fingers move the table from my bed.

What to do? Don't know what she's to do. Terry, thank God! Delighted to see her.

'Hello, Minnow.' Come early for the weekend?

'Hello, Jif! Look what I've brought you.' She brings a plastic shopping bag over to me. 'Fresh scallops.'

'Lovely.' I try to sound enthusiastic. Fairly weak. Used to be a great favourite of mine.

'I'm going to cook them for you. With a special sauce.'
She's come to do the cooking to give Teil a break.

360 mg MST tonight. Six pills. I count them out and Teil
checks them. I take tonight's dose. Put a further dosage in a small
bottle, ready for the morning.

We watch *Merry Christmas, Mr Lawrence* to take my mind off
things. About life, if that's what one could call it, in a Japanese
prisoner-of-war camp. Pain under control for the moment.
Mine, not theirs. They were in considerable pain. The Japanese
are unbelievably cruel, it would seem.

March

All that morphine. Still entrenched in agony. Don't know *how* to resolve the problem. Remains very much an issue. Try Coproximol. Creaming. Usual means that contrive to get one through. Everyday remedies don't have much effect on this far from everyday kind of pain.

Pleasant enough food, completely overshadowed by a sense of helplessness, of hopelessness, in the face of inexorable pain. How much should I endure today?

Talk round and about it. Teil rings Worthing. Duty Doctor. Other authorities and quasi-authorities. Plump for a further MST tablet. Teil suggests taking some of the liquid Diamorphine reserve. Advises I simply take a 'slug' to deaden immediate pain. MST is slow release. Not sure. What does Teil know? None of the medics suggest this solution. Could it be fatal?

That's not the only quandary either. Running out of supplies. Saturday morning. Nearby chemists are afraid to stock this type of drug because of break-ins.

'Just as well they know us locally. I've asked the chemist to arrange for more MST with their morning order, and rung the Duty Doctor to write a prescription. I'll go and see to it shortly before noon. Just made it all in time.'

The prescription's a special one, for dangerous drugs. Only Teil's allowed to collect them. Concerned with complicated legal matters, here.

It's worrying. One can't necessarily obtain the drugs, let alone ensure they work. Teil's organized it. How would I manage on my own? What would my life be like? It's ghastly enough even now.

Not an entirely idle question either. Teil returns with the drugs, looking fairly groggy. Announces she simply has to get to bed herself. She's feeling unwell. Reinforcements have been called in. Madeleine and Colin are taking over.

Another new Marie Curie this evening. Unclear what for. Not young, but all dressed up – make-up, high heels, dressy blouse and skirt, covered by a nursing overall.

'What would you like me to do?'

I don't know what she's supposed to do. No Teil to tell her. Can't remember. Panic. What if she turns me the wrong way, like those two at the Durstone? Days of agony to follow. What if she drags me down the bed? Can't stop her. Weak. Fragile. Helpless. Exhausted. In too much pain. Teil, the only person I can really trust, is ill. Can't defend me. Fight for me. Insist for me. I don't want this stranger in my room.

'Sorry about the clothes, but I'm going out tonight.' Rueful smile.

I don't smile back. Don't care about her plans. Care about my comfort. Terrified she'll get things wrong. Summon all the energy I have. Direct her into harmless activity.

'If you could bring my washing things and toothbrush.'

'Yes? Where do I find them?'

My God! I've got to give her directions? Don't need this. Prefer to be alone. 'I'll call my daughter.' Minnow. Strong, young, competent Mad. She'll safeguard me.

The nurse fiddles about, washing my face and hands. I suffer it.

'Could you see to my father's bedsores?' Mad isn't sure how this is done. Nor, really, am I.

'The Sprilon spray,' I direct, annoyed with Mad for mentioning the matter. Appalled. In case the woman does the wrong thing. 'I'll lean over.' I haul myself over, using the monkey-pole. Pray she gets on with it. The sprung mattress makes me insecure. I could fall off the bed. No cot sides.

'Does that feel right?'

'I can't feel, I'm afraid.'

She sees I'm paralysed. A nurse, isn't she? Why doesn't she *know* what to do? What's she for? Where's Mary? Why hasn't *she* come? I don't like this woman!

'I think that's right. Anything else you'd like me to do?'

Go. GO! I want you gone. And don't come back. Dismiss her. Fast. 'No, thank you. Thank you very much.'

'I'm due back on Monday. See you then.'

SUNDAY, 2ND MARCH

Colin suddenly appears in the middle of the night. 'What's the problem, Dad?'

'Problem? I'm fine, thank you. Anything wrong?' Something up with Teil? She's seriously ill?

'The loudspeaker woke me. I thought you called.'

Not intentionally. I remember a dream, nightmare perhaps. I must have shouted out. Shall I tell him it was a mistake, a dream? Try to invent something? I haven't the mind to fabricate anything. Prefer the truth in any case.

'Sorry. I didn't call on purpose. A dream, I think.'

'I'll just sit down a minute. I feel a bit dizzy, getting up so quickly.'

It's becoming quite absurd. I don't want to propel my son out of bed. Bother him. Make him feel dizzy. Don't want to be a burden in this way. Hate it. Helpless to alter it. I'll sort it out as soon as Teil's recovered. This will not do. I cannot live, knowing I have a fatal disease, and see my family made ill around me. I've no interest in that at all.

'Right. I feel better now. Shall I cream your back?'

That's filial duty taken to its limits. I try to stop the tears from flowing. Turn my face. 'That would be very nice.'

Trust my son to do this properly. He's gentle, quiet, practical. Makes a good job of it. I feel a little better, but guilty. This is appalling. I tried so hard to be a good father. Now I'm burdening my children. Thank God Richard is out of reach. I know he suffers anguish on my behalf, but physically he's safe.

'Better get back and try to get some sleep. Turn the machine off your end.' How can I spare these two? A nursing home. Go to a nursing home.

'I'll put it out into the corridor. Then I'll only hear if you actually shout for help.'

'Right. Thank you.'

He's gone. I reach up and turn off my end of the alarm. What's it matter what happens to me? Heart attack. Fall out of bed. So what? Perchance to die. . . . Prospect of the latest Marie Curie tomorrow makes me wish I would.

Teil pops in early. 'Sorry. I feel ghastly. Some sort of gastric flu, I think. I'll stay in bed today, as the children are here. I'll be over it by tomorrow, I'm sure.'

She stays a little, relaxing in the chair. A golden time. So short.

Teil's clearly pushed herself too far. Now she's ill. Don't want her ill. No use to me even if I were selfish enough to want it. Can't protect me if she's ill. No one else. To understand my needs. I'm too weak to ask for what I want. Relied on Teil when I was fit! How can I do without her now?

I'm sick with anticipatory worry about the nurse.

'I'll sort out the nurse for you, Jifda. Don't worry. I'll see to it.' My daughter will protect me. Courageous, efficient, energetic. She'll go in to bat for me. I can't. Simply can't. What will she think of me? An abject, shivering coward? 'No problem'. Dear daughter. I need your love. Your strength of character. Your will to help. And you are giving them. Have I deserved such children? Have I deserved this disease?

Jean Sturbow. I hear her penetrating voice reverberating down the long corridor. 'I like it when they're peaceful' I overhear. Is that Teil answering her? What's she doing, up again? 'Such a privilege to have been here. There's a nurse coming this evening?'

'Yes. She's due at five.'

'No need to disturb him much.'

Door opens. She comes in and does virtually nothing. I do feel rather off. Some sort of cold, just to help matters along! A little chesty. Not up to food.

Everything's somewhat hazy. Floating feeling. Teil. Teil in the room. And Mad. Neither of them talking. No TV. No radio. No video. Odd. Just sitting by me. What are they doing? Can't make it out.

Suddenly feel better. Scene clears. Less congestion in my chest. Even feel like something to eat. 'I'm hungry,' I hear myself saying. 'What's for lunch?'

'We've had lunch, Jifda. It's nine o'clock.'

'What would you like?' Teil's standing by me, stroking my hair back from my forehead. Like? Can't think about that. Just food. Food I enjoy. 'I'll find you something nice.'

She's feeling better already? Good. That's good.

MONDAY, 3RD MARCH

Liz on a Monday? Odd. Different from usual prescription writing.

'Can you lean forward slightly? Just a little listen to your chest.'

I do have a sort of cold. Same as Teil, I suppose. Some sort of fluish cold. No need to fuss. Not likely to get worse while I'm in bed.

'Have you got a cough?'

'Not really. I'm just a bit wheezy.'

She finishes fiddling with her stethoscope. I don't like the feel of it along my back. 'I think we should take a sample of the urine,' she says, straightening up. 'Shall I prescribe antibiotics?'

'Jeremy's always said he doesn't want that. He wants to allow things to take their course.'

'I don't think it'll be all that long now' I hear her murmur, turning towards the door and going out.

What won't be long? Diagnosing the urine for cancer? What of it? Already know about that.

TUESDAY, 4TH MARCH

Mary today. No strength to speak to her. Knows I'm feeling off. Usual soothing self. Terry with her. My favourite nurses. I couldn't be in better hands.

'Would you like me to arrange for another Marie Curie nurse tonight, Mrs Warburg?'

'We won't bother, thank you. I'll manage.'

Thank God for that!

Liz again! 'Just thought I'd call before I'm off on holiday.' Assembles prescriptions. 'We could start on a hundred milligram pills. That'll make it easier for you to take them.'

Good old Liz. What a good idea. Five pills instead of eight. A drop in the ocean of pills, now . . . feel so weak . . .

'How's the cough?'

Cough? What cough? 'Better, I think.' All I can manage.

'Shall I give you something for it?'

More drugs? Don't think so. Teil brought it up only yesterday. Would I wish to take antibiotics to stop a chest infection? In other words, would I wish to stop, deliberately stop, pneumonia killing me off? No, I would not. Best way to go. Better than renal failure, I suspect. 'I think I'm perfectly all right. Quite enough pills already!'

'Just as you wish. There's no obligation.'

They go off. I hear them chatting in the hall. What's all that about?

'No . . . yes, yesterday . . .'

'Not all that long . . .'

'. . . my son . . . Boston.'

'. . . not yet. . . .'

I hear the front door shut. Were they talking about contacting Richard? Am I dying now?

'What was all that about?'

'Liz says you've got an infection in your chest.'

'I know that! So what? Just a bit of flu, isn't it?'

'I dare say. But you *were* rather poorly yesterday, as Mary puts it. And over the weekend, you know.' She sits down beside me, on the chair she's placed alongside my bed. 'Actually, Mad and I thought you were going to die! But you didn't.' A smile lights up her face. 'As a matter of fact, you suddenly rallied and demanded food. We thought it very funny . . .'

'Didn't feel as though I was dying.'

'Liz thought there might be a possibility of a chest infection getting the better of you. Apparently one of the nurses rang her and said she thought you were definitely going. Now I know what all that privilege stuff was about. I wondered what that meant.'

'That's why she came again today?'

'Partly. And to offer you antibiotics for the chest infection.'

'Bit late, wasn't it?'

'We told her, right from the start, that you don't want to prolong things.'

Both of us are still pretty groggy.

WEDNESDAY, 5TH MARCH

Definitely an infection in the bladder. Bungs up the catheter. Terry turns up with antibiotics. Type worked out by the lab. Isolates the organism and prescribes the correct antidote. All done by computer, no doubt! Medicine by remote control.

'What are you writing down?'

'We're just keeping notes, to make sure we don't miss out on anything.' Terry brings the note to show me.

'I know what you mean. I've got a chart here. Tells me what pills to take, and when.' I'm pleased with my system. Cross out a section each time I take pills. Difficult to fit new ones in. Have to concentrate. Got to do it, otherwise things will accelerate.

'Try to drink at least five pints a day,' Terry keeps urging me.

'It's not that easy to fit in, you know. There's this bulge in my tummy . . .'

'I know. Just try. A bit at a time.'

Two Highland Spring bottles by my bed. Hold one and a half litres each. One diluted apple juice, the other water.

Notice Teil and I talk less. Often just sit. Hold hands if Teil can get near enough. Say nothing much. A word here and there. Nothing much to say. Just want to be left alone with each other. Calm. Loving. Silent.

THURSDAY, 6TH MARCH

First knitted doilies in the post this morning for Teil's new book. Displayed on a red velvet cushion. Good to see them.

'I've made a start on writing up the Diary for you, so you can look at it. See if you want that approach. Try a little editing.'

Nice to see the Diary taking physical shape. Can't do any editing. Too weak. Tomorrow, perhaps.

Back's kicking up again. Gone to 600 mg MST. 'Quite a good dose' Worthing admitted last time Teil was in touch.

Mutter a good deal to myself now. Morphine, Teil says. All nonsense really. Words come out without my authorizing them, so to speak. So to speak! A jumble of muddled syllables. Words turned round, mixed up. Reminds me of Mad learning to speak at eighteen months. 'Ban ette!' she'd pressed us, over and over. Eventually light dawned. Her blanket. She wants her blanket. Same now with me. Think a word, and out comes jumble. Teil has to guess what I want.

And my body. Feels as though it's floating. I can see it, ethereal, on the bed. I'm up on the ceiling, looking down. It's buoyant, as though on water. Someone outside. Who's that?

'Cur whe rawdains.' I see Teil looking for a clue. Point at french windows. 'Durr ve dawcains!'

'The curtains? You want me to draw the curtains?'

'Yeh.'

'But it's still light outside. Still lovely.'

'Daw ve dainsur. Man. Vere'sh a man. Shideout.'

'There's no one . . .'

'Vere'sh a man. Shtaring ahme.' I can see him outside quite plainly, a dark, black figure with a cloak. Just standing there looking in at me. I don't like him staring at me so. I want the curtains drawn.

FRIDAY, 7TH MARCH

The room's changed somewhat, I've only just realized. A bedside table has gone, replaced by three chairs, their backs forming a barricade against my falling out. It works, but makes it harder for me to reach belongings for myself.

I used to be in favour of euthanasia, voluntary euthanasia, in cases such as mine. It's against the law, not an option. I've rejected suicide already. Would I ask for euthanasia, if it were available? Not at present. Life is still sweet, however bitter-sweet. I still enjoy myself, relish Teil's company. I like Mary, appreciate Terry. Revel in seeing the snowdrops, and the sun, outside my window. Gratifying to think about the Diary. I might still be around for publication! I bask in just being, lying here all on my own. Why not? So I'm immobile, can't do many of the things I used to do. I can still think. Live in my imagination. And can read, though I don't want to. Can listen to music. Occasionally do. But live in my mind – my body simply houses it. The pain is tiresome, but more or less under control. The nursing bit only takes an hour or so a day. Why should I die just yet? I'd like to see my grandson in. Jeremy Hillier. I'd like to hear his voice.

SATURDAY, 8TH MARCH

Pain breaking through again.

'I'll try to get in touch with Worthing. He might be at home.'

'He hasn't anything further to contribute.'

'I'll ask him about my Diamorphine idea. It worked, the time you tried it, didn't it?'

She's back in no time. 'He says try it. For instant relief, so to speak.'

She brings me what she calls a 'tot', about 20 mg in a little water. Horrible taste. I really don't like it. But it works. Relaxes me sufficiently to get over the extra pain. Eventually I feel comfortable.

'I'll ring the Health Centre and arrange for some more.'

So here I am. Tons of morphine. The stuff does make me gaga, but apparently there's no other solution. Either morphine works, or you've had it. What happened to all those promises of different sorts of pain control? All whistling in the wind.

I'm fortunate to have GPs who allow me any amount of morphine I require. Worthing tells us there are some who refuse to prescribe the stuff on the grounds that it may shorten their patients' lives. *What* do these doctors think they're talking about? What, in fact, has it to do with them? Who asks them to make moral judgements? In the last analysis, how much morphine I take is my affair, no one else's. Only I can judge what's right for me. I can listen to Teil, listen to Worthing, listen to other opinions, but in the end I have to make the decisions.

I've got a little job! Teil's learned how to wash the sheepskins. The essence of the matter is to brush through the almost dry fleece. I don't mind that sort of job. Like it. Makes me feel useful. Contributing. I can manage only a little at a time. Worked out Teil can do the central bits quite quickly. I finish off the edges, the slow bits, the little bits. Team effort, as so often in the past. Teil displays our final achievement to Nurse Kalmett. The fleece looks almost new. She's impressed, I think.

Urine problems. Rita Locksley arrives, as though on cue. Rattles on a bit. Rather a loud voice but heart of gold. Apparently hides her feelings under that forthright exterior.

'Can you get the urine to come through?'

'We'll have a bash.' Well, a juggle anyway. Nothing at first. See it trickling through; not fast, but it's coming. 'Just give us a ring if you have any problems.'

I see Teil look at her sideways, know she intends to call the Duty Doctor out, and not a nurse, if the tube blocks up again. At least the urine's clear. Light yellow; no blood, no gunge. So why's it stopped? Who knows, or cares? Just let them unblock it somehow.

Small shots of Diamorphine control the pain. Drift amiably through the day.

'I'll settle you down early.'

Not tired. Only nine. Well, can't be helped.

'The ruddy thing's blocked up again.'

We jiggle and we juggle. No good. Firmly bunged. The doctor, or not the doctor? Teil rings.

'If you could help me.'

Teil is Sheila Dorian's willing, but somewhat nervous, assistant. The young doctor is pleasant, smiling, but her hands shake. I know she's apprehensive, new to the job. 'We'll need scissors.' Feel slightly alarmed. 'And some boiled water. We should have sterile water, but I couldn't get hold of any. I think we'll be all right.' We? They, maybe. But will I? What if I get another infection? 'It may stream out rather fast when I remove the old catheter. I think we'll need a shallow container.'

'Will this do?' A bright orange, rectangular plastic dish. A cat's litter-bin!

'Very good. Yes.'

Nearly eleven by the time she's gone. Too tense to go to sleep. Talk for an hour or so. This will not do. We have to find a place for me before the end of April. Teil can't survive like this indefinitely.

'I'll ring Alec Turnpike in the morning. He might know a place Liz hasn't come across. She's new in the area, after all.'

Don't want to go, but feel there isn't any choice.

MONDAY, 10TH MARCH

Ask Teil to see to pillows. She adjusts them. Within half an hour they need readjusting. She tries again, and yet again, tiring rapidly.

'Ring Alec Turnpike.'

Strange. Most difficult part of being a patient is to try to work out how to ask for help. Ask too much, and the medical profession gets narked. Ask too little, and you can't get the service it isn't at all unreasonable to request. This tightrope to be walked. For patients. For their families. No one wants to push the medical profession. Even if one couldn't figure it out oneself, they let one know soon enough how put upon they are! But there's a limit to the thought one can give one's medical adviser. An illness such as mine needs help. They've undertaken to be helpers. That's their job. So let them do it.

In fact the doctor shows no signs of irritation. 'Well, there's Frogmore,' he says at once. 'That's where most people in the area go.'

'Frogmore? But isn't that a NHS hospital? Do they have single rooms?'

'NHS, yes. But they do have one or two single rooms. Amenity beds. I'll give them a ring and see what I can do. I'll get back to you.'

And he rings back, a mere hour later. 'Frogmore can offer you a room, a single one on their upper floor, this afternoon.'

'This afternoon?'

'Yes. Took a bit of pressure to get it for you, actually. The room's free now. Talk it over and ring me back.'

We talk. And talk. And talk. The strain of it. The bleakness of the situation. Teil's most reluctant to send me off again so soon. I'm most unwilling to stay here in this condition. A burden. Making her ill. Possibly killing her! We'd prefer to leave the hospital solution for a couple of weeks more. Perhaps they'll have another room then, or perhaps they won't. Possibly our vacillating will prevent them offering us a room again. Teil goes to talk to Alec.

'All settled?' I feel noble, allowing her to arrange it.

'I couldn't do it. I've arranged to meet the Matron and look at the set-up, but I've cancelled for the time being.'

'I don't want that.' I can't let her go on. She won't last the course. I'll be left without her at the end. 'It won't be any use to me, your getting ill as well. I've got to go.' Quite emphatic, considering how weak I am. 'Ring him back and say we've changed our minds.' Almost like my old self. Have to go. Know that.

Alec hasn't cancelled yet. He understands our problems and our difficulties, a common dilemma for people in our predicament.

I'll go tomorrow. Feel virtuous. Chivalrous. Made a decision. An important resolution. For myself. Still capable of looking after my wife. Still a human being. Not just some vegetable, lying here, incapable of thought, of choice, of judgement. Still in charge.

Frogmore is within fifteen minutes' drive from us. Twice-daily visiting is feasible. Teil contacts the Sister in charge. Meets her to see the room.

'She sounds really nice, warm and sympathetic. Less starched than most people in her position. But, as we didn't take the upstairs room immediately, and a downstairs one has "become available", as Sister Kinder delicately put it, we'll have to settle for that.'

Well, there it is. Tomorrow I go to Frogmore. Teil rings Alec to organize the transport. Free, this time. On the NHS.

Awful night. Worried sick. What am I doing, playing at honour? Haven't I got enough to contend with? What's the point of Teil looking at the rooms, for heaven's sake! It's how the staff behave that counts. Will they treat me properly? I had Donald's protection at the Durstone. Now I'm on my own. The sterling Liz on holiday. Wouldn't trust Tom, let alone Alec, to bat for me. I'd say I'm shit scared, but it's hardly an appropriate term!

Teil's early, thank God. Uneasy herself, of course, in case she's sending me to my death. Death in a tinpot hospital. Death where we might not be together. Sending me off to the unknown. No wonder she's looking strained.

'You can't just lift him. He's got cancer in his spine. It's dreadfully painful. Have you got a canvas you can slip under him? That's what the other ambulancemen used.'

'A canvas?'

'A sort of tarpaulin sling. You put it under the patient and lift it rather than him. Keeps his spine supported.'

'I know, Bert! That green thing.'

And they produce a rather basic version of the tarpaulin stretcher the private ambulancemen had used, worn-looking, stained, without handles.

'He's a big one, George. Heave on the count of three.'

Teil gave me a Diamorphine dram half an hour ago. Just as well. They try, of course. But they jarred me on to the stretcher. I wondered if they'd make it at all. No handles to help them.

'When will *you* come?' I suddenly realize I'm off to this strange place alone. Who'll see I'm properly installed?

The men are solicitous, take my suitcase. I don't want anything else at present. No TV, no radio, nothing. Want to see what it's like. I might not stay.

Teil's beside me, two sheepskins in her arms, as the men lower the stretcher from the ambulance. 'Room Two,' a plump, elderly nurse in grey instructs the ambulancemen.

Stretcher trundled along the corridor. The room is large and airy. Light, too. The bed's prepared. A nurse in blue is standing by.

'I'll just put the sheepskins on the bed,' Teil's explaining to them. 'We've also brought a support pillow, just in case.'

We don't want to antagonize the staff. Want to ensure my comfort as best we can.

'Some people like them, I know,' the nurse in blue is saying. Can see she's in charge, from her bearing. 'We find they're not really necessary.' Judicious tone. Trouble to come?

'Shall I unpack the suitcase, Staff?' The nurse in grey looks towards the nurse in blue. Staff nurse, in charge when the Sister isn't here.

'We'll leave that for the moment.' Somewhat curt.

Teil's arranging the pillows according to the gospel of the chief physio. They lift me on to the bed, I notice blood on the canvas. The trip has opened up the Durstone bedsores, almost healed in just a few days at home. What about blood on the sheepskins?

'My husband's bowels haven't been evacuated today,' Teil's telling the Staff Nurse. 'I've made a list of the drugs he takes, and brought sufficient MST for the first twenty-four hours. He takes them at six-thirty, morning and evening.'

The Staff Nurse smiles, a little sideways smile. Late twenties? Early thirties, perhaps. Trim figure. Neat waist encircled by her nurse's belt. Straight, jet-black hair cut in a page-boy. Welsh lilt. Staff Gwynne. Smile still on her lips, but a determined mouth. As the smile fades I see the mouth shut tight. Her eyes survey the scene. She turns to me. 'A cup of tea?' A flicker of a smile returns.

Tea. Oh, God. I can't stand tea. Or coffee. Food. I'd forgotten about food. It might be ghastly here. Grimace into a smile. 'No, thank you.'

'Coffee? Fruit juice?'

'No, thank you very much. I won't have anything.'

'If you're sure.' She turns to Teil, eyes slit. 'We'll leave you to unpack him, then.'

'Thank you very much for everything,' Teil's saying as they leave.

Large, winged, vinyl-covered 'easy' chair under the window. Upright chair in one corner, complete with a foot-rest. 'I'll bring the trolley to put on your right,' Teil's saying cheerfully. 'And the TV and the radio . . .'

'Not today. I don't want anything today.'

'They seem very pleasant. I see there's an aerial point and a plug. I'll arrange some sort of muffling for the ripple mattress. It sounds like a monster!'

A rather superior type of ripple mattress. Monkey-pole. Bed's very good. Relatively comfortable. Cot sides extremely useful for moving from side to side. Plenty of pillows. Much better cradle than the Durstone one.

Teil's off. Gives me a chance to rest after the move. I lie alone in my strange new surroundings, not uncomfortable, but forlorn. Jittery. Anxious. Tense. Don't know why. Some sort of warning signals exploding in my brain. Nothing to put my finger on. Unbelievable clattering outside. Tea-trolley.

'Cup of tea?' Tiny shrimp of a woman, no more than four foot ten and very slight. Deep creases in her weather-beaten face betray late middle age. Her white-overalled figure is half-way through the door.

'No, thank you very much.' I raise a twisted smile.

'Coffee, then? Biscuits?'

'No, really. I'm not hungry.'

'All right, dear.' Smiles at me compassionately. 'I take orders for supper in the mornings. I've had to choose for you today. There's soup. And egg or cheese sandwiches.'

'Any brown bread?'

'Only with the cheese.'

'The cheese, then. Thank you very much.'

Nibble at the supper. Soup's tinned. Mousetrap cheese. Bread's brown, not wholewheat. Drink hot chocolate. Pudding's some sort of synthetic jelly with synthetic cream. Teil offers me one of her wholewheat watercress sandwiches. Don't want to eat, or be seen eating food from outside.

Door opens. No knock. Staff Gwynne enters, stands at the

bottom of the bed. 'I thought we might have a little chat about your bowels.' What about my bowels? She wants to do them now? 'We like to use suppositories. Perhaps you'd like to try that method.' Teil's glancing at her, not much concerned. She expects me to turn this down flat. I'm not up to saying anything. 'It's much better for you than manual evacuation. That's quite risky, you know. It *could* perforate the bowel.' Hasn't, in all this time! 'Suppositories work in half an hour or so. We put them in, leave them to work, then clean you up.'

'You mean a bedpan?'

'Well, we try. But sometimes just the incont pads.'

Teil understands she has to speak for me. 'I think a bedpan would be rather hard for my husband to sit on. He's terribly thin, you know. He's barely got any flesh on him. And what about the bedsores? They might well get worse.'

'That's all right. The pads will do.' Dismissive. Turns away from Teil. 'I know you'll find it rather tiresome at first,' slightly smiling at me, 'but we can help you regulate your system. Then you can really be in control. So much better for you.'

'In control?'

'Yes. We can teach you how to control your system. Lots of paraplegics learn how. It would be much more convenient for you. Why not have a go?'

Paraplegic! Never thought of my paralysis quite like that. I'm a paraplegic. Something of a shock. See Teil steel herself on my behalf.

'I realize my husband's paralysed as well as having cancer. But it's not the same thing as paraplegia. He has cancer in his spine. That makes it very delicate and excruciatingly painful. Paraplegics don't have that type of pain.' Teil's unimpressed with the nurse's position in the medical hierarchy. She's solicitous for my welfare. Much concerned with that.

'Don't worry, Mrs Warburg. We'll look after him.'

See the firmness of the mouth. The eyes go cold. The shoulders brace.

The most disconcerting part for me here is the lack of a telephone connection. No doubt I can survive two weeks without the phone. Teil will be here at ten-thirty.

Not too bad a night. I'm not crazy about people shining torches in my face in the early hours, checking if I'm OK. Tends to wake one up. What's it matter if I'm not? Covering themselves. Nothing to do with me. Order lunch. Chicken, boiled cabbage – only fresh vegetable offered – then some sort of pudding. Not quite the Durstone menu.

Nothing's happened about my bowels. Lots of chat, no action. Staff Gwynne came at seven this morning. Maintained she'd see to it directly. Still nothing's emerged. Should I ring? Have they forgotten? Ah, here they are.

Half-hour wait, that's all. Put me on a commode. Rather too hard. Took three of them to get me on to it. Very nervous. Will have to ring to ask them to put me back into the bed.

Two hours before they take me off. Nothing's transpired about the bowels. Thank God Teil's coming. Can't cope. She'll have to have a word.

'Hello, honey, I've brought the trolley.'

'I told you not to.'

'You can't just lie here in a catatonic state.'

Why not? I feel numb, half dead. Just want to doze, sleep the time away in here. How soon can I get home again?

Spend my time saying 'No, thank you' to almost everything at lunch. Teil says she'll bring sandwiches for me tonight.

'I don't want you to. It'll upset them.' They might not like it if she brings food for me and I'm seen to turn theirs down. Wish she'd leave me to it.

Been lying on this incont pad for hours now. Can't help the state of bedsores. Wish they'd just disembowel me. Don't care whether they perforate my bowel or not. What does it matter? Incredibly anxious. Nothing emerging but expect it to. Teil will have to sort it out.

'I've brought you some lovely fish and a little rice. And some fresh salad and fruit.'

'Don't let them see it!' Notice her press her mouth shut. 'I'll pretend it's mine if anyone comes in.' And almost at once: 'I'll just see if I can tame the ripple monster, shall I?' Not sure about that either. 'It's a much bigger one than the one we're used to. And the bare room makes it reverberate.' She uses Colin's method. Cuts down the noise a bit. 'I'll just go and have a word with the nurse on duty about this bowel business.'

'I've talked to the nurse in charge. A very pleasant, elderly lady. She says they have to have a doctor's permission to evacuate you manually.'

'Why didn't Turnpike warn us?'

'I've no idea. This must happen all the time. How could we possibly know about it?'

I knew Turnpike wouldn't look after me properly. Liz isn't back till Monday week.

Can't do the Diary here. Someone may be listening to what I say. I'm sure the place is bugged. May write a few notes. They won't be able to read my writing. Anyway, won't do so while I'm in the room, I'm pretty sure.

THURSDAY, 13TH MARCH

Lying here, fretting, expecting my bowels to act, and they do not. Badly in need of a tranquillizer. Have to ring for a nurse. She has to arrange for pills: two of them to see me taking them. An hour's time-lag.

Wish I hadn't been so bloody noble. Wish I was at home. Teil's always telling me I'm far too nice. Maybe she has a point.

'We've come to sit you in the chair, Mr Warburg, to help your circulation.'

Three of them lift me from bed to chair. Very painful. Take three pills to help me endure it. Teil will see they don't leave me too long. Can ring, but don't like to make a fuss.

[*151*]

'Alec Turnpike says he'll sort the bowel matter out right away,' Teil reports.

It should be seen to any time now. Thank God for that.

Teil's here for three hours in the morning and four in the late afternoon. Only thing to live for. Leaves at eight for an early night.

Perhaps the ghastliest night since the beginning of this intolerable illness. Thought I'd already plumbed the depths. Not true. The suppositories suddenly work. Tons of faecal matter, oozing all around me. Revolting. The stench! I ring the bell. This time the nurse brings reinforcements. Two others, quickly. The kindly, elderly one. Two young ones. Door opens to admit yet another nurse while all this is going on. She stands beside me.

'You've got a grandson, Mr Warburg! Isn't that lovely?' Shit! 'Your wife's just phoned. Everyone's doing very well. Your daughter-in-law is perfectly all right.' Covered in shit to hear my grandson in. Bugger this bloody disease! No Teil to share the news with. No Richard on the telephone. Just all this filth around me. Pain, smell, blood and even tears.

'Are we hurting you, Mr Warburg?'

'No.'

'Are you comfortable now?'

'Yes.'

'Can we get anything for you?'

'No.' Just piss off. Let me be. I'm better off without you.

The whole repulsive performance is repeated three more times. Fuck the lot of them! Who's going to get me out of this? When can Teil have me back again? How long, my God, how long?

FRIDAY, 14TH MARCH

Coming here has been a disaster. Four times last night, and now more of this ghastly faecal mess. What was I thinking of, getting myself in here?

'I took the opportunity to tackle Sister Kinder about the bowel evacuation. You've met her now, haven't you?'

'She seems rather nice. Very gentle and friendly.'

'I think she is. I couldn't believe she'd allow this suppository business to go on, but there's something we aren't *au fait* with.'

'What's that? You mean this nonsense about perforating the bowel?'

'No. To the best of my understanding, it's nothing medical. The reason they're using suppositories on you is nothing whatever to do with illness, or bowels, or doctors. It's to do with the nurses' union.'

'The nurses' union?' I was only dimly aware that nurses have a union.

'Yes. It's against union rules to evacuate bowels manually.'

I can't believe I'm hearing right. 'They have union rules to say how patients are to be treated? I thought nurses are supposed to follow doctors' instructions.'

'Only within the guide-lines laid down by the union.'

'So this business of getting Turnpike's permission was neither here nor there?'

'Nothing to do with anything except using up my energy, and putting us off. They're not telling us the truth, as usual.' We've been dismayed before, but I don't believe we have been as shattered as this. Presumably this is the reason Liz did not suggest this place. She was a nurse before she became a doctor. 'I'll ring Turnpike as soon as I get home. I'll work out something to get you back again.'

'You can't take me in this state. It'll kill you off, too.'

'I can't deal with it in the state they've got you into, no. But I'll sort it out.'

'Their big aim is to make life even bloodier than it is already for really sick patients.' If I sound bitter, it's because I am.

'We'll see it's in the Diary. So that other people know. There's no way I'd have sanctioned your coming here if I'd had any inkling of this. Are we to suppose that Turnpike didn't know?'

'Does he know anything?'

'Not much. Anyway, he was so busy telling me you'd be in a coma within a day, and dead within three days, he probably didn't consider it worth discussing.'

'Killing me off again, was he?'

'Naturally. I took no notice this time. Bloody useless.'

'Nurses' unions, indeed!' Alec had snorted when he heard about my circumstances. 'I'll get Tom Quigley on to them. He's got a way with him. He'll charm the nurses.'

He'll need an unusual amount of charm, in my opinion. More, I suspect, than he can muster. Because when Staff Gwynne came in this evening she all but cut Teil. No smile, no cheery greeting, as before. Just a bare 'Good evening', slight nod, turned to me, busied herself and left us. Tom Quigley charm her? Willing to bet he can't.

SATURDAY, 15TH MARCH

Terry's come to see me! Overwhelmed she should think of visiting.

'You shouldn't be in here,' she's saying, outraged. 'A man like you. It isn't right.' Can only silently agree. Not clear, though, what particular attribute makes it unsuitable for *me* to be in Frogmore and not for someone else. 'A brain like yours,' she continues, readjusting my pillows in the way she does at home. 'Can't expect you to put up with being here.'

It isn't, to be truthful, my brain I'm worried about. I know that, in effect, I'm in the power of people whose capacity to analyse is less adept than my own. Even in my present state. Not sure that's relevant. More concerned about my bowels. I tell Terry about that. Her indignation is complete.

'That is outrageous. Haven't you got enough to put up with? I'm going to tell Doctor about this as soon as I get back to the Health Centre.'

'You think Turnpike will be able to do something about it?' Hasn't, so far!

'Turnpike? I mean Dr Tom. He'll see to it. He's very good at seeing to things here. He's got a way with him.'

That bit again. Must be something to it. What with Teil and Terry both getting at him, presumably he'll give it a try. Meanwhile I'm at the mercy of Staff Gwynne, whatever anybody says. I can't defend myself, to all intents and purposes. I can't force her to evacuate my bowels manually. Can refuse suppositories if I can find the strength. Let nature, whatever that might be, take its course. At the price of faecal matter building up inside me.

'I'm completely in her power,' I insist to Teil.

'Like being in a concentration camp, you mean.' Going a little far perhaps. Fairly true that one can see how the horrors of a concentration camp might develop. 'Exactly what I'm always saying. Very dangerous to assume only Nazis are capable of inhumanities.'

A cosy little country hospital, set in the gentle West Country. The elements are here. Undeniably here.

Teil and Mad arrive during my lunch, bearing a bottle of champagne with glasses to celebrate Jeremy Hillier's arrival.

I can't stop *them* drinking. Don't want to myself. What will the staff think? Staff Gwynne, what will she think? Worse tortures than ever if she thinks I'm some sort of alcoholic. Can't even keep off the drink in hospital. Hardly likely to know I only take the odd glass of wine, at most.

'You don't have to drink a great deal, Jifda. Just a sip for the toast.' Madeleine's getting annoyed. I'm between the Devil and the deep blue sea. Reluctantly accept a small glass. Toy with it. Taste a little. 'Won't be a minute. Just going to the loo. . . .'

'I don't want this.' Hold the glass out to Teil. 'Pour it down the basin for me.' She doesn't argue. 'And put the bottle away in that bag. And the Thermos. I don't want them seeing me eating or drinking anything they've not supplied.'

Teil doesn't say anything, just puts the things away. I have to live here. I'm the one who has to take the consequences.

'Hello, Mr Warburg. How are we feeling?' Staff Gwynne sweeps in, smile fixed. Keeps her back to my wife and daughter. Leans over me. Painstaking. 'Shall I just plump your pillows for you?' Hardly need her when my wife is here! And if she's so keen on helping me, why all this charade about the union?

'Hello.' From Teil.

No response. Black hair tossed slightly, so I know she's heard. The smile broadens to a grimace on her face. 'How's the lunch? Can I bring you anything else?'

Curiously overdone concern. What's she on about? I banter vacuously, worried about the smell of champagne on my lips as she leans closer still. When will she go? Suddenly, as swiftly as she came, she's gone. No word to my two visitors.

'Bit tricky, isn't she?' Mad says at once. We haven't said that she's Staff Gwynne. She has no way of knowing who it is. 'She might, I suppose, have spared a couple of seconds to say hello to us.'

'Obviously nurses' union rules don't allow fraternizing, or even sororizing, with relatives,' Teil says immediately, grinning. 'I dare say she's heard I've been on to the doctors about her damned suppositories. So she doesn't like it. So bloody what. I'm stopping her if I can, and that's that.'

'I wish you wouldn't be quite so bellicose. I'm sure she's only doing what she thinks is right.'

'Thinks is right? Right to torture someone who's already tortured with disease? Right to insist on bloody union rules in a case like this? Come off it!'

If the place is bugged, as I suspect it is, what will they do to me next? I've got to shut her up.

I turn to Mad. 'How's your new job?' I don't understand it, can't follow the ins and outs. And if the truth be told, I don't care. It's too remote from what's left of my life. Glad she's doing what she likes. She burbles on. I'm getting exhausted. 'When are you coming back?'

Mad's quick to spot the unsaid meaning. 'You mean you want us to go now?'

'I expect you've got better things to do.'

I don't actually like being visited by more than one. Teil and I just commune. I'm not up to this. They go. I sink back. Blessed oblivion of sleep.

Pretended tiredness last night. Mad insisted on 'doing something'. Tapes, TV. I don't want to know.

It's quieter at weekends. No cleaners. Ambulatory patients go home. Staff Gwynne's off. Staff Cheerpling takes her place. Early thirties. Efficient, but a soft, gentle face. Mouth curved into a smile. Lips full and rosy red. Fine blonde curls halo her head. Her hazel eyes gaze at me sympathetically. I take to her. Union member? Don't know. Thinks I shouldn't be here.

'We're here to help you,' she declares. 'That's our job. If you're at home, don't ever worry about asking for support. That shouldn't stop you going home again.' It's not as simple as that. Have to decide when to ask for help. We're as modest as we can manage. Even so, help's not always willingly forthcoming. Tone can be judgemental. We're very sensitively tuned. 'If you get it wrong, that's tough. The Duty Doctor's there to help you. They're well paid for it, you know.' She straightens out the bedding over the cradle. 'It's dishonest to take the money and then moan about being called out.' A novel point of view from someone in the medical profession!

Teil and Mad arrive.

'Hello, Mrs Warburg. Is this your daughter, Mr Warburg?' No problem, apparently, in greeting them. They've brought food. I might just add some to my hospital meal.

'I see the monster's tamed a little.' Teil kicks the box the ripple mattress motor's in.

'Goodness. I thought that was your store of bottles!' Staff Cheerpling laughs.

Bottles?

'I've used an empty Highland Spring box,' Teil explains.

'Water! I thought it was a store of wine, or something even stronger!' For heaven's sake. They think it's a store of liquor. She doesn't seem to think that bad. 'Good idea for him to have a drink or two,' she jokes as she leaves the room.

'I've worked out how to have you home,' Teil informs me, looking like a cat sated on clotted cream.

'I don't see how.'

'By persuading the Health Service to let me have the right equipment. I've seen how the hospitals do it. I can do all the work these people do for you, apart from actual nursing. The Community nurses do that anyway.'

'How can you? It takes hordes of them here!'

'They're just doing a job. Mine's a vocation. All I need is a proper, modern hospital bed. Then it's easy.' How can she survive this damned illness of mine? 'I'm going to get you out of here at the earliest possible opportunity. I have to be the judge of when that is. None of them can judge for me. I'm simply going to ignore them all.'

'You'll kill yourself.'

'Not true. I'll be ill unless I do what I consider right. I'll simply persist until I've assembled what's essential.'

We want me at home in such a way that Teil can manage. Be with each other as much as possible. No visitors. No tapes. No TV. Just alone together for what time remains.

MONDAY, 17TH MARCH

Noises off again, with a vengeance. What Teil calls a 'screamer' next door. Tend to think of her as a 'shouter'. Anyway, disturbed patient. Her door's left open. Her shouts can be heard all over the hospital, by me at any rate.

'Harold! I want Harold! I want him now!' Over and over again.

Then, later: 'Will someone *kindly* come and explain what I am doing here?' She might well ask. 'What is this place? Where am I? Harold! I want Harold!'

She keeps this up for hours. Eventually stops. When Teil arrives, she's asleep. Worn out or drugged? Her door's still open. Teil sees a man sitting by the bed. Harold, presumably. Poor Harold.

'Look at that! I can reach my feet.'

'Very impressive. Does it hurt?'

'No. The physio lady says I can get some extra mobility if I do the exercises.' It's almost impossible to believe.

'It's the bed. Because you can hold the sides, and the mattress isn't sprung.' Teil's faith in physiotherapy is limited.

'She says she'll have a "slide" made for me, so that I can slide from bed to wheelchair and back again.'

The more I do, the easier at home. I'll work at anything for that.

Greater level of mental awareness and lucidity. Helping with physical requirements. Appalling depression, catatonia almost, of the last few days is lifting. More cheerful. Two bright young nurses come in. Say they've been before. Can only hazily remember. Suddenly find myself considering their 'beautiful' bottoms. What importance such previously trivial matters assume in here! That I should think such things at all.

Full gram of MST now. An ocean in itself. Teil asked Turnpike to prescribe more.

'I'll add one or two extra hundred milligrams, if required by the patient,' he'd assured Teil.

He actually prescribed 1000 mg. No choices. I didn't feel I had the option to refuse. Teil isn't here at early morphine time.

The drug certainly changes one's perceptions. Feeling of receding. Dates. Days. Objects in the room. Different state from the non-ill state. Perceive it but cannot convey it. Just different. Vague. Feeling of fluidity. Nothing stable. A shifting, unfocused world.

Teil's annoyed at too high a dose. 'That man's always overdoing things,' she complains.

Knock. Sister Kinder. 'Just come to have a word about the suppositories.' Smiles encouragingly at us both. 'I know we're not getting a satisfactory result. But there's a different kind. I think you'll find you won't have any trouble with that one. It works quickly, within half an hour.'

Surely that's what they said before? Or am I getting muddled?

'Isn't that what you said before? My husband would really much rather be evacuated manually, you know.'

'I do understand. But we have some problems with that. . . .'

Know it won't be that simple. 'I'll try the new one.'

I can see Teil's eyes narrow, lips purse. She's not here, doesn't have to take the rap!

A man's come to change the curtain-rail in my room. Nurses decide I can't be left to enjoy the intrusion. Sit me in a wheelchair. Dress me in the clothes they insisted Teil supply a few days ago. Promise to take me for a walk.

'Oh, dear. It's rather nippy, isn't it?' No sooner has she wheeled me a foot or two outside than the nurse wheels me back.

'I'm not worried about the cold. I'd love a walk.'

'I don't think that will do.'

She wheels me in and shuts the door on the sunny day outside. First time I've seen the hospital corridors. Not exactly inspiring. I'm placed in a side corridor among the empty wheelchairs. Left alone, looking out on to the car park. Can see other patients sitting in the sun porch leading off the corridor. Old. Very old. But better off than me. Stuck here. Forsaken. A place reserved for flotsam and jetsam no one knows what to do with. Fit in well, I suppose! Very angry. Furious. What right have they to treat me like this? Am I a piece of garbage? Don't the sick need human dignity?

Suddenly Teil's here. She returned this afternoon and found my open door and empty bed. Man working there. No one to say what's happened, no nurse around.

'Do you know where my husband is?' she'd asked, aghast. A catastrophe?

'I think the gentleman's in a wheelchair.'

She wanders down the corridors. Finally spies me, still alive.

'I wondered where you were! They've dressed you up. Did they take you for a walk? What are you doing in this odd place?'

'Two steps, and then they said it was too cold.'

'Too cold?'

'The nurse said it was rather nippy.'

'So what? You're dressed, aren't you?'

'Too nippy for her, presumably!'

'I'll take you! Let's see, how does this thing work?'

'Don't! Not without their permission!'

'What's it got to do with them? *I'm* going to do the pushing.'

'No, I don't want it. I'll just stay here. You go. Leave me to it. I'll just stay here. An outcaste. Untouchable. In a corner. Not even fit to be with other patients.'

'I expect they thought you'd rather be alone. This is probably the only place for that.' What does she know about it? She isn't here, doesn't have to stand the racket.

'Ah, there you are, Mr Warburg.' Could I be anywhere else? Can I move myself? 'We'll get you back to bed now. The curtains are all ready for you.'

'Shall I take him for a walk first?'

'I'll go back to the bed.'

Enough of this. I want to be in bed. Teil chatters on. I want to be at home. In bed at home.

WEDNESDAY, 19TH MARCH

Ridiculous. Of *course* the new suppositories are no better. Same sort of problems. Same disgusting results. Same repellent consequences. Martyrdom. Pure torture. No other word for it. Gwynne woman's responsible, I know. Nothing I can do about it. Pretend I don't loathe her because, if I didn't, she might get up to all kinds of other torments. Completely in her power. Teil

[*161*]

can't help. Terry can't help. Tom, precisely as I suspected, wasn't able to do anything.

Teil's latest strategy is to enlist Liz's help. She's back. Returned on Monday. Teil rang her first thing. Liz wasn't exactly enthralled! Only just kept her temper, Teil reports. But Teil persisted.

'I need better equipment at home. A proper hospital bed, not like the one they sent before. A modern one, with a proper back-rest and cot sides. Above all, cot sides. Without them I simply can't manage at home. With them Jeremy's safe, he can't fall out of bed, *and* he can help by using the support they give.'

'I do agree.' Point, apparently, taken. 'I'll contact the Nursing Officer.'

'And you'll sort out the bowel business?' Liz might, just might, have a chance of doing that.

'I'll do my best. Their attitude's absurd, of course. I'll do what I can. That's all I can promise.'

Liz. Surely Liz, concerned for my welfare, forthright, brave, surely Liz can solve the problem?

She stands at the bottom of my bed, listening to my rambles, Staff Gwynne at her side. I feel obliged to mitigate the problems because, in the end, it's Staff Gwynne who'll deal with me. If I antagonize her, she might do anything! I've turned into a whimpering idiot. A funk.

'You find the suppositories difficult?' Liz asks, trying to be co-operative.

I shirk the truth. 'Not too bad.'

A smile from Staff Gwynne, almost a sneer.

'And the MST? I gather it's rather knocked you out. After all, it *is* twenty-five per cent up on your previous dose.'

'I think I could use less of it.'

'I'll see to that. Anything else?'

I try to think. Will Staff Gwynne get at me if I suggest going home? Risk it. 'Is there any problem about my being at home?'

'None at all. A good idea.' Brisk, clear-cut. What about Teil's health? Not Liz's concern. 'Well, if there's nothing else?'

'I can't think of anything,' I lie.

There are several points I'd like to raise. They forgot to bring my MST this morning. I finally remembered myself, two hours late, when the pain started up again in earnest. Physio lady promises to come, and doesn't. Nurses put me in a chair and leave me longer than I can manage. I'm forced to have the suppositories and attendant pain, and mess, and smell. That's what puts my wife off. Don't like the way they forget to close my door, against the constant clanking, thudding noises in the corridor. Say none of that.

No change suggested about the suppositories.

THURSDAY, 20TH MARCH

Absolutely enormous bunch of flowers from Richard and Ruthi. Teil brings it in.

'They'll put it in a vase for you . . .'

'Take them away.'

'But . . .'

'Take them away. I don't want them. Looks like a funeral.'

'But you like lilies . . .'

'Not any more. Just give them to the hospital. I'm sure the other patients will enjoy them.'

Don't want flowers any more. They look like wreaths to me, especially lilies. Very odd. I used to think longingly of being given lilies. Waited hopefully each birthday, hinted quite often. And no one gave me them. Now they're always sending them. I don't want them any more. Lilies mean death to me.

I have this enormous bulge in my abdomen. No one will say what it's about. All insist it's loss of muscle tone. We believe it's caused by soft tumours in that area. Assume they don't like to say. Know they don't like to mention unpalatable facts they can't do anything about. No one will tell us what the signs of my condition worsening may be. I'm in the dark. Completely in the dark.

I've decided it's not useful for Teil to come in the mornings. There's always something frightful going on. Decide she should come around three-thirty or four. Stay for the evening. Better all round.

Don't do much. No electronic entertainment. Not even much chat. Just sit. Well, Teil tends to walk about. I sit or lie. Can't walk. Teil tells me any interesting news about the business. I tell her what's been happening here. She gets annoyed with me for not defending myself. How can I? I'm in their power. She can't take this on board.

FRIDAY, 21ST MARCH

Teil arrives early, thinks Liz might come today. Sure enough she does.

'How's the nine hundred milligram MST?'

'Better. I don't feel quite so gaga.'

'And what about the physio? How's that coming along?' Liz has always been keen on physio.

'The hospital seem to think they can get Jeremy much more mobile. The physiotherapist says she can organize a slide, so that he can use a wheelchair. That would, of course, make all the difference to his life.'

'Yes, of course.' No sign of interest.

'It would be worth his staying here until that's worked out.'

'Yes.' Considering how keen she is on physio, she seems curiously unkeen on the slide. After all, if I'm to live several months more (*pace* Turnpike!), it would make an enormous difference.

'I understand the Artificial Limb Centre can fit him up with a wheelchair.'

'I don't know anything about that.' Oddly unenthusiastic. 'Well, if there's nothing else. . . .'

She's gone, leaving a sort of disappointment.

[*164*]

Day of the big move. It's actually happening. I didn't believe it when Sister Kinder broached it. Something they'd like to do but don't get round to. Like the slide. Or giving me a bath. Or taking me out for a walk.

Sister Kinder first thing: 'We're moving you upstairs today. At one o'clock, as I promised.'

Wonder of wonders, everyone on time – Sister Kinder, Staff Fervens, one of the Irish brigade, Teil and Col. All zero in promptly at one. They help move my wheelchair into the lift, up to the new room.

No problems. New room's much the same as the old one. Well, exactly the same. Tap doesn't drip as much. Better view. Rolling, grassy hills instead of the car-park. Very pleasant. No new curtain-rail. No TV aerial point. Same sort of bed. Teil and Col fetch my trolley, my clothes, my bits and pieces. All very exciting!

And Mary Houlder's come to visit me. How touching! Kindly, motherly soul. Trying to make conversation. I'm exhausted already. Not doing very well.

'My goodness, when I came to the room and saw the empty bed, I thought well, where's Mr Warburg, then?' She thought I was already dead! Not yet, Mary, not yet! 'So I was glad to see your wife. And how are things in here?'

'Very nice.' I'm not going to say anything else. What's the point? She comes here all the time. No point in running down a place which does its best.

We sit, the four of us, attempting small talk. Teil sees I've reached my limit.

'We'll leave you to it, dear. Back at around five. Give you a chance to sleep off all the excitement!' I need that. Indeed I do.

'I'll be getting along, too, then,' Mary says.

All depart. Blessed peace.

And then – another treat. Almost a miracle! Sort of thing that's heaven for me now. Sister Kinder comes and does a manual. Very effective, by all accounts. Doing it herself. Other nurses refuse. Staff Gwynne. What will she say? I'll meet that problem when it comes. She's off duty for the present.

Manual's made me feel human again. I can hardly thank Sister Kinder enough. The relief of it! No sitting, petrified that things may 'happen' while I have visitors, while I'm in the bed without an incontinence pad, while I'm having a meal . . . just blissful. Can manage in here if they do the manual. Can she go on doing it? What happens when she's not here?

Teil's also overwhelmed. Sets out the macrobiotic food for the evening. A celebration dinner. 'She's absolutely wonderful. She's really thought about you, hasn't she? What with this room and everything.'

'Yes. Funny, isn't it? It all depends on the sister in charge in the end. Nothing to do with doctors, nothing even to do with unions! The sister in charge is what counts.'

It's quieter up here. No clanking trolleys. Just the quiet thump of ambulant patients with their walkers outside my door. TV lounge two doors along relays its programmes. More acceptable than the 'shouter', even if, in the end, there's not much difference. From my point of view.

SUNDAY, 23RD MARCH

Really sound sleep. First time since I came. Teil and Col for lunch. Quite fun. Must be excruciatingly dull for Colin. Sunday papers. He can read those.

Bored. Of course he is. Suggests the crossword. No good at those, even normally. And now? A crossword? Absurd. Can't begin.

'That tiresome motor's kicking up again.' Colin is fiddling with the cardboard box.

'I know, I've tried to calm it down. It just won't work.'

'Could you leave it alone? I don't mind it.'

'It's not just noisy, it shakes the whole room!'

'Forget it. I don't care.' I wish they'd leave my things alone. Don't want them fiddling with appliances in here. Now Teil's messing about with it.

'There! That's better. At least it doesn't vibrate.'

'You'll damage it.'

They ignore me. I don't count, simply don't count. Not even to Teil.

I don't want anyone but Teil to visit me here. What can I do with them? Just Teil. Quietly. Not mending gadgets or talking. Simply beside me.

'When did they last change the urine bag?' *Must* she go on about things? Why not leave them be?

'Forget it.' I can't be bothered, don't want hassle. Jiggling with it. Bladder washes. Doctors. Want to be left in peace. I see her biding her time.

'I'll be off then, Dad.' Difficult for the poor lad. He doesn't like this place any more than anyone else does. No idea what to do when he's here. I feel for him. Yes, time to go.

'Nice of you to come, Cockle. Very nice. Hope you have a good trip back. Hope business continues to do well.'

Time for Teil to go. Nurses assure her they'll keep an eye on the urine. Bladder wash. Duty Doctor – another bloody Sunday! No advantage in being here, then. Doesn't keep us from having me home. But what about the bladder wash? Could Teil do that?'

MONDAY, 24TH MARCH

'I'm afraid the slide isn't ready yet,' the hospital physio informs me. 'It does take a little time to get it done.' Naturally. Stupid of me to think it would be ready. Instructs me on moving from side to side. On lifting my bottom off the bed. I try. Strenuous. Arduous. Takes all my energy and concentration to move a tiny bit. Is it actually worth all this?

'Could I really *use* a slide?' Presumably she knows. If not, what's her function?

'I don't see why not. Thousands of paraplegics do it.'

That bloody groove again. I have cancer. Cancer, woman! Not the same as a road accident. Is that really so difficult to grasp? 'I have cancer of the spine.'

'I'm sure you can do it.'

That's beside the point. Question of trade-offs, isn't it? Is it worth risking making things worse for the possibility of making things better? Who is going to answer that question properly?

'The Artifical Limb Centre said they'd be in touch,' Teil tells me.

True, and amazingly quickly. They ring Frogmore while Teil's still here. 'We'll send someone down,' they say. They will? The NHS will send someone down specially to see if I can use a wheelchair? Incredible! Do we really have a service as magnificent as that?

TUESDAY, 25TH MARCH

The Nursing Officer this morning: 'I hear you'd like one of our beds to use at home.'

'Yes. My wife thinks she can have me there as long as she has the right bed.' I try to collect my thoughts. 'You sent one before, but it wasn't modern enough.'

'Yes, quite right, we did. I had a look at it when it came back. Not too good, I admit!' He laughs heartily, as though he'd played some sort of joke on us. 'What exactly d'you need?'

I can't work it out. 'Could you talk to my wife? I'm not precisely clear.'

'What days does she come?'

'She's always here by four, at the latest, every afternoon.'

'See you at four, then.'

And off he goes. I can't tell him what we need, can't evaluate facts in my mind. Too difficult. Need notes. Haven't made any. Wish people wouldn't ask me. Can't answer them. I'm ill, too ill to answer them. Even forget to tell Teil about the visit.

There's a sudden, loud, peremptory knock. The door opens almost immediately.

'I'm Michael Parring, Mrs Warburg. Have I seen you at church?'

'I do go to Holy Trinity, yes.'

She's taken off guard. She doesn't remember seeing him! Is the place staffed exclusively with Catholics?

'Thought I'd seen you at mass.' Catholics tend to stick together. He'll do his best for us, I'm sure. 'About this bed. I think I've found one for you. Not quite like the ones in here, I'm afraid. We can't quite rise to those. But better than the last one.'

'With cot sides?'

'We can get cot sides for it. There's provision for them.'

'Can the bed be raised and lowered?'

'No problem there.'

'Fabulous.'

'The lorry foreman will be in touch about delivery. And I've got the artificial sheepskins in hand. Just have patience.'

The lengths to which the NHS goes to help are quite remarkable. We'd no idea. Of course, we understand. Saves them money if I'm looked after at home. Still, if someone at home is willing, it's best all round. We're very grateful for the support.

WEDNESDAY, 26TH MARCH

Turnpike's come across a new drug to help with bone pain associated with cancer secondaries. Some complicated name. Irrelevant. He's given us the drug company write-up. Advertisement feature!

He's not pushing me into using it. Liz is coming tomorrow. I need to be in hospital to have it administered. The drug itself is in pill form, but one side-effect is nausea. They plan to inject me with an antinausea drug, make sure I don't have any problems there.

I've no idea whether to try it or not. Nor has anyone else! Just something one might try. Cut down on the vast amounts of morphine. Even now. Could it make me worse?

I suppose it's kind of them to try to help me. It also means I have to think. I find that increasingly difficult. Strain. Not so much the thinking. Making decisions. Can't summon up the energy. Marshal the pros and cons. Not ready to abdicate decisions. I certainly don't want them made for me. No easy answers.

Easter in hospital. Well, so what, really. Don't make much of Easter at the best of times. The children declare themselves beyond such things as hunting Easter eggs. I used to enjoy hiding them. Even last year we had a hunt. Traditionally, I hide the eggs. Everyone else looks for them. Teil always wins. She's terribly competitive about it – she and Richard. The rest don't even try after those two have collected half a dozen apiece and no one else has found a single one! Even so, Teil always wins against Richard, in spite of his sharp eyes. Odd. Always did, even when we had parties for young adults, before we had the children.

'. . . the urine block work out?'

'Urine?'

'You're miles away!' Why should I stay here? I can roam the past in my imagination. The future looks too bleak. 'What happened about the catheter in the end?'

'They called Sheila Dorian out.'

'We can do that at home. I'll have to learn to do a bladder wash.'

Sister Kinder happily co-operates. 'It's very easy, Mrs Warburg. I'll show you.' And she proceeds to demonstrate.

'I think I'll be able to do that.'

We're getting ourselves attuned to my coming home. Not on Easter Tuesday. Too quick for us. We need another week.

'D'you think it will work?'

'I don't know.' Liz is no wiser about the new drug than we are.

'I suppose it's worth a try.'

'I'll order it, then, shall I?'

'Yes.' Idle to pretend that I'm not terrified. What am I getting myself into now? What for? Why don't I just carry on with the morphine?

'If the drug works, it would help with the wheelchair business.' That, I gather, is what Teil's been hoping for. The drug might stabilize my spine sufficiently to make it possible for me to attempt the slide and the wheelchair.

'It's a thought.' Liz simply isn't prepared to take any part in that affair.

GOOD FRIDAY

Good Friday. Good? It's not significant because I'm not a Christian. I believe in God, but not in Jesus being the son of God. Anniversary of the Crucifixion. Blasphemous, I suppose, to think in terms of that for myself. Curious, though. New drug starts today and finishes on Sunday. Three days, nine pills. Wish I could think in terms of Resurrection!

'Here we are, Mr Warburg. Just take the pill, and I'll give you the antinausea injection. Let's see. In the upper arm, I think. It won't hurt.'

True. I can hardly feel it. So terrified, I'm numb in any case. Almost sick with anticipation of nausea. Pretend to smile. 'I'll be racing down your corridors in a wheelchair next,' I say. Anything to hide my fear.

'We'll have to organize a race with Mr James!' Sister Kinder banters back, intent on getting the needle in. 'He's getting good at using one.'

No effect that I can feel. No nausea. Nothing. Early days yet.

'I've brought you some lemon sole, cooked in the sauce you liked so much last time.' Minnow tries so hard to think of things to do for me. 'And I've brought you the Mahler you said you'd enjoy. *Das Lied von der Erde*. Berliner Philharmoniker. On tape. Shall we put it on now?'

'Thank you very much. All right.' Reluctant. Suppose I can put up with it. Makes it harder for me to understand what they're saying. 'Not quite so loud.' Fiddle with the fish. Can't really enjoy it.

'How was the pill and the injection? Do you have any nausea?'

'No. It's OK.'

'Any effects at all?'

'Not that I've noticed.'

Mad prattles on, trying to get me interested – films she's seen, theatres she's been to, reviews of the latest books. I can't follow her, let alone take an intelligent interest.

'Let's do the crossword.'

'Oh, all right.'

Surprised I should agree. Teil's right, of course. One can just pretend to think of answers to clues, just sit there and pretend to think of them. The other day I got one by mistake!

HOLY SATURDAY

Wholly charming. Small basket with tiny eggs. An Easter present from the Friends of the Hospital. Somebody, or bodies, have made these little gifts for the patients who aren't able to get home. Winsome.

'Have you had an Easter egg, Mr Warburg?' It's the little shrimp, the one who brings the menu, such as it is, and offers tea – breakfast, mid-morning, lunch, teatime. She's always cheerful, always tries to get me something.

'Not yet. After lunch, I think.' I'll have to ask Teil to eat them. Can't manage it myself. Gratifying, but effort's too great. Never liked those little sugary eggs.

'Not much for lunch today. Cook's off.' Cook's a young lad, fresh out of catering school. Not bad. But not good either! No matter, it's tins now.

'There's tomato soup, scrambled eggs and peas on toast. And jelly. No choice today, I'm afraid.'

'That sounds very nice.' I can attempt eggs. 'Can you do brown toast?'

'We'll try.'

No problems with the pills or injections so far. No effects of any kind. Might just as well not be happening. That's what I suspect. Neither one thing nor the other. Waste of time.

Wife and daughter. Lunch in a Thermos. 'Eat some of these eggs,' I instruct them, instantly.

Teil puts two or three in her mouth. 'How touching. Who are they from?'

'Friends of the Hospital.'

'Really? That's charming. How reassuring that people like that exist.'

'Some of the staff came round in funny hats earlier on. Paper hats, and dressed in amusing ways. A sort of carnival act. Some of the kitchen staff, and the porters and so on.'

'They came to see you?'

'Yes, one or two. Not too many. They know I'm very ill. But they didn't leave me out! The nurses thought them incredibly funny. I suppose they were. I'm not quite up to it.'

'We've brought some shandy for you, Jifda.'

'Shandy?'

'To make a change for you.'

'I'll pass on that.' I thought I'd made it clear. I don't want any alcohol in this place.

'It's good for you to drink it. Sister Kinder says shandy's a good idea. A different taste, not just water. Why not give it a try? You might enjoy it!'

'Sister Kinder says it's all right?'

'Yes! This isn't a prison, you know.'

'Come on, Jifda. I'll keep you company.' Mad pours a tumbler for each of us.

[*173*]

'Happy Easter, Jifda!'

Easter Sunday. What's that to me? Nothing at all. Tempting for some, I suppose. Eternal life. I do believe I'll live on, in some form.

'Happy Easter. How was church?'

'We left just before the last hymn. I can't take people's questions or the looks. I'd really rather not talk about the present situation. Doesn't do us any good. Diana says she'd love to visit you.'

'I don't want anything like that.'

'Maybe when you're at home. Very kind of people to offer. If you feel like company . . .'

'I shan't.' What on earth would I want with company? What can I say to people in this world? I'm not part of it. In the twilight zone. Perhaps purgatory is a better word, since there's pain, anguish, even agony. Agony in the hospital. No garden for me!

'Special lunch today. Breast of chicken, boiled potatoes, and a salad.' Don't want it. Don't want to eat anything. 'Any problems with the new drug?'

'No. Nothing's happening either.'

'I suppose it might take a little while. A week or two.'

'Nonsense. It's a waste of time.'

'Let's have a bit of the Mahler, shall we?' Mad sounds bright and cheery. Too bright.

'It's too noisy.'

'Shall I read you some of *The Sunday Times*?'

'I'm not interested in the papers.'

'Richard rang. They're all very well. Little Jeremy's keeping them up all the time. He needs feeding every hour, apparently. Because he's so small. So Ruthi is exhausted.'

They don't stay too long, thank goodness. Feel tired again already. Only Teil later today. All I can manage.

No physio lady. Bank Holiday. When will they bring the slide? We've decided I should go home tomorrow week. The hospital physio comes only on Mondays. Decide to leave on Tuesday. Chance to help me. How else can I learn? Can't visit me at home. No desire to contact field-marshal physio again.

Wonderfully quiet this weekend. Teil's gone to explore the rooms Sister Kinder mentioned. Says they're really good.

So, generally, they do have room? Presumably we're talking about upstairs. Nursing me up here possible. Never ring unless I feel obliged to. If they hadn't made all this trouble about the bowels, I'd never have bothered them at all! How do they think we manage on our own?

Amazingly, we have Alec Turnpike to thank for Frogmore. Hate being here, but know the place is essential as an escape route for Teil. We both agree: better than a nursing home.

Back to routine. That's what I like. Just plain routine. Nothing new. Nothing unusual. Nothing special. Just existing, dealing with my ghastly body, is all I can undertake.

April

'The mainstay's in place. The hospital bed's installed!' Teil's eyes light up with joy.

'What's it like? Adequate?' A really good bed's essential. I'm dubious about their supplying one.

'Bedrock! Much more modern than the one we had before. There are cot sides. And an excellent back-rest.' She's positively breathless with pleasurable anticipation.

'I've put our Dunlopillo mattress over the NHS one, just to make sure it's soft enough for you. But, because I can't manœuvre the back-rest if the second mattress is right up to the back, I've got that extending beyond the base. I'm rather pleased with my solution. I've pulled out the metal grid meant for holding bedclothes and slipped the two small mattress ends from our cot bed under the Dunlopillo. That's made the bed about two feet longer!'

'It all sounds terribly complicated.'

'Not now it's done. I'm really thrilled with the set-up. It means you won't be cramped. We can have you further forward. I simply arrange the back-rest in a useful position and rearrange the pillows as before, but much more efficiently.'

Not sure I can get the hang of all that. Very practical. Ingenious, even. She'll sort it out.

'I'm absolutely thrilled.' She puts her arm around my shoulders and hugs me. She really wants me back?

'Of course I do. I know Liz and the nurses all thought you should be at home, but they don't seem to know what makes it possible. On and on about more nursing help, home help, chats with nurses. They'd just be extra burdens, as far as I'm concerned.'

'I know, I tried to explain.'

She rabbits on. Not at all like her. 'I know exactly what's needed now – a functional bed with an integral back-rest, cot sides, a monkey-pole, at least six natural sheepskins, three machine washable ones, and about eight pillows. And a cradle. I haven't got that yet, but it's on order.'

'I hope they can get one like this one.' Old-fashioned, curved shape. Keeps bedding off my feet, but view isn't too impaired.

WEDNESDAY, 2ND APRIL

A visit from Worthing! Very good of him. He's never been to Frogmore. Pleased to see it. Nothing further to contribute. Just reconnoitring. How things are. Whether the new drug's helped. Not that I've noticed.

'D'you think it's sensible for me to attempt to slide myself on to a wheelchair?' Take the opportunity to test out another opinion.

'Anything that makes life more interesting is worth trying.'

Not what I asked. No energy to pursue the subject.

'Worthing was here today.'

'Really? That *was* nice of him. I know it's out of his way. Did he say anything about Brenda?'

'Her doctor won't allow a hospice nurse to visit her any more.'

'What d'you mean, won't allow it?'

'Worthing must have the GP's say-so to visit, otherwise he's not permitted to advise.'

'Even when he's been before?'

'So I gather.'

Incredible. Terminal patients are completely at the mercy of their GP. How can one judge how a given GP will react before one is ill? Thank God for Liz. What would have happened to us without her? I think Teil might have had a breakdown by now and I might be in even worse straits than I am already. Now everyone's doing all they can. No pressure. Giving me all the drugs I need.

How can anyone decide to withhold basic rights of pain relief from another human being? On whose authority? Dependent on the GP? That clearly won't do!

THURSDAY, 3RD APRIL

Zeroing in on Tuesday, 8th April. Home-coming. Truly. I hardly dare believe it. Can Teil really contrive that?

'I've told you. We have to try.' She's getting quite impatient. Such confidence!

'What if you can't?' I always anticipate the worst.

'Then we'll have to make other arrangements.' A shrug. 'I'll organize something with Sister Kinder. I'm told it's often done.'

'You mean a specific booking?'

'I'll talk to Sister Kinder. Tomorrow, when she's on duty.'

There's a vigorous, incisive rap. Not used to people knocking. Don't reply.

'Come in,' Teil calls out.

Small, dapper man stands there. Late forties, roughly.

'Mr Warburg? I'm Dr Kahn, from the Artificial Limb Centre.' They've sent a *doctor* all this way just to see me? 'I've come to see if you can use a wheelchair.'

'That's very good of you.'

'Not at all. Let me see, I've got some details here.' Wades through familiar routine. History of my tiresome illness. Doesn't take long. Quick brain. 'Now, let me just examine you.' Looks at my appallingly disfigured body. At my spine. 'Grasp my hands. Use your full strength.' Still muscle in my hands. My wrists. They've always been powerful. Captain of fives at school. 'Possible. Not very strong, but adequate, I think.' Not very strong? *Not* very strong? My wrists? What is there left?

[*178*]

'You're satisfied he can use a wheelchair?'

'I believe so.'

'D'you think he can use a slide?'

'I don't see why not. Anyway, get them to teach him. Have a go. Nothing's gained by not trying! They'll lend him a chair to start with. Once he can manage, we'll send one in his size.'

'You don't think it's too dangerous for him to try?'

'No, I don't think so.'

'In spite of the cancer in the bones?'

'It shouldn't make any difference.' We thank him. 'I've never been here before. Interesting. Well, goodbye. And good luck!'

Will I *really* be able to use a wheelchair? Find it hard enough to sit in a chair.

'It's your only way to some sort of mobility. You might live a long time yet. I know it's a bit risky. I don't think Dr Kahn really knows anything about cancer. Usual thing. His speciality is wheelchairs – well, whether patients can use wheelchairs or not. You have enough strength in your arms and wrists at the moment. So, once your physio lady has shown you how to use the slide, we ought to have a stab at it.'

Monday. Physio lady's day. That's why I'm staying till Tuesday, so she can show me how to use the slide. Then take it home. Community nurses will lend a hand. Terry says so.

FRIDAY, 4TH APRIL

Couple of little taps on the door. Sister Kinder opens it. 'Oh, hello!' Teil straightens up from bending over me. 'I was just looking for you. I thought we might have a little chat.' Comes in, stands at the bottom of my bed, idly looking at the charts there. 'I see that everything's planned for Tuesday. Any problems?'

We'll never get it all together. Absurd to think we can.

'Everything's set at home. The bed's installed, we've got a ripple mattress and a monkey-pole . . .'

'Good. Have you got a stand for the collection bag?'

'No, we haven't. We just pinned it on to the mattress, before.'

'I'll send one along. You're all prepared? Quite happy about everything?'

'I think we are. Just a tiny bit worried in case I find I can't cope, after all. I'm sure I shall, but just in case . . .'

'He can always come back here.' That's what we want her to say, what we've been waiting for. Everything else is simply trivia. 'I tell you what. I'll keep the room for two days. If you find you just can't manage, we'll have it ready for Mr Warburg to come back to.'

'Can you really? That's fabulous! Really marvellous. What we need is knowing we have a safety net. It makes us feel calmer.'

'One of the rooms across the landing might be better. Quieter. I'll see what I can do if Mr Warburg does need to come back.'

'We really do appreciate all you've done for my husband. You have been wonderful!'

'It's nothing. We do what we can. I wish we could do more.'

'I'm so grateful to you for seeing to the manual evacuation.' It's primarily Sister Kinder herself who sees to it. And the elderly Staff Nurse, occasionally, when Sister Kinder isn't on duty. The union members won't touch it. Won't touch me! Bless Sister Kinder. I shan't forget her kindness.

SATURDAY, 5TH APRIL

'The catheter's blocked again. I don't think I can come home. It isn't sensible.' It's not going to work out. How can I think of going home? Absurd.

'I know how to do the bladder wash. I'll watch the nurse again this time.' Trying to soothe me, but she's not a nurse!

'What about moving me about? It takes three of them to do it. How can you possibly do it on your own?'

'I won't need to. I've told you, I've mobilized the bed.' All that again, but will it work?

'What about the bedsores?'

'You'll have cot sides. I can spray Sprilon with the best of them.'

'How can we possibly handle the wheelchair?'

'Let's see what happens on Monday. We can always forget that. All that fuss, and they haven't bothered here.'

'I don't think we'll pull it off. I don't want all the hassle of going home and then coming back here again.'

'We'll be fine.' She always dismisses problems. 'Stop panicking. We'll try, at least for a day or two. And if we can't make the grade, Sister Kinder will have you back.'

No option for me, as usual. Let it go at that. What choice is there?

SUNDAY, 6TH APRIL

Bladder wash cleared the tube yesterday. Clogged up again today just as I'm getting attuned to the move. Mentally, that is.

Should I consider suicide after all? Would that be the proper thing to do? Like Koestler? Made a pact with his wife. Don't think Teil wants to die because I'm dying. Don't want her to. My work would simply disappear. Children can't look after it. Too complicated. And not their business.

Anyway, the Diary should be written. Not because it's mine. To help the many people in my situation. I owe it to them. Originated the idea. Achieved a good deal of useful work. Teil can finish it. Will have to. Can no longer tape comments. Make a few notes. Mostly convey my reflections to Teil. Gives a purpose to the life that's left me.

Egg sandwiches again. White bread. Nice to be home for wholewheat bread!

Two bladder washes do the trick. Not difficult. Even I could do it.

MONDAY, 7TH APRIL

Last day at Frogmore, for the time being. Perhaps I'll never return? Unlikely I shall.

Waiting for physio. Slide day. Uncertain about trying it. Have to, otherwise no chance of mobility. No other way of transporting me on to a chair and back again at home.

'Hello.' Woman's not carrying anything. 'Slide ready?'

'I'm afraid not.'

NOT? So how am I going to use it? A sham, as ever. Led up the garden path. Never intended to make a slide for me! Can't take that long. Just pretence. All that nonsense about getting me mobile. Bowels under control. Helping me to help myself. Just so much blather. Just so much shit! I'm in their power.

'You could come in and we'll show you how to use the slide when it's ready.'

How much longer d'you need to make one? You've had four weeks. Six months? When I'm dead and frazzled?

'Shall we do some exercises?'

'I think not.'

Bugger off. What good are you? To hell with exercises! What does this woman know anyway? Nothing. Nothing at all. Nothing about cancer, that's for sure. None of them do. None of them know about the sort of bloody cancer that I've got. Spontaneous remission if the kidney's taken out! An old wives' tale, more like. One case, Lazenby said she'd read about. One case! Bloody hell. Amateurs.

I'll go home. Stay at home. There's only Teil and me. The children try. They've their own lives to lead. There's her and me. Help from some of the nurses. And Liz. But actually it's up to us. I'm going home. Want to be there. Immobile, but at home with Teil.

TUESDAY, 8TH APRIL

Today. *Home!* Certain I'd never see it again. Contemplated finishing it all. Quickly. Never mind how. Just shall I? So far my answer has been no.

Strange, really. Only last year I read Exit's *Guide to Self-Deliverance.* Approved of it. Obvious, isn't it? Finish now, with dignity. Save Teil the months of looking after me, and my children the spectacle of watching me die, slowly, tortuously, embarrasingly. Save me the agony.

Don't want to. Astonishingly, I don't want to take or lose my life. Glad there's no Euthanasia Bill through Parliament. If there were, I'd be even more suspicious of the people who look after me than now. The implications of depending on a GP for the final say! I'd think each pill designed to kill me, not assuage my pain. Each nursing act carried out to shorten life. Each doctor's visit an assessment. Is it worth taxpayers' money to keep me alive?

I want to go on living, even though I can't move from my bed, can't work, can't control my excretory functions. I can hardly enjoy food, books, TV. All the same, I want to remain. Today I'm going home. I have reasons for living!

They've done their best here, I know that. Not good enough. Many promises. Few fulfilments. Done things against me. Suppositories. Shan't forget those, or nurses' unions. Do people know what nurses' unions mean? Of course they don't. The Diary will alert them.

'Is the ambulance here?'

'Not yet. Let's find something to do.' Mad's trying to amuse me. Stories about her job. I just want to go home. Suggests listening to tapes. I want to be with Teil. Reading me pieces from the paper. Not interested. Don't care what happens in politics. It's after two. Where are the ambulancemen? 'Let's play a card game. How about cribbage?'

'Too involved.' Can't add. Snap? Ridiculous! Can't play that either. Too quick. The crossword. Cross word. Can think of a few for the ambulancemen. It's four o'clock! Have they forgotten me?

'I'll go down and see what's happening.' Mad opens the door and Sister Kinder's there.

'Sorry we're running a bit late today. A bad road accident, I'm afraid. The ambulance is being used for the victims.' Kindly smile, as always.

Half-past five. Back at home. Ecstasy. At last in my own house, in our dining-room. View of our garden from french windows. Teil's cooking. Euphoric. My wife and daughter round me. Heaven.

WEDNESDAY, 9TH APRIL

Peace. Such peace!

Amiable company for breakfast. Dandelion coffee, whole-wheat toast, a little honey. Served on the Siena. Enchanting.

'What d'you think of the set-up?'

'Very nice.' Obviously spent a deal of time and trouble. Not clear what on. Just the bed, isn't it? 'Point is, can you cope?'

'I'm sure of it. Anyway we've three days to find out.'

'And then?'

'And then I'll ring Sister Kinder and see if she can offer us a permanent safety net, some way or other. I'm sure she'll do her best.'

'A safety net?'

'The *chance* to get you off to Frogmore if it's absolutely necessary. I think that's what I need. The possibility, and then not use it.'

'You can't go on indefinitely.'

'I think I can. Second wind.'

Got my wife back. She's looking after me.

THURSDAY, 10TH APRIL

Nurse Kalmett sees to bedsores. Need spraying twice a day, or more frequently. Frogmore has not improved them.

'Why do they always get worse in hospital?'

'They've no idea how to treat them. We'll have them round in no time.' Aims Sprilon, quickly and expertly. 'Could you spray once or twice a day, Mrs Warburg?'

'Of course I can, now that we've got the cot sides.' Nothing to it. Lot of fuss. Hardly the sort of thing that requires expertise in nursing. 'No need for anyone to come again just for that.'

'You'll be all right if someone comes just once a day?'

'We'll be fine.'

Are they loading too much on her? Will she get exhausted again? How can she stay the course? Everyone says it's impossible.

'Should you have taken that on?'

'I'm fine. Stop worrying!'

Usual catheter problems. Teil does a bladder wash, and it works! Could do it myself. Nothing to that either. Are we really set? It's possible. I think it's possible.

Today I go back to Frogmore or the room's gone. Am I killing my wife? I don't want to harm her in any way.

'What about time off for you?'

'I'll go and visit Medora for a weekend. Just for a change. Mad can take over.' Her aunt in Sussex. They get on well.

'Of course.' Not too soon, I hope. Could Mad really look after me?

'Mad's perfectly competent. I'll show her what to do. If I can do it, she can too.'

'Hardly the sort of thing I want my daughter doing for me . . .'

'She's offered. She says she's only too pleased to do something constructive. Let her. She'd like to give real help. It's not always easy, you know. Think of poor Richard. Too far away. It's difficult for him to live with that.'

'I suppose so.'

My daughter see to bedsores?

The proposal from Sister Kinder turns out better than even we could have dreamed of.

'Would you like me to arrange a room as soon as possible after you feel you could use a break?'

'Is that feasible?'

'Of course. Just ring me up. I'll find you one.'

We can hardly believe our luck. It's the safeguard we've been praying for. On the NHS. If we're in trouble, they'll rescue us. Could we ask more?

'Sister Kinder is Joan of Arc,' Teil says.

I think we're happier now than we've been since this ghastly illness was diagnosed. Settled. Able to arrange our own lives the way we're used to.

SATURDAY, 12TH APRIL

It's the twins' birthday. Hard to believe that twenty-nine years have passed since Teil produced twin sons. So long ago. Yet I remember the day very well. Wrote *Richard II* on the second crib!

'There you are, Cockle. A birthday cake!'

'Thanks, Mum. See you remembered my favourite.'

'Talk of the Devil's Food Cake, as they say!'

'We'll give the Tock a ring, shall we?' Expensive, but it's their birthday. 'Hello, Tock. Happy birthday! And many of them!'

'How are things?'

'Well, I'm back, as you can hear. Cosily ensconced. My own private phone Teil had put in. A splendid new bed, with all mod cons. Yes, I'm very well equipped!'

'Good.'

'Your brother's here. Anna's on duty, unfortunately. And Mad's in Cannes at the Video Festival. We're celebrating here. We'll drink your health. What are your plans?'

'Well . . . surprise party last night, and tonight we're going out. All three of us.'

'You're taking Jeremy?'

'He enjoys going out.'

Twenty-nine years. Enchanting sons. Blue eyes. Curly blond hair. Like little angels. A smiling pair, easy to raise. Now showing a warmth and attitude it would be hard to better. The next time they're together will be at my deathbed.

SUNDAY, 13TH APRIL

'Can you take over for a weekend in May sometime, so I can visit Mad?'

'Be glad to.'

'There's a good store of everything. It's virtually a mini-hospital!'

'I can always come with Anna.'

'Something of a buswoman's holiday for her.' I don't want Anna. Know she's a doctor, used to illnesses like mine. Young woman to me. I don't want her looking after me. It's bad enough with my daughter.

'She won't worry about that.'

A tranquil, almost normal Sunday. Teil and Col in church. *The Sunday Times*. Lunch. Tea. Colin goes off to Anna.

MONDAY, 14TH APRIL

Terry appears to be my personal nurse. It's always she who comes, except on Thursdays, her day off, or at weekends. I take to her. She seems to care, to be genuinely concerned about me. I'm still a human being, not a sack of potatoes, even if I can't move much more than that. I have feelings.

I'm always reminded of Shylock's speech. To be ill with cancer is just a little like being an outcaste, like the Jew that Shylock was. People tend to regard you with a certain . . . discretion, hesitancy. But I might say, almost as Shylock said: 'Hath not a cancer victim senses, affections, passions, as a well man has?' Indeed he

[*187*]

has. 'If you prick us, do we not bleed? if you tickle us, do we not laugh? if you poison us, do we not die?' We do! We do! 'And if you wrong us, shall we not defend? If we are like you in the rest, we will resemble you in that.' We shall. Indeed, the Diary will defend!

Occasionally I feel cut off from normal human contact. But I'm still here. Perceive. So what I care about is people round me who show concern.

I seem to doze much more. Assume I'm about to make some notes and suddenly find I've just woken up. More signs of discomfort, too. I shan't mention that to Teil just yet.

TUESDAY, 15TH APRIL

'Guess whom I met shopping.'
'Jennifer?'
'Staff Gwynne! I didn't recognize her, of course. She was out of uniform, wearing jeans. I heard someone saying "Hello, Mrs Warburg" behind my shoulder. When I looked round I couldn't see anyone I know, but this woman was looking at me. Eventually it dawned on me. The jet-black hair. Not in a page-boy any more. A different style. Permed, but glossy black.'
'Amazing that she greeted you!'
'Yes, indeed. "How's Jeremy?" she said. I said you were getting along. What else is there to say?'
'Nice of her to ask after me, I suppose.'
'Hmm. I also met Beatrice. She keeps saying she'd like to visit you. People just don't seem to understand. I told her you can only be visited for, at best, a quarter of an hour. She said she doesn't mind at all. But, of course, I'd have to bring her out and take her back. I'll do it if you'd like that. It would make a change for you.'
'It doesn't interest me.'
'Perhaps you'd prefer Eileen. She's very quiet, and she knows what it's like for someone to be very ill. After all, Eric died only three years ago.'

'I think that might be better. After mass, perhaps. Just for a very short time.'

I don't need company. Extra strain. Already turned down my brother David. Know he doesn't want to come. Can't stand illness.

WEDNESDAY, 16TH APRIL

Pain's definitely worse again. Taking 1100 mg MST twice a day. Still not enough. 'If the drugs don't get you, the cancer must.' Remember New Orleans. Jazzy. Mint juleps.

Teil contacts Worthing. No answers other than upping the dose. Something tells me not to. Hardly because I'll be an addict when I recover from this illness! Not going to. Know that. Addiction makes no difference. But there's a still, small voice telling me to beware.

Of what? Don't know. Do know that, however circumscribed my life, I wish to continue it. Enjoy myself. That sounds insane. But I do. Look forward to Teil joining me for breakfast. Relish our meals together. Our time together. Stays longer now. Don't exactly *do* anything. Spend time companionably. Quietly. Consult a good deal about the Diary. My feelings about my illness. Teil makes a few notes. Hard to tape. Confusing, all those buttons to press. Recorder's heavy, too.

I'm a nuisance, I know. Use up resources, people's strength. Useless. Can't contribute. Teil says that isn't so. Says that, whatever I might not be able to do, I still cherish her. In sickness and in health. And I do. Value her. Of course I do. That hasn't changed. Tender my love. Offer my affection. My admiration. Something I still give. Thank God for that.

THURSDAY, 17TH APRIL

Discussion with Liz today. One of the new breed of doctors. Doesn't merely dismiss alternative medical practices. Uses homoeopathy. Evaluate relevance of acupuncture in Western medicine. Isn't the discourse which enthralls me. Pretty indifferent to all medical practices at present! None of them can help me. Except make morphine available to hold the pain in check. No. Real pleasure is that Liz considers me worth talking to.

Know the nurses respect the fact that I still think. Liz is a different kettle of fish. Gratifying she exchanges ideas with me as though I'm normal, not just a patient. Doesn't talk down to me. Makes me feel alive. Turns down coffee. But seems content, if not exactly keen, to talk.

'Before I forget, I have a message from Staff Gwynne.'

'Staff Gwynne?' What is this? Is she trying to persecute me here, at home?

'She specially asked me to remember her to you.'

'Staff Gwynne did?' She feeling guilty?

'Yes. She seems to have built up a special relationship with you!'

So there was more to the antipathy between Teil and Staff Gwynne than I realized at the time? I remember now. She said, 'You can wash him if you want to, you know. He's *your* husband!' To Teil. Several times. I know Teil wondered what she was talking about. Perhaps she fancied me?

FRIDAY, 18TH APRIL

Teil's visiting Medora. I always thought her lucky to have a relationship like that. Always wanted a friendly aunt myself. Family, but not lived-with family. Like my visits to my grandmother every week. We were her favourite grandchildren, my cousin Deirdre and I. She liked me best. 'She positively adores you,' Ma was always saying, bemused. Never herself, apparently, understanding this passion.

It was always sole or chicken for lunch. Doctor's orders. Just stewed fruit for dessert. 'Will you take cream?' my grandmother would ask me wistfully, and ring the bell for Maud to bring it in. She died on my birthday. Heart attack. Insisted she'd never see me again when I made my farewells, leaving for Wisconsin. The only near relative I really liked. Well, Deirdre, too. I could trust my grandmother. We talked. She listened. She admired me. At least I've got the 'Bluebell' pastel now. I like looking at it.

Mad's taking over. Good of her. Insists she's glad to. I don't like it. It's not proper. Feel inadequate. Can't do anything for her. Not even understand the complicated structure of her work. Politics. Problems. Can't take it in. Don't want my children remembering me like this!

I know Teil must go occasionally or I'll end up in hospital again. Two days alone with Mad.

'We'd better demonstrate the spray as well,' Teil says. 'Are you up to leaning over?' I'm up to it. Don't know what my backside looks like. Suspect it's pretty bad.

'No problem there.' Not for Mad maybe, but there is for me. Choice between a stranger nursing me and my daughter ministering intimately to my body. My daughter!

SATURDAY, 19TH APRIL

Mad counted the pills for me last night. Checking again. Can't be too careful. Dangerous drugs after all!

Draws the curtains, asks what I want for breakfast. Always the same – brown toast and dandelion coffee.

'Could you cut the toast into triangles?'

'Of course, Jifda. Just tell me how you like it and I'll see to it.'

'I don't like the big cup.'

'I'll change it for you.'

'And don't forget the new bottle of water. I'm supposed to drink a lot.'

'I know, Jifda. I'll get it for you.'

'The pillows aren't right. I've got a diagram of how they should be. Two upright against the back-rest. Then two across . . .'

'I know, Jifda. Lean forward and I'll see to it.' Important.

Doesn't grasp the difference it makes. Slightest deviation and my back begins to ache. 'How's that?'

'I can't tell right away. It seems all right.' Terry can see to it.

'Would you like some more coffee?' Trouble is, she fusses. Teil just gets on with it. Can't work out what I want. Teil knows. Haven't the strength to ask. Just wait till Teil comes back. Terry will help me wash. Tell her I'm not feeling up to it. What's the time? Terry's late. Saturday's difficult. 'Shall I bring your wash things while you're waiting?'

'I'll wait till Terry comes.'

'Shall I cook you something special?'

'No, don't worry about the food. It doesn't matter.'

Not as hungry as I used to be. To think I ate those huge amounts only last autumn. Not even keen on chocolate biscuits now.

No Terry. A weekend nurse.

'Shall we watch some TV?'

'Must we?'

I find it noisy, fall asleep and can't follow the programme. She's bored with me. Why doesn't she just go next door? I don't need company. She feels obliged to stay.

SUNDAY, 20TH APRIL

Not a good night, Teil being away. Know Mad does all she can. Still feel anxious. Takes a lot of trouble with the food. Just don't care. Asks me what I want. Don't know. I want Teil back. Will she have to send me off somewhere? I can't face that now. Like it here. Quite content to live here, doing what I can. All right, not much. Can listen. Sounding-board for business deals. Inspect the doilies as they're knitted. I still contribute!

'Shall we do a little physio before I go to church?'

I think the physio makes me worse. 'Not now. Later, perhaps.' Very good of her. Tries so hard . . . wish she wouldn't do so much. 'You don't have to wait for Teil to get back, you know.

You can leave any time. I'm perfectly all right. I've got the phone in case of an emergency.'

'Don't worry about me, Jifda. I'll be fine.'

Why shouldn't I try to help my daughter? Last time we'll be together on our own, I strongly suspect.

Teil's back already! It's only six o'clock.

'How was it?'

'Enjoyable. As always, with Medora.'

'How is she?'

'Blooming, enjoying her cigarettes!' Medora smokes like a chimney, something like twenty a day. Forty if she can afford it! No sign of cancer. Nothing at all.

'Still thriving on that?'

'Apparently.'

Extraordinary woman. Bit eccentric, really. Funny thing, we can't stand each other in the flesh, but we respect each other. At a distance.

MONDAY, 21ST APRIL

'Elizabeth is on the phone. She's asking if she and David can come over for an hour. They won't stay long. Just to come and say hello.'

'But David can't stand illness.'

'Apparently he'd like to come.'

'I suppose I can hardly refuse.'

'Of course you can. Just say if you don't want them. I'll see they're not upset.'

'It would be churlish. Make sure they know that I get tired easily, that I can't talk for long. Or to more than one person at a time.'

'I'm sure they'll be discreet, as ever. Elizabeth is quite aware. She'll steer David in the right direction.'

'When?'

'They thought Wednesday.'

'I have no other appointments!'

My relationship with my brother David has not been entirely satisfactory. Mostly Ma's fault, though not of course entirely. He bullied me when we were children. She didn't really stop him. He tried to be the man in charge. I wasn't having any! So we clashed. Nothing unusual in that, of course. No doubt it happens in most families where the first boy is six years older than the third. Even later, when we shared a flat, he still tried it on. I put a stop to that! And later still he believed Ma's innuendoes. I told him not to. He wouldn't listen. Didn't tumble to Ma till recently. Never was as bright as me!

I'll never be without my mother in this world. I so much wanted to! But she goes on and on, and I'm declining fast. Perhaps the next world will be free of her.

TUESDAY, 22ND APRIL

Good deal of post. Enjoy opening the letters. Nice to find a cheque in nearly every one! Like presents at Christmas.

'All done?'

'Yes. Ayliffe here today?'

'She is. Tuesday's always a good day. The weekend post to see to.'

'She could come and say hello if she wants.' I haven't seen Ayliffe for weeks.

'I'm sure she'd be delighted.'

'After the nurses have been. I don't want her involved in any of that.'

'Of course not. I'll tell her when you're ready.'

'Hello, Ayliffe.'

'Hello, Jeremy.'

She's always cheerful. Remarkable. Don't think I've ever seen her glum. She can be sharp at times, but she's never dismal.

'Have a chocolate biscuit.'

'Lovely chockie bs!'

In many ways we speak the same language. Both been to public school. She hated it as much as I did. Teil always says she doesn't know what we're talking about. We share the attitudes and mores instilled by those awful schools. Understand each other's references.

WEDNESDAY, 23RD APRIL

'David and Elizabeth are ringing around noon to make sure you can manage a visit.'

'That's very thoughtful of them.'

They arrive on the dot. Teil brings them in through the french windows. Fine day, though a little cold, I gather. Snug enough in here.

'Elizabeth and I will go next door,' Teil says at once.

And there we are, two brothers, more or less strangers. He's mellowed. Doesn't try to bully me! I'm told he's none too well himself. Heart trouble. Is it coincidence that all three of us became seriously ill somewhat early on in life? Hew had MS since the age of forty-eight. Just made his fifty-eighth birthday. Died, I believe, two days after it. Don't think I'll make mine. Perhaps I'll die two days before. More likely two months. And now David. He's sixty-three, of course. Much older. But still, not old enough to die. And he's got heart disease. After all that royal tennis? World champion several times. Exercise enough for anyone, I should have thought.

'Ma's excelled herself again.'

'I heard.'

'She's even quarrelled with Elizabeth.'

'That's quite some feat. But she's up to it, I gather, in spite of little strokes, and bouts of epilepsy, to say nothing of periods of depressive illness.'

'She'll outlive us all.'

'I don't doubt it for a moment. She's outlived Hew, she'll outlive me. You're our last chance.'

'She's got it in for everyone – Liz, Thane, Karin, the lot.'

I used to rail against my mother. Not now. I'm not really interested. I no longer get worked up. Don't allow her to contact me direct. Write her notes, roughly every fortnight. Masterpieces of nothingness. Talk about the garden, weather, state of public events, trips I've been on. Nothing you can put a handle to. That could be misinterpreted. That could give information. Nothing at all.

I visit her twice a year, at Christmastime and in May. Near her birthday. Force myself to go up to London. Take Mad for protection. She's brilliant at it. I won't have Teil involved.

'D'you have to keep to a diet?' I try to interest myself in David's life.

'I'm supposed to. Liz keeps me up to it.'

I like Elizabeth. Contrary to what my mother's always put about, I think she's very shrewd and capable. Marvellous wife to David and, by all accounts, a wonderful mother. Comes in and changes over with David to have a chat with me. I enjoy that.

THURSDAY, 24TH APRIL

I was never in any way emotionally involved with my father. Hardly likely with a father who did positively nothing for me. He did a fair amount against me, on his own admission.

'I owe you an apology,' Fred announced the first time I visited him after Pamela's death. This was quite unexpected. 'I didn't in any way behave like a father to you.' Thin. Old. Hunched back. Crouching in his chair. Still smoking. I tolerated in him what I don't from anyone else. *'Force majeure.'* He meant, presumably, his second wife. An irresistible coercion, excusing fulfilment of fatherhood? Fred stopped by his second wife? So he left my mother for Pamela (whatever story Ma may tell). No doubt Pamela aided and abetted him in that. Nevertheless, it was hardly entirely up to her that he not only neglected his paternal duties: he also positively put me down quite often, when I was young and vulnerable. After all, the big publisher, still high on the crest of publishing Orwell, known for his somewhat unexpected bravery in standing trial at the Old Bailey for publishing *The Philanderer*. And winning! He did not try to win *me*. Tried to lord it over me. I'd have none of it. Even so, I remember being ridiculously pleased when he apologized.

Pathetic to be so pleased at this short acknowledgement by a virtually dying man that he'd not done too well. Not his fault anyway. Hobson's choice! And, though he'd done nothing for me, he expected me to visit him from Somerset, just for an hour or so. 'Can't manage more. One of those things.'

He gave me his pen. His pen! He'd written his autobiography with it, presumably. Not bad non-fiction. But what has his pen to do with me? He gave his Orwell-inscribed copy of *Animal Farm* to Rosenthal. Left money to Elizabeth. Nothing to David. Or me. *Force majeure!*

Odd. Only one to recognize *A Woman's World*. Know they all thought him past it. I don't think that's true. He wasn't overly taken with rest of my work, but he had a nose for fiction. Not the sort of thing you lose with age or infirmity. Either have it or you don't. 'Your book is a triumphant success,' he wrote me. I have the letter still. 'Original (very), exciting, well written, with a sad but (I suppose) an inevitable ending. One regrets the break-up of the marriage.' His one true gift to me.

FRIDAY, 25TH APRIL

'I had a long discussion with Jennifer today. People haven't a clue about terminal illness. They have some nutty idea of someone lying in bed with a fluish cold. Absolute rot about God's will, which drives me up the wall. What sort of a god would will such a disease as this on anyone?'

'I suppose I might deserve it.'

'I think that's pernicious rubbish. *Deserve* it! What sense does that make? Millions of people might merit all kinds of dreadful punishments, but it's evident they don't get them. Some of those piously hypocritical remarks make my blood boil.'

'I wouldn't let it get you down too much.'

'Like people who thought women are meant to suffer in child-birth, if you remember. No anaesthetics in case you interfere with the wonderful laws of nature, and other insane arguments. Same thing.'

'Not quite, perhaps.'

'Sound precisely the same smug cant to me.'

I can understand why she's fed up with people's attitudes, particularly the ignorant ones. Don't think they mean any real harm. Just mistaken. I haven't the energy to discuss it. 'They just mean to be kind.'

'Then preserve me from kindness.'

'I really think, you know, that I must take some measure of the blame.'

'You? You take blame? Whatever for? If anything, you tend to be too good, too bloody noble.'

I feel so helpless to do anything for her. Leaving her in the lurch. Leaving her to it. Don't mean to. Either for her sake or for mine. It's happening all the same.

SATURDAY, 26TH APRIL

Richard and Ruthi on the phone. Haven't the energy to talk. Sound so slow, so dull, almost half-witted. Not that I can't think. What I can't always do is express my thoughts.

'I'll fill them in on the news and then get back to you, shall I?'

Teil goes off to her office to take the call. Can vaguely hear the litany of events. Can hear, but I'm not listening. All so tedious. Time for an end.

'Can you manage a few words?'

'Just hello, goodbye.'

'Richard's already passed his patent agent's exam. Clever of him, isn't it?'

Have trouble remembering what it is that Richard's doing now. Ah, yes. Taking a law degree. Extraordinary! Never expected that. Intelligent, of course. Never expected him to leave his science research. Still does a little on the side.

'Hello the Tock. Hello Frock. And how's the Flock?'

'Noisy. Keeps us up at night.'

'That'll pass soon.'

Remarkable pair. Show such concern. They've offered to bring Jeremy Hillier over for me to see. Can't allow that. No strength. Beguiling in theory, not possible in practice. Sweet of them. Really not on. Not much with babies at the best of times. Tubes of toothpaste. Similar to me!

Teil takes the phone away. Can hardly hold it to my ear.

SUNDAY, 27TH APRIL

Eileen sits down gingerly in the armchair while Teil is making coffee. 'How are you, Jeremy? I'm sorry. What a stupid question. You look very cosy.'

'I'm fine, Eileen. How've you been keeping?'

'Very well, thank you.'

We both lie, keeping up a social front of nothingness. I know she's frail and feeling empty. Poor old Eric died three years ago. She's not really over it. Don't think she ever will be. She isn't young, and wasn't when he died. Not used to dealing with the world. He saw to everything. But she's survived. Manages to keep her end up when it counts. Good for her!

'I expect you're still working, aren't you?' Eric was a writer too. She knows that it's one's life. Understands. Nothing really stops one. Only cancer!

'Are you back to painting?' Must get away from my problems.

'Just a little. Rather slowly, I'm afraid.'

'But you are doing it? That's good. I'm glad.'

Her pictures are remarkably strong in character, exactly the opposite of Eric's somewhat delicately rendered ink and wash. Not what you'd expect from her at all – bold, strong shapes in startling, vivid colours. Representational, but not photographic. Not outstanding, but not bad.

We drink the coffee. Already feeling overdone. Teil looks at me, gets up to collect the cups, and simply gathers Eileen up to take her home. As we thought, I can't enjoy, or even tolerate, visitors. And Elieen must be the least exhausting person we know.

Can no longer directly communicate with people. Too far away from the world even to talk to Eileen. Between life and death.

MONDAY, 28TH APRIL

Teil takes the phone and soothes our willing, but uncomprehending, daughter. Not that I don't want her to visit. Can't cope with her. With anyone. Can manage nurses because I have to. Even with them I hardly speak. Days of banter seem to have passed. Always maintained: once I lose my sense of humour. . . .

Can't talk on the phone. What shall I do on my mother's birthday, coming up in May? Teil says forget it till it's on us. Suppose she means I might be dead by then. And so I might be.

I've very little left, yet don't want to die. Might just be a setback. Felt better before. Takes all my energy to swallow pills. I keep a schedule for them.

'Twelve MST. You check.'

'Quite correct.'

Teil puts them in the little screw-top bottle, place that's easy for me to get at. Have spares in case I drop the bottle and can't reach it.

'Shall I cut up the potatoes?'

'That would be best.'

Will she have to feed me soon?

'You look rather pale. Are you specially tired?' Liz. Routine call.
'I suppose so.'

'Bit anaemic, I think. Perhaps we ought to do a blood test.'
'What for?'

'To see whether you should have a transfusion to help with the anaemia. And there might be other problems . . .'

'You mean go to Frogmore?'

'I don't think they can do a transfusion there. I think it would have to be a larger hospital.'

We've been through this before, Teil and I. Worked out that this situation might arise. Had the same experience with Teil's father, Ralph. We rushed to see him in a clinic near Vevey. Remember Vevey from before, on Lake Geneva, near the dungeon at Chillon. Went there with George to a conference for linguists, representing the English Department at UC during my days at London University. Ralph lived in Lausanne then. We went to see him.

'He's dying. He's obviously dying. Why are they *forcing* him to have a blood transfusion? He says he doesn't want it.'

Teil couldn't see why they should force her father then, any more than she can see why anyone should force me now.

'If we didn't give him a transfusion, he would die,' the *professeur* in charge explained to me. Once you're in their clutches, they do what they want. Not interested in what the patient says. Even though we were quite ignorant about cancer then, we could see that. Now, so much more experienced, I certainly won't allow myself to be taken to a hospital. Absurd idea.

Teil puts my case for me. 'He doesn't want a blood transfusion. It would mean, as you say, going to a hospital, travelling in an ambulance for twenty-five miles, staying there a few days and travelling back. He might well die in the process. Away from home. He doesn't want to know.'

'That's perfectly all right. I'll tell the nurse to do a test, then you can decide. No one will force you to go.'

Even Liz doesn't quite understand. I don't want a blood test.

I've no wish to learn about any possible problems. What I don't know about, I don't have to make decisions about. Simple as that. Won't have the blood test. If the nurse tries to insist, I'll call Teil. She'll protect me.

WEDNESDAY, 30TH APRIL

Pain's getting through again. Definitely. Don't really want to increase the morphine dose. Haven't much choice. Lying here in pain doesn't achieve anything. Might as well lie here without pain – well, in relatively mild discomfort. Drugged. Some choice! All the wonders of modern medicine, and what do we end up with? The opium poppy! Known for I don't know how long. Nothing to touch it.

Think the pain's increased because of the possibility of hospital. Odd. Not really worried about dying now. If I'm honest with myself, I know I'm going to be dead soon. I'm worried about the process, and where I am. Don't want anyone to hasten my death, or to suggest ways of prolonging my life. It's my affair. And if I want advice, I'll talk to Teil.

May be a hopeless burden to myself, and others. Well, primarily to Teil. The nurses and GP are doing their jobs. Whether they minister to me or someone else is neither here nor there. As for being a burden to myself, well, I still enjoy myself. Astonishing but true. In touch with nature through the french windows. Communicate with Teil. We analyse the situation from a general point of view.

'But what about the infringement of your liberty? You're stuck here day in and day out.'

'That's something else.' Interesting now. One of our conversations. We might have been discussing someone else entirely. A case of exploring motives, going deep into the human psyche. 'It may be hard. I can't pretend it isn't. But you're still here. You can still talk to me. You can still offer me something no one else can. You're still, essentially, you. That may not be true of other people. I wouldn't know. But I know it's true of you. Strange as

[*202*]

it may appear, you comfort me. It's you who'll help me through the grief. It's you who are doing that.'

'Have I told you that I think you're wonderful?'

'It's just the way I feel.'

My wife still wants me. I can still help her. I'm still unique. My cold, still body feels a sudden surge of life charge through its veins.

May

'Could you lift the bedding off the cradle and look at my legs?' I can feel the toes moving! Definitely.

'Do they hurt?'

'I can feel my toes moving. Are they?'

'Not that I can see. Are your feet hurting?'

'Nothing to do with that. No! It's just that I think there's some movement in them.' She can't seem to catch on. Maybe I'll be able to walk again!

'There's a patch which seems rather raw. Are you cold?'

'Cold? No, of course not. It's quite warm in here.'

Now what? Must there constantly be more problems? Am I going to get gangrene in my legs and have to have them amputated? Gangrene can kill quite fast, I think. I'll refuse an operation.

'They're just a little sore. It's nothing to worry about.' Nurse Kalmett clearly thinks I'm over-reacting.

'It isn't gangrene?'

'Gangrene? No.' She carries out the chores quickly, methodically. Not talkative.

'What did she say to you?' She might not tell me if it's something serious.

'She doesn't think it's anything of any consequence. Just a sore they missed. They probably washed your feet and left a bit of damp between the toes, that's all.'

'Something's always going wrong.'

'Your bedsores are doing very well. Actually, they're almost healed. It's quite remarkable. Those sheepskins, and the Sprilon, really work.'

Teil rambles on. I'm not listening. My toes feel as though they're moving. I'd like to move them, and my legs. I'd like, just once, to walk around the room. Totter around the terrace, perhaps, just one more time before I die.

FRIDAY, 2ND MAY

'You haven't forgotten Spalding's coming today?'

'Must he?' I don't want him to see me in this state. He wouldn't want to see me either.

'It's the weed-killing. It's already very late. I just can't find the time to do it myself.'

'I don't want him seeing me like this.' She's insensitive, sometimes.

'He won't come round this way. I'll tell him to leave this area. He'll just do as I ask.' It used to be me who told Spalding what we want done in the garden.

'What about the path outside this room?'

'I'll see to that myself.'

I welcomed my stints with Spalding. We got on, he and I. Occasionally he called me 'boy' – friendly West Country term for a man. Not what it means in Standard. Refers to me as 'the boss', sometimes 'the gaffer'.

'I've got him clearing the ditch down by the new golden elder hedge.'

My job to tell him what to do! Don't want him coming near me. Embarrassing for both of us.

Funny thing. Last year, when he was hacking away, smoking his frightful 'fags', I guessed he'd got lung cancer. Smokes like a chimney, but he's flourishing.

Medora chain-smokes even more than Spalding. In her seventies. No sign of cancer.

Just me. I've got this awful illness. Never smoked. Hardly

drink. Careful what I eat. Exercise. Why have I got cancer? Because my mother smoked when I was young? Because I'm a worrier? Because I deserve it?

SATURDAY, 3RD MAY

Lovely out. One of those beautiful early May days. But May stands for Ma. Her birthday soon. What shall I do?

'Inform the aunts, I would think, so they can tell her you can't get up to London.'

'They'll give the real reason away.' She doesn't imagine they wouldn't relay such news, does she?

'I don't think so. I'm pretty sure they'd rather not. Who'd want to tell her?'

Why should Ma care? She must know how I feel about her and, however much she kids herself about her feelings for me, she must dislike me too. Human nature. Not that I think she ever really cared for me. Don't think she knows what caring is. Talks about it constantly. That's easy. Buys presents. That's easy too. No, I don't see her grieving much. Or about David. When I *did* mention severe backache, she simply ignored it. Talked about herself. What else? Constant troubles with my mother. She can't act on what she doesn't know – that's been my strategy for the last twenty years or more. Well, more like thirty-three. When we came back from the States I saw her for what she is. Never cottoned on before. When I saw, or rather heard, her again, I understood.

SUNDAY, 4TH MAY

I resent the fact that so much of my day is spent sleeping. I hardly need to sleep my small amount of life away! All this

tucking me up and tiptoeing about. It quite irritates me. I'd *rather*
be woken up by people once they get back from wherever
they've been. Takes me almost fifteen minutes to come to properly. Drugged sort of sleep.

MONDAY, 5TH MAY

Bank Holiday. Strange, when the house is empty of everyone
except the two of us I almost manage to forget I'm ill. And so
does Teil. She comes and sits in the easy chair. We talk just as we
used to do – about our writing, its progress, marketing tactics,
sizing up the chances of success, future projects.

'What about *A Call to Arms*?' I know it's good. I worked hard
on that.

'I'll finish that. After all, it's two-thirds done.'

'And who will be first author?' Of the first joint novel we've
drafted.

'You, of course. You've written most of it. I don't think I need
change that.'

'I wouldn't like to think you'd put my name first if you've
virtually written it.' Possibly Teil would think she should give
credit where it isn't due. Because I'll be dead.

'I wouldn't do that. It wouldn't be proper for me to palm off
work I'd done under your name. That would be dishonest.'

'But I wouldn't like to miss out either.'

'I'll make sure the credit's distributed as fairly as I know how,
whichever way seems right. I know you wouldn't like it any
other way.'

'So what about *The Macro Factor*?'

'I don't suppose I'll ever do it.' I can understand why she's off
that book. I'm saddened all the same. 'I've got more print-outs of
the Diary entries . . .'

'I can't do much. I've still got lots to get through.'

'I thought you might like to read them.'

'Not just yet.' Can feel an element of depression creeping in.
Not clear why. Been unusually cheerful most of the time. Why

now? What's changed? Another wet day. Bank Holiday! Nothing to me.

What am I doing here? Not getting anything done. Existing. No point. Can't even read the Diary.

TUESDAY, 6TH MAY

A rather curious spasming this morning, sort of minor convulsion through my body. What's it up to now? And hiccups. Still going as Teil brings my breakfast. Her eyes look bleak. Doesn't say much. She knows something I don't? Sign of impending death? Been told what to look out for?

'I don't think hiccups are anything in particular. I've heard of people getting them and doctors can't stop them. One often wonders what they *can* do!'

'They fixed the shingles.' She's altogether too anti-doctors.

'Liz did, yes.'

'So maybe she can fix the hiccups.'

'I'll give her a ring.'

Teil doesn't like to ring her. Feels she should.

'I'll come out later,' Liz says. Tiresome to bother her. Can't stop the hiccupping.

Still doing it when Liz arrives right after surgery. Is something up?

'There's nothing I can do for that. I think it'll go soon.' She's being kind, presumably.

'He also had a sort of spasm in the early morning.' I wasn't going to mention that. What for? 'A sort of shudder through his body. Is it something to do with the bulge in his abdomen?'

Liz prods around. Obvious to me she's no idea what the bulge is. Nothing to be done. Prescription rites. They leave while the nurse finishes her chores.

'I told Liz you were feeling depressed. She said you have good reason! Anyway, she said she'd be glad to help chemically, if you wish. She's written a prescription.' Another one? They'll soon take the place of meals! 'I can get it for you and you can have a go.

You're under no obligation, of course. It's entirely up to you. She said it *might* have some effect on the spasming and the hiccups – relax the muscles or something.'

'I may give it a try.'

Like the injections in the hospital, it'll probably have no effect. Same with the hormones, that useless episode. So now depression pills. Well, why not? The more the merrier.

Nothing more about the blood sample, thank goodness. Won't give that a try. Time's running out, I'm sure.

WEDNESDAY, 7TH MAY

Can rule out depression pills. Knock me out completely. Dozed all evening. Slept through the night. Still drowsy now. Absolutely no point in that. Enough oblivion to come, presumably. If not, so much the better. Meanwhile prefer to feel depressed than not to feel at all.

Am I dejected by the approach of death? Don't think so. Lived with the knowledge that I'll die soon for quite some time now. Over a year since I first felt those clawing tentacles clutching my ribs. Always sensed I'd get cancer. But those gripping pains were different. That *was* cancer. Deep down I knew that death would claim me in a year or so. Tried to forget it. Pushed it away. Even when the kidney tumour showed quite clearly on the X-rays. Believed MacKnife that I still had at least a year or two, possibly five, or even ten! Hoped myself into it, allowed the operation, went along with that useless X-ray therapy. A mutual delusion society, between the doctors and myself. That's why they keep their distance, why they behave so heinously. They know they're impotent.

Can't understand why they don't tell the truth if one asks them to do so. Repeatedly. Specifically assures them that one wants to know. Lazenby was always countering that just because one is reasonably intelligent, and asks to be told the truth, doesn't mean one is ready for it when one hears it. What makes her think she knows? The arrogance of it! Took it on herself to be the judge of what I could manage. Deliberately misled me. The treatments were clearly not for me. May help the medics with research, keep the records straight. Must be seen to have done everything possible, no matter whether it was the best course for the patient.

Many people instinctively don't go to doctors if they suspect their case is beyond medical help. Once on the treadmill, it's hard to get off. It's not only a lack of guts, though they might be in short supply. All that double talk makes it difficult not to be bamboozled. Disease is hardly conducive to clear thinking. One is, after all, ill. Taxes what energy one has. One's aghast, horror-struck, possibly numbed with fear. Hope kindles, springing eternal, more or less. So when the doctors lie, and there's no other word for it, they commit a crime against the patient. It's not their business to decide what people can, and cannot, shoulder. What do they know about it? Simply projecting their own view. A premise of people who are well, whose job it is to heal. And when they can't? Feel menaced.

THURSDAY, 8TH MAY

Drugged feeling's finally worn off. Still *compos mentis*. Not interested in living without that. Point at which I'd welcome euthanasia.

Tricky, though. Who's going to administer it? How? Quaint idea that two doctors could assess the case. How can anyone but the patient judge the circumstances? Some arbiter, in some office, deciding whether a case is right or not? Hardly what it's all about. No. Either the patient's provided with the wherewithal and does it for himself, or it's not on.

One scarcely likes to trust a doctor, or a pair of doctors, even. They're notoriously prone to mistakes. Sort of gaffe one prefers to make oneself. Nor do I fancy some euthanizer, Ku-Klux gowned, injecting me in order to kill me off. Don't want what amounts to an executioner standing at my deathbed. I'd rather have death come when the time is ripe, whenever that may be. Prefer to trust to luck that someone will be with me, preferably Teil. One of the children, perhaps, not some stranger sent to do the deed.

What sort of person would that be, anyway? However much one speaks of mercy killing, it's still an execution. May have been murderers who were keen to hang. Doesn't affect the way the hangman feels about his job. Or the person who switches on the current for the electric chair. Or even the soldiers in the firing squad. It's too deliberate an act. Quite different from turning off the life-maintenance machine. Patient's alive only because of the machine. Very often the brain's dead. Simply a question of removing something which keeps some body going mechanically. Can't compare that to deliberately finishing a life still under the individual's control.

Not that I want to put death off. I don't. I'm ready now, in the sense that I can't function. Life for me is creative writing, for which I freely gave my time. I can no longer do that, so I'm content to die.

Means leaving Teil to it. Feel guilty about that. She's entitled to the reasonable expectation that I'll share her life for many more than the thirty-two years we've had together. Doesn't have the *right* to it. I'm sorry to be leaving her – my greatest sorrow, apart from my unfinished work. I've done what I could to be a good husband. Hope she won't be too grieved – or too relieved! – at my death. A year or so of mourning, perhaps. Then hope she'll have a full and varied, happy life. Wish that for her, and for my children too. Tried to be a good father. Finished now. Can't give more. Come to the end of what I can do.

FRIDAY, 9TH MAY

Col taking over for the weekend. Teil off to London. I'm anxious she won't be able to stay the course.

'I'll take a weekend break every now and again. That'll be enough. I'm fighting fit! Don't worry, I'm not going to let you down. I'll keep you here. If I need help, the children will support me.'

'The children have their jobs.'

'I'll get a night nurse if we need one. Mary Houlder. We'll pay her privately if necessary.'

'What if things go wrong this weekend?'

'Col knows where I am. Mad would drive me back at once.'

'But can he carry out what's needed?'

'Of course he can. He need only ring the Duty Doctor. And he's got Anna too! I know he'll get her bleeped, and she'll talk him through any problems while he's waiting for help.'

'Will two nights away be long enough for you?'

'I'm OK. Truly. I'm only going as an insurance policy.'

Not so much the disease now. Of course that's terrible. Used to being ill. Hard to remember a time when I was not. Now scared I'll be shipped off to hospital. Completely in their hands. Do all they can. Part of the trouble. Feel obliged to override the patient. Do too much. If there's a crisis, no leaving one in peace to die. Rush life-saving equipment to the patient's bed. Medical staff where one would wish to see one's family. Not in Frogmore, perhaps, but in the larger hospitals. Don't want to know. Can Teil hold out? Am I killing her? Who will look after my work if she dies? Who'll write up the Diary?

SATURDAY, IOTH MAY

'What shall I make for lunch? I've brought some lovely fish I thought you'd like.'

'That would be very nice. Don't prepare too much. I don't need much to eat.'

'What sort of vegetables do you prefer?'

Don't know what to answer. Not interested in meals. Too

many pills! Food makes no sense. 'Just cook what's easiest for you. I'm not very hungry.'

'Shall I stay with you?'

'If you've got work to do, you carry on.' Don't need company as such. Like to know someone's about the house, that's all.

'I can help Mum to sell the Vicarage. She won't want to stay here. It's too big for one.'

'Probably. But she might want to stay. Don't try to push her.' Must say a word or two on Teil's behalf. People misinterpret her wishes.

'Of course not. I'll just help if she wants me to.'

'Your mother's an unusually able woman. Remarkably independent too.' Marshal my thoughts, for Teil's sake. 'Naturally, she's a woman, a human being, of a particular type of character, nature, temperament. Obviously I should wish you to help her as much as possible in her bereavement. I should also wish you to understand that the greatest help you can give her isn't necessarily the kind you might expect. I think she'll want, in fact need, her privacy. Right from the start. As much, if not more, than compassionate, caring and congenial company.'

'I understand, Dad.'

'Obviously try to help her in the way she evidently wants. Not always in the way that you, and maybe others, might think or feel she ought to want.'

'I know what you mean.'

'People might think she "should talk it out", or not be left alone so much, or some such ideas. So please, just respect and abide by her wishes, whatever others may say, however strange or unusual in the circumstances they may seem to you. Perhaps – I hope and expect – you will find no difficulty in this. But I'd like you to bear in mind what I've said. I know you'll try. I'm sure you'll lovingly achieve.' Exhausting. Hope I've conveyed my meaning, for Teil's sake.

'I'll remember. She talks about going to live in Sussex.'

'Yes, we thought about living there together.' But now we shan't. We shan't live together anywhere, except in spirit. I'll always be with her in spirit. As, thank God, she will be with me.

Teil on the phone. 'Any problems?'

'We're doing very well. Col's made lots of lovely food, most of which I haven't been able to eat, unfortunately. But delicious morsels. How's George?'

'He sends his very best wishes. Says he's so sorry he never made the trip to Somerset.'

'Has their house changed?' I helped them buy it.

'Very little. The neighbourhood has. Lots of new houses. But still reasonable country round about.'

'And you went down to David's?'

'And saw a film, yes.'

'See you later, then.'

'See you soon. Love you!'

'Me too.'

She's back tonight. Can she really visit all these people, fit in a film, everything? Suppose it shows the difference between us. For some years now I haven't been able to contemplate such a full social weekend. Simply could not undertake it. In retrospect, the signs of illness?

'Do you feel rested?'

'I'm fine. Honestly. I keep telling you. Second wind or something.'

'I could go on for months! They all say so.'

'Perhaps.'

'You mean you think I won't?'

'I mean I keep an open mind, rely on intuition. We've had so many estimates. All different. All wrong! Except for Lazenby's. We shan't know about hers till August.'

'There's a limit to the amount you can put up with. I'll have to go off for a bit.'

'There's a limit anyway. Time. We believe in time. We know it's all too short.'

'You mean *you* think I haven't got all that long.' She thinks I can handle knowing that. 'I don't mind.'

'It's not exactly that. It depends what you mean by long. But certainly, compared with our marriage, not that long. I might as well make the most of what is left.'

'You'll have a breakdown.'

'What makes you think I'll be better off without you than with you? I'm used to looking after you, even before the illness. How will I survive without you, as well as without looking after you?' She doesn't often cry.

'You'll have my work.'

'I expect I'll need it.' That's what drew us together in the first place, what's kept us so close ever since, I suppose. She's always said she considers my work an asset, not a hindrance. Always maintained that supporting those who're trying for the highest in creative work is worth the effort. Worldly success is neither here nor there. Suddenly she grins.

'You know what Jennifer suggests? That I go to a beauty farm! Sweet of her. Little does she know that that would be nothing short of purgatory for me.'

'You wouldn't enjoy it, being pampered?'

'I would not. I prefer this any day.'

Colin tried to get the pillows right, but couldn't. Teil sorts them out expertly. My back feels better right away. She'll be here to help me, even beyond the grave.

TUESDAY, 13TH MAY

Nurse Kalmett today, much to my surprise. 'I'm just going to take a blood sample. Just a prick. It won't hurt.'

That's why she's come! 'No, thank you.'

'Nothing to it, really. It won't hurt.'

'No, thank you.'

'Dr Walsh-Comfitt asked me to . . .'

'I know, she mentioned it. No, thank you. I don't want a blood sample taken.'

'But if you need. . . .' Suddenly Teil's here. Either she left the loudspeaker of my 'baby alarm' on, or she's psychic. 'Good morning, Mrs Warburg.'

'Hello. We haven't seen you for a long time.'

'No. Your husband's saying he doesn't want a blood sample taken.'

'That's right, he doesn't. No point. He doesn't want a blood transfusion. And he doesn't want to know if there are any other complications.'

'Then you won't be able to say whether you'd like treatment or not.'

'That's right, we won't know. That saves a good deal of decision making.'

No comment, and no more attempts to persuade me.

'Nurse Kalmett tells me you refused the blood sample?'

'Yes. As we said, we prefer not.' News certainly travels fast. She must have reported straight back to the Health Centre before Liz started on her rounds.

'Of course, that's perfectly all right. Any problems? You don't feel too tired?'

'No, I feel very well. Just this little local difficulty with my back.'

No smile. Even if I felt unwell, I wouldn't let on. What for? Nothing to be done for me. Things might, quite inadvertently, be done against me.

WEDNESDAY, 14TH MAY

Unexpected letter in the post. My brother David. Don't think I've had a personal letter from him for perhaps forty years. 'It was great to find you so well (or possibly just so brave!). I thought the visit eminently worthwhile and hope that you both felt the same.'

Brave. He calls me brave! Probably the highest praise he can bestow. Came to visit me. Is it possible he feels something for me after all? I'd like to think so. Yearn to think so. Not just because I'm ill. I prefer to be liked. Crave it. Yet I'm not – generally liked, I mean. Respected, often. Looked up to, sometimes. Loved, evidently by my family. But liked? Know Teil likes me. Not sure about anybody else.

Now David's ill again. His GP seemed unconcerned. Elizabeth insisted he be admitted to the local hospital. They pronounced him fine. Gave him medicines, placebos perhaps. Lasted a few days. Then another relapse. Do these doctors know anything? This time a major London hospital. 'The spell in St George's seems likely to be longer, on two counts: (1) the intervention of the Bank Holiday, and (2) a determination by the medics to make haste slowly. I am sure that they are right and plan to be patient – up to a degree anyway.'

Ma's ill as well. Said to be dying. Don't believe it. Nothing to go on, except my psyche. Told me no chance of my outliving her. Right, of course. She's absolutely determined to survive till ninety at the very least. Don't doubt she will. No longer a matter of concern to me. A race, David calls it, between the three of us. What's wrong with us?

THURSDAY, 15TH MAY

Teil's taken to sitting with me in the afternoons. Desultory chat about the Diary. Teil has ideas about the structure. Hear her, don't connect. Leave that to her. My job to get material across. All I can do. Discuss which publishers to approach.

Tearful again. She's often tearful now. 'Sorry, I don't know why I'm being so stupid.'

Teil holds my hand. Hard to get any nearer to me. Separated by cot sides, sheepskins, pillows. Above all, by the disease. Sits on the chair next to me, as close as we can get.

'I've taken down quite a good film on the video. Shall we put it on?'

[217]

'In the afternoon?'

'Why not? Pretend we're going to the pictures!'

She draws the curtains, puts the video on. We watch some film. 'Popcorn? In the best American tradition?' Last time I did that in real life we watched *On Golden Pond*, with Fonda clearly dying as a man, not just in the part. Went to see it with Richard and Ruthi in Boston. Large popcorn-maker in the centre of the foyer. Ruthi made popcorn for me here. Lovely popcorn. I'm glad Richard has Ruthi.

FRIDAY, 16TH MAY

'Is that better?' Even Teil can't always arrange the pillows properly.

'It will have to do.'

'I'll fetch some Diamorphine.'

Pain's started in again. For heaven's sake – on fourteen MST pills twice a day. A flood of opium.

'Next time Liz comes I'll ask if they do higher dosage MST.'

'Higher?' Crazy to think of even more.

'There must be others. . . .'

Others? What others? The cup seems to be in her hand, and yet it's on the table. It can't be both. Am I hallucinating? Try to sort it out, bantering as best I can. 'You're trying to keep the cup from me, aren't you?' Bad enough that I have to drink from an invalid cup. There seems to be no reply. Better stop talking. Obviously too much, since there's no answer. Why doesn't she respond at all? I'm talking quite a bit. Can't seem to stop. She always said the morphine made me talk too much and hushed me up. Now that I can hear myself doing it, there's no reaction. Is she annoyed with me? Worry about that with people, especially Teil.

And here are David and Elizabeth! How did they get here? French windows? Didn't know they were coming again. Carry-ing flowers from their cottage garden. Hydrangeas. Charming. David's come to see me. Well done, David!

'Did that help?' She can't be annoyed. She's looking quite concerned.

'Help?'

'The Diamorphine. Did it help?'

'I think I feel more comfortable.'

Think I do. Not quite sure. Don't feel pain. More a numbness, a light-headedness. Where have David and Elizabeth got to? Why doesn't Teil answer? I must drink from the cup of life. The cup is dancing now. Floating up from the table, dancing in front of me. Twirling around. A red skirt twirling. Singing. 'Singing in the Rain'. Gene Kelly singing in the rain. My favourite musical is *My Fair Lady*. Magnificent. Could watch it for ever. Teil's holding the cup to my lips! Thought that it was dancing.

'Take the cup away. I don't want any more.'

SATURDAY, 17TH MAY

'Take notes. For the Diary. It's important. Things are very strange now.' Sensations I have never had before. 'My feet feel like clogs. Well, as though they're wearing clogs. Hard on the outside. Like stone or brick. Well, maybe more like wood. The feet themselves feel fine. Presumably they haven't actually changed?'

'I can't see any difference.'

'It's very strange. My feet seem to be running round the place, but somehow in a container. Not attached to my body at all. My feet are dancing. Cavorting all on their own. They've escaped from the container.'

'Container?'

'That's what it feels like. A sort of box.'

'Does it feel pleasant?'

'The dancing's fun but my feet ache. Quite severely. Like a solid piece of log. They feel the pain quite badly.'

'I'm sorry.' Tears starting up again. Not that bad. Didn't mean to imply it was that bad.

'It's fine at the moment. Quite fun, really. Tap dancing.' I look at her sitting in the chair. Not always easy to tell whether I've said something, or just thought I've said something. Look at her eyes, her face. No sign she's heard what I've just said. Must try to get across it's not that bad. Surely I'm speaking now? Can hear my voice quite clearly.

'I'll have to get on to Worthing about a pump. Syringe driver. The stuff isn't working properly by mouth apparently.' She still hasn't heard. She's worrying now about my having pain.

'All the stuff does is make one feel odd. It doesn't stop the pain.' No sign she's heard. Try again: 'It's quite fun, really. Tap dancing.' This time she hears me. Her eyes smile slightly, but the mouth stays pulled down at the corners. Sad. The worst of it is leaving her alone, alone to face my death. 'Will you be all right?'

'I suppose so. Don't worry about it. I'll carry on. You know, very competent and all that.' Watery attempt at smiling.

'Not quite a question of that.'

Not so far gone that I can't work that out. She'll manage from a practical point of view. Of course she will. Better than I ever could, if the roles had been reversed. What about emotionally? What can I do about it anyway?

Can see out of the corner of my eyes. Don't have to move my head. Can pretend I'm not looking and see precisely what is going on. Will I see after I'm dead? Will I see Teil?

'I'll see to the Diary. Visit Richard and Ruthi.'

Normally quite accepting of death. Sometimes do feel angry. I'd like to go to the States. Would like to see Jeremy Hillier, be a grandfather, play with him. Would be good at that. Good with toddlers. Why should I die now, so early? Why should I? Don't want to.

SUNDAY, 18TH MAY

Body feels as though it's lying in a coffin. Know it isn't. Know I'm still here, because of the attack. The legs are now attacking me, marching up towards my head. But they've been caught. The big toenail's caught on the brick wall! That's stopped them.

[*220*]

Not that it does much good. The Communists have taken over now. The changes have already taken place, whether I want them to or not. It's all over. Minnow tells me not to worry. She says Ma's here, but that it doesn't matter. And the aunts. Can't see them. Know they're here.

Wake up sweating when I think what's happened. My movements tend to be involuntary now. Makes no difference what I want my body to do. Leads a life of its own. A life? It leads a life? Perhaps the world has changed. Nothing seems sharp, it's all diffuse, almost out of focus. My body's still, immobile, as though already in its box. Objects around it move. The room spins round. The bed is on a roundabout, swinging in circles. Can see it all. Not there any more. Out of the body. Dressed as if I were still in bed, but I'm not there. Watching what's happening.

Teil's here. Drew the curtains, brought the breakfast. Of course I know she's here. Heard her before she came!

'Are you awake?'

'Of course I'm awake!'

'Honey? Are you awake?' Can't seem to get her attention, like a small child trying to get the parents to understand. 'Would you like something to drink?' Watch her face. Something has got across. If I think about what I want my body to do beforehand, it usually does it. Programmed, like one of Col's computers. Programmed it! 'I'll help you drink it.' Why help? I can hold the cup!

MONDAY, 19TH MAY

The world's more like itself again. Vividly remember my father telling me how, 'coming round' from a heart attack, he had 'looked on the world and found it good'. Very much impressed me at the time. Now, some years later, 'coming round' from being befuddled by drugs, I know far better what he meant. I, too, have looked on the world and found it good.

Good! In spite of atrocities. Inhumanities. Wickedness. Not that I found it bad before. But I find it far, far better now. Good in the sense that God is good. Which is, perhaps, to say that the world is God. And is not better than it is simply in so far as it rejects God.

Strange. Feel reasonably well. Generally quite content and cheerful. Not at all afraid of dying. Don't feel I'm likely, in some sense, to be changed by it. Take it I'll always be with those I love. Available. For advice. For discussion. As a sounding-board. If wanted. All I can do now. Less than it used to be. Intrinsically doing what's required. Essentially there for them. To contact me. Can still do that.

'What about some ice-cream? From the health shop. The genuine kind.'

'That sounds inviting.'

'Should go down easily, and it's quite nutritious too.'

'Terry said something about a complete food in a tin.'

'Yes, I bought you some. Try it. A little, perhaps.'

'All right.'

'The chemist said it's only available on prescription. Then I realized it isn't. I'll talk to Liz about it tomorrow.'

'We don't need it on prescription. We can afford it ourselves.'

'Of course, if you prefer. Shall I make some dandelion coffee?'

Can no longer chew that easily. Teil makes a meal and I leave most of it. She doesn't seem to worry. Don't like causing unnecessary work.

TUESDAY, 20TH MAY

'Hello! We weren't sure you were coming today.' Liz.

'Sorry. Very inconvenient to turn up at lunchtime.'

'Whatever suits you. Anyway, can't say I'm all that hungry.'

'My husband is finding it quite difficult to swallow. Should we switch to liquid food?'

'Good idea. I'll write a prescription for you.'

I told Teil we'd buy it ourselves. What's she on about? We don't need charity.

'And is there a two hundred milligram MST?'

'Let's just check.' Pulls out the book of words. There isn't, apparently. 'Are you having difficulty swallowing?'

'No, no difficulty.' Another of Teil's hobby-horses. I *can* swallow!

'But there might be. I'm nervous about what happens if it does become harder. I've been on to Peter Worthing about organizing a syringe driver. He agreed at first. This morning he said the powers that be had told him not to bring it until my husband can no longer swallow. That would be a bit on the late side, in my view.'

'I don't think you need worry. We can give him injections while they set it all up.'

'I know you can, but it's not as good. That's four-hourly, isn't it?'

'It's not a problem. We can teach you how to give them.'

'Four-hourly throughout the night as well?'

'You really don't have to worry. We'll make sure you're all right. We'll give you all the support you need. I don't think he'll have any complications about swallowing. He looks fine to me.'

Feel fine. Quite well, in many ways. Just this little local trouble with the cancer. If it weren't for that I'd be quite spry. Don't know why Teil is fussing so.

'I don't actually want to learn to inject you, with morphine or anything else. I'd be afraid of killing you.'

'I'm sure it won't come to that. I feel fine.'

'You keep saying that. It's high time for the syringe driver to be in place. I can tell. I'm going to ring Worthing and ask where I can buy one.'

'Buy one? Why can't we use theirs?'

'Because, quite obviously, they're not going to let us have theirs until it's too late. I may not know much about medicine, but I do know about life. If you're worse, I may not be able to set up medical gadgetry. I'm emotionally involved, you know! They all seem to think I'm some sort of useful robot. I prefer to be prepared.'

'What can you do with a syringe driver? Afterwards, I mean?'

'The hospice can have it when we no longer need it. A contribution.'

'But don't they cost a fortune?'

'I don't know. I don't care. I can't do anything to help you get well, but I'm not having you in pain.'

She's quite angry. Don't know what she's so stirred up about. I'm sure they'll all do their best. They'll manage very well.

'Anything at all you'd like to eat?' Hope she calms down now. Want tranquillity. Peace. A gentle, relaxed atmosphere.

'A bit of scrambled egg, perhaps?' Won't take much preparing. In case I can't eat it when it comes to the point.

WEDNESDAY, 21ST MAY

Terry looks a trifle concerned today. Perhaps Teil's right after all. Maybe I am deteriorating? Whatever Liz may say. Hardly expect Liz to get it wrong. But still. . . .

Quite content. Equable, even. Lived the way I wanted to live. Done much of what I've wanted to do. Enjoyed doing it. More than most people, even if they live longer, can usually maintain. Had plenty of time to leave my affairs in order. Made sure that Teil won't have unnecessary hassle on her widow's plate.

Wary about the actual manner of dying. Obviously. Don't like to think of losing my mental faculties. Lost my bodily functions. Prefer to die with my mental ones intact. Not so worried about pain. My impression is that pain control is something they're getting very good at. Nursing staff will administer it. More concerned about not being kept alive officiously. Don't want my life needlessly prolonged, to an unduly painful or merely vegetable existence. Something which any reasonable human being would regard as intolerable. Don't want that. Clear I can rely on Teil to ensure this doesn't happen. As long as I stay here, at home. Says she can guarantee that. Can she last out?

I pray she can.

What causes cancer? No single reason, presumably. Don't believe it's *just* caused by stress. More in the area of a particular kind and degree of stress. Quite different from the ordinary kind. See it more as being gripped in a vice between the claws of irreconcilable conflict and intolerable despair. Caught between an apparently insoluble, or inadequately soluble, situation and a hypersensitive persona. I am an individual predisposed to guilt and anxiety, whether these are merited or not.

Now understand why I contracted, and still have, cancer. This knowledge will make it possible for me to put into practice measures that will enable me to defeat the disease. Not by surviving it, but by making use of the new illuminations my illness has given me. Insights into other people. Clarifications in relation to my work. My sickness has made it easy for me to be free of culpability or dread for the first time in my life.

My equability in the face of cancer, at the time I knew I might have it, and now I know I do have it, is an aspect of my view of the purpose of the disease. As a way of removing myself, if needs be, from a life which I did not, and do not, regard as essentially or sufficiently worthwhile and rewarding. And, above all, I realize that, at last, I am provided with an adequate justification for taking the means needed to overcome this state. Without censure. Without dismay. Without trepidation.

A definition, then. *Cancer* equals *oblivion*. A malignant growth, which tends to spread and reproduce itself, it corrodes the part or parts concerned, and generally ends in death.

Sometimes cured by diet. SODiet!

SATURDAY, 24TH MAY

My cancer is a form of profound melancholia. Get rid of the dejection – as I now can, probably *because* of the cancer – and I get rid of the cancer. My feeling and view now is that, if all things are reasonably equal, I am bound to recover from this disease. To be more healthy than ever before! Recover in spirit, that is. Not in the body. I've even written a poem about it.

Cancer – The Crab

I've always liked crab –
the meat, that is
makes me feel good
the iodine
makes me sleep soundly
no waking in the small hours
perhaps that's why I didn't run
feeling it settle on the seashore of my body
clamping its claws about my bones
catching me
alive
eating me
to death.

When I first saw that huge incision scar, I felt just a little like the 'lady' who has actually been sawn through by the resident magician!

SUNDAY, 25TH MAY

'You look a bit poorly, Mr Warburg. Are you feeling unwell?'
'I'm all right.
'I'll ask Doctor to look in tomorrow.'
'No need. I feel tolerable. My wife can always ring the surgery.' Don't want all this interference. Might drag me off to hospital. Teil might not be able to stop them. Want no treatment. If it's time, so be it. Not afraid to die. Let's distract her. 'How are the bedsores?'
'Not bad at all. As a matter of fact, your skin's in wonderful condition.'
'The sheepskins!'
She looks at me reflectively and nods. They like Teil to help

them now. Two of them moving things under me, about me. Why do they suddenly need two?

'You've done very well on the nursing.'

Well, why not? Have all the time in the world to look after myself. Try to do the creaming as they say. Not as often as I'm supposed to, but I try. Feel guilty if I don't!

So tired now. So worn out. Perhaps I should have had a blood transfusion. No, don't want that. Means a trip to the hospital. Didn't help Ralph. No transfusion. Nothing. Just stay here. Peaceably.

With Bean. W i t h . . . B e a n i e. On our own. Just as we used to be.

MONDAY, 26TH MAY

'Try getting fifteen pills down. I know it's difficult. I'll put them on the back of your tongue.'

Teil's trying to be practical. Helps me get the pills down. More and more pills. Pills and pills and pills and. . . .

Something's up. Pain's got worse again. More than that, feel a big congested, chesty. Can't breathe as easily as I could. Not really a cold or a cough. Odd feeling of suffocation in my chest. No point in talking to this nurse. Just an underling. Teil has to tell her what to do.

'Blast! She's absolutely useless. Forgotten to take the specimen.' Wish she wouldn't get so stirred up. What's it matter? See her look at me. Voice changes, softens. 'Would you like another drink?'

'No, don't bother. I'll just have a nap.'

'A little ice-cream before you go to sleep?'

'No, I'm just tired. Don't worry about me.'

Poor little Bean all on her own. Done everything I can. Can't help her now. I'll still be with her . . . I know I'll still be with her.

Dark already. It's night already?

'I'll just draw the curtains, just for a little while. Would you like some fresh air?'

'It's rather cold.'

'I thought you might like some fresh air. It gets rather close in here.'

'Just for a minute, then.'

Doze again. All I seem to do.

TUESDAY, 27TH MAY

'Can you lean forward, so that I can listen to your chest?'

'I don't think . . .'

'Are you finding it hard to breathe?'

'No, not really. I'm rather tired.'

'The anaemia, I expect. Have you got a cough?'

'I don't think so. My chest feels rather constricted. Congealed. Congested, I mean.'

'Yes. Not too bad, I think.'

'I tried to get the address for the pump. The syringe driver. Worthing hasn't rung. D'you think you could get it for me?'

'Of course. But you really needn't distress yourself. We can teach you how to do the injections.'

'I don't mind buying a syringe driver. I can give it to the hospice when we don't need it any more.' Very diplomatically put!

'I think they're rather expensive.'

'It's neither here nor there.' Usually so careful about money, too. What's she thinking of? 'He's got an infection, hasn't he?'

'A bit of one. Nothing to be concerned about.'

'Shall I tell my son in the States to come?'

'Alert him if you like. Nothing critical. I think he'll be all right.'

Not yet. The time isn't yet.

Infection's getting worse. Liz didn't offer antibiotics. Didn't ask. Rather leave it. Not looking too good. Lost my appetite completely. Lost my sense of humour.

Teil's alerted Worthing again. Not that he doesn't want to help. The hospice won't let him bring the machine until I can't swallow. Can still swallow. No problem really. Why does Teil worry so?

Terry's back. Glad to see her. Does everything quite slowly. Don't like to hurry. Some of them rush. Can't manage things quickly. Need to take my time. Need time. Time. There isn't enough time.

Always sleeping now. When I wake up Teil's sitting in the chair. Just there. No lights. No TV. No radio. In the chair. Boring for her.

'You don't have to sit there. I'll be all right.'

'Yes, of course. I like being here.'

'You'll get over-tired.' What shall I do if she can't hold out? Could be months yet. Liz doesn't think I'm in danger. She said not to get Richard.

'The loudspeaker's on all the time. I take the outlet round the house with me. I can hear. Even if you whisper.'

Outlet? Loudspeaker? Oh, the baby alarm. Just like being an infant. Others ministering to one. Everything via other people. Birth and death. Very near each other. Same thing, really. A birth into another world. Don't believe there's nothing. Can sense there's something . . . something.

THURSDAY, 29TH MAY

'D'you think this is it? D'you think I'm actively dying, as they say?'

'I don't know. The nurses say you're "very poorly", whatever that may mean. Liz says she thinks you'll pull through.'

'I know. But do you?'

'I don't know. Possibly not. I'm not too sure.'

'Will you be able to write the Diary?'

'Yes, I'm quite sure I will. Be glad to. Give me something I can do for you.'

'You can do your own work.'

'Yes. No one to share it with. That's going to be the worst of it. No fun. No fun at all.'

She'll miss me. Glad she'll pine, even though I know it's grief for her. Want to be mourned. Don't want to die and be forgotten. Want them to lament my death. Miss what I was to them. Don't just want to die and be forgotten. Nothing to show for it.

FRIDAY, 30TH MAY

Is this it? Has the cancer got me? Well, not the cancer. An infection, as expected. In the chest, I gather. Or the kidneys. They haven't taken a specimen. Possibly it could be that, for all they know. And who does know? No one's prepared to say, yes, you're dying. Why not? Had long enough to get used to the idea!

Cancer. The Big C. Got John Wayne, though he tried to fight it. I've tried to combat it. Teil tells me not to fight too hard. Says it's counterproductive. Maybe. Fight if I want to fight.

What causes it? Must try to figure out the origins for those who live after me. Maybe it's different for other people. For me it may well have been that I was *afraid* to display my creative talent to the full. Terrified of showing, let alone using, it. In relation to my mother, first and foremost. 'Put him down a peg or two!' she always tinkled. Ringing in my ears. An expert tinkler. Most certainly succeeded at it. If you can call that sort of thing success. Put him down. Stop him. Kill him!

And my father. Not that much better. Left me at the age of two to tender mercy of my mother. *Force majeure!* Of course. Pamela's jealousy as well. Two of them.

My siblings too. My brothers. Not Hew as a boy, but later. Obsessed with my being better academically. Didn't care. Nothing to me. He could never pass exams. Was that my fault? Never held it over him.

They frightened me to such an extent that I compromised my talent, especially in terms of worldly success. Hid it in all kinds of ways. Writing under a pseudonym they wouldn't know. Making my work obscure. Inaccessible. Unpopular. Deviant even. Writing only for a small minority – a minority of one, to be precise! Well, maybe Teil as well. And the children. Preferred to show only my academic talent. The lesser one. Unimportant to me. Gave up my university appointment. Left. Hid in the wilds of Somerset so that I could escape into myself. Is that what caused my cancer?

SATURDAY, 31ST MAY

Pain's getting worse again. How can it? With those massive doses of MST.

'Try to get the pills right on the back of your tongue. They'll go down more easily.' Swallowing's getting difficult. Don't eat at all. Now even drinking's a problem. How can I get six pints a day down me if I find it hard to swallow?

'I . . . w a n t . . .'

'Some ice-cream?' Why does she finish what I want to say? Can't know what I intend. Like to complete my own sentences!

'I . . . w . . . a . . . nt . . .'

'Are you in pain? Would you like some Diamorphine?'

'I . . . w . . . a . . . nt . . . w . . . a . . . .' Perhaps pointing is better. Want my notepad. Why can't she grasp that? See her look along the finger, then back at me. Still hasn't got it! Why not? Obvious I want the notepad. Said so several times!

'. . . n . . . o . . . te. . . .'

'The notepad?' Bring my hand down. Feels rigid. Everything feels hard. Like wood shavings. Stiff. Even the sheepskins. 'I'll get a pencil.' Didn't ask for one. Why's she interfering? Want to decipher what I've written down. My lists. Want to see my lists for today.

'I . . . c . . . a . . n . . . mm . . . a . . . ke . . . m . . . y . . .
o . . . wn . . . r . . . e . . . q . . . u . . . e . . . s . . . t . . . s.'

'I just want to make sure I fetch what you want to have.'

'. . . s . . . s . . . p . . . e . . . ak . . . f . . . or . . . m . . . y . . .
ss . . . e . . . l . . . f . . . I   c . . . a . . . n . . . s . . . a . . . y . . .
i . . . t . . . m . . . y . . . s . . . e . . . lf.'

I still want to speak for myself. I don't need an interpreter. I can
do it. I'm not that far gone! It's just all this morphine she keeps on
giving me.

June

SUNDAY, 1ST JUNE

'A r e n 't . . . y o u . . . g g o i n g . . . ?'
'To church? No, I think I'll skip it today.'
'Why? . . . I'm . . . f i n e . . . f i n e . . .'
'I don't feel like it. It's a lovely day. I'll open the french windows, shall I?'
'N o . . . n o!' She looks surprised. Can't she see that man looking menacingly at me? The one with the parrot hook. Don't want him staring. So threatening. Doing the rhynes, I suppose. Why's he in our garden?
'I'm just unlocking it for the nurse.'
'I . . . w a n t . . . i t . . .'
'Shut. I know. You want it shut. I won't open it.'
'I . . . c a n . . . f i n i s h . . . m y . . . o w n . . . s e n t e n c e s.'
'Of course, honey. Sorry.'
'I . . . can . . . finish . . . my . . . own . . . sentences. I don't need anyone to do it for me.' I'm still here. In charge of what I say.

'We won't bother him much. Just wash his face a bit. He's nice and peaceful. We won't disturb him.' Why's she keep harping on? Not like her to be so subdued. Teil tries chatting, but she's oddly quiet. What's her name? Jolly one. Loud. Talkative. Not that you'd know that today! 'I'll leave you my home number. If you need any help, just give me a ring. No trouble. I'll be glad to come.' Off.
Well, that's nice. Peaceful Sunday. Just the two of us.

[*233*]

'Bean!' An age. Why doesn't she come? Said she can hear me whispering. 'Bean!'

'Just coming!'

'There was an enormous plop.'

'A plop?'

'As though something exploded inside me. Below the navel, on my lower left side.'

'Is there anything you'd like me to do? Are you in pain?'

'No pain. Seems to be all right now. Nothing to do.'

'A drink?'

'I don't feel like drinking.'

'I'll just give Liz a ring in case there's something which ought to be done.'

'I don't need anything. Just thought you'd like to know. For the Diary. Leave the pad here. And the pencil. It was a major and substantial convulsion. Didn't you hear anything?'

'Only your calling me.'

'Like a crack in my mind.'

'Is it still going on?'

'The crack? How could it? But it might start again.'

Feeling of vague anticlimax during the convulsion. Of disappointment. A sense of the possibility of dying. Of leaving a good world. Departing on such a ridiculous note. Like one clown farting at another. Breaking up. An impression of cracking up. My body fragmenting. My mind popping. Yet Teil's only registered the smaller spasm like a kind of quivering. Bigger than the earlier one, but still only a shudder. No noise at all. Audible all the time to me. Amazed Teil hasn't heard anything. Incredible. My body crackling. Disintegrating.

Gone off. Other matters to attend to, presumably. Because she thinks this is it? D-day? Dying day! Death day! Don't think so.

That rather large protruberance in my belly's settling down now. Just wind, as I suspected. Could help to disperse that frightful distension. Eliminate it. Help me relax a little. Pretty uncomfortable tumescence. Asked them to do something about it. Can't, apparently. What can they do? Flatulence. Dispersal of gas. Just like a baby. Maybe I need burping after eating. Reason I can't eat. Or drink. Air taking up the space. Probably not near death within hours, or even weeks, let alone minutes! Just hot air!

I'm both relieved and put out at the same time. Fed up with all this terrible physical wreckage. This awful discomfort. Pain. Dependence on others. Jaded. Only way out. Yet relieved I'm still here.

Not quite that wearied. World's still there, and it is good. Not necessarily better than the world to come, whatever that may be. But blessed. Feast on the view. Love Teil. Appreciate her beside me. Write notes. Watch. Always the observer from outside. . . .

'Best not say too much. Hearing's the last thing to go.' Terry. Gentle Terry. Why shouldn't I hear? Afraid Teil will say I'm departing now. Teil doesn't know. If she did, she'd say. Honestly. Never lies to me. Relationship is built on trust. Confidence between us that we'll tell the truth. Know she won't change that at the last.

'He had quite massive convulsions earlier on. They're much smaller now. Almost trivial.'

'I see. How do you feel? In yourself?' That odd phrase again.

'All right. Didn't mean to bother you. I'm sure you've got much more deserving causes than mine.'

'He's finding it hard to swallow. Did you contact Worthing?'

'I'll see to it directly. Perhaps a liquid tranquillizer might be easier. Move him on to it gradually.'

Out of the room. Can hear very well. Terry's right. Hearing's acute.

'Shall I send for our son?'

'No. No need for concern. Just alert him in case there's any deterioration. The infection's not that bad.'

'Is it in the kidney?'

'Perhaps. In the chest as well. Kidney failure's not a bad way to go.'

Front door bangs shut.

TUESDAY, 3RD JUNE

The spasming is very distressing. Not simply intermittent twitchings. Constant, continuous, convulsive shuddering. Torturing my frame. Body all aching and racked with spasms. Sometimes a big one. A sort of jump. As though I'm being propelled into space. Followed by little ones. Endlessly tremulous. Everything jerks. My hands shake. Can't stop them. Can't speak properly. Lips displaced involuntarily. Intended mouth movements badly impeded.

'G . . . r . . . i . . . te . . . t . . .'

'I'm writing it down, honey.'

'L . . . e . . . u . . . r . . . y.'

'I'll make sure it's all included.' Teil still understands what I'm saying. For the Diary. Write it down . . . write it . . . down. . . .

Exhausting. Wake from a sort of sleep. More a trance, since I hear what's going on. Apparent sleep. Eyes mostly closed. Hands clasped behind my head, to keep them still. Stop this insistent movement. When will it end? Must it finish like this? Couldn't I be at peace?

Liz brings another tranquillizer. Hopes to calm all this activity.

'I'm sorry. There's nothing I can do. It will pass soon. Just something temporary. No need to worry.'

She really believes that? Knows Richard's in Boston. Would she really not warn us if she knew that I'm in the process of going? Now?

Mary. Madame Curie for the night. In Teil's chair. Opens the french windows wide. Cold. Want them closed. Can't communicate. Words jumble . . . constantly moving mouth. Don't want to wake Teil. Don't want windows open . . . too wide. . . .

Mary here all night prevents Teil coming early. Eagerly anticipate that. Nothing against Mary. Just isn't Tiel. . . .

Teil helps me drink the liquid food. Brings ice-cream. Childhood again! Slips down. Like apricot best. Teil spoons me medicines.

Liz. Again? 'I'm off for a couple of weeks on Thursday.'
'Veer're oo goin'?'
Pause, and then she registers. My mouth still twitches. Not as badly as before.
'Cornwall. Just down to Cornwall.'
'We wenn noo Walcor. Voley conny.'
Aghast look.
'We went to Cornwall. Lovely county,' Teil translates.
'Voldervol vish. Pelporr fish.'
Frowns, completely uncomprehending.
'Wonderful fish. Polperro fish,' Teil interprets. 'We went to Polperro one winter.'
Liz smiles reassuringly, humouring me, indulging the little child.
'I've ordered oxygen. They'll bring it later on. There's nothing worse than a choking feeling.' Why would I choke? Taking pills? 'Sorry there's nothing more I can do. I'll be in again tomorrow.'
Will I see her again? Or tomorrow?

Nurse evidently shocked at my appearance. Clearly thinks I'm on my way out. Now. Can tell.
Difficult to swallow. Maybe I'll be on the liquid hard stuff soon.

[*237*]

Shudders calming down. Thank God for that! Can speak clearly again.

No urine samples taken. Let the bugs take over! If the chest don't get you, the kidney must. Who knows? Not they!

Young man, carrying a heavy, cylindrical object. Oxygen! To help me breathe, Liz said.

'Just try it, honey. See if it helps your breathing,'

Don't like it. What's it for? Don't like the mask. Mask of death. . . .

THURSDAY, 5TH JUNE

Hospice agrees about syringe driver. Fine. Brilliant. Equally, there isn't one available for me. Great!

Teil's on the phone all morning. 'Can't you leave it to Worthing to sort out?'

'Evidently not. And the local medics probably know less than I do.'

Apparently I'm quite ill. Can think easily. Can even talk, very slowly. Teil irritatingly completes my sentences, but accurately. Instruct her for the Diary. Keep records. Important. Reminders. How else will she know what it was like for me?

Alec instead of Liz. Otherwise complications if I exit and Liz is away. Brisk. Not much to say. Well, what is there to say? Prescribes morphine for the syringe driver. They guess how much. No idea.

Terry again. Antinausea injections. Teil's bought a syringe driver. Arriving tomorrow. Won't have to swallow pills. Automatically, continuously, injects morphine. Heroin.

Is Terry here? Or Mary? Hard to follow what's happening.

'Liz says she thinks he'll pull through.' Teil's trying to decide whether to inform Richard.

'Still touch and go, though, isn't it?' Terry openly disagreeing now. Cares. Wants to help us get it right.

Touch and go? She saying this is it?

'Am I dying now?'

'I don't know, honey. Terry obviously thinks you might be. So does Mary. Would you like me to ring Richard?'

'I don't want to disturb him for nothing. I don't want him to come if it jeopardizes his career. Only if he wants to come. It's not for me . . . if he wants to come. Must have the chance . . . I'd love to see him if he wants to . . . love to see him . . . see Richard . . . see the Tock. . . .'

'It's getting late. No Marie Curie to inject you. I'll have to give you the antinausea by mouth. Can you try?'

'If it's good for me.' If it keeps me going!

'Good? It'll stop you being sick. That would be bad.'

'I'll try.'

Rumbling in my throat. Rasping, rattling sound. Liquid trickles down. Feel need to spit it out. Splutter, cough, then catch my breath. React as though choking to death. Teil takes the babycall. On our own. Better that way.

FRIDAY, 6TH JUNE

12.30 a.m.

'Where am I?'

'At home, honey, with me. Alone together. Just the two of us.'

'Am I dying?'

'I don't know, but I think so. The nurses think so. I've rung the Tock.'

'Is he coming?'

'Yes. Perhaps on Saturday. Maybe later today.'

'What day is it?'

'It's night. It's early in the morning. Friday.'

'Will you be all right?'

'I expect so. Don't worry about me.'

'I'll have to go to hospital . . . you won't be able to cope.'

'You're not going anywhere. You're staying here. At home. I'll stay beside you.'

'Will you manage to write the Diary?'

'I'll make sure I do.'

6.30 a.m.

'What's going on? Where's Minnow? Is she coming soon?'

'Very soon.'

'And Cockle? Where's the Tock?'

'What's happening? Where's Terry? What's the time? Are you taking notes? . . . The Tock . . . time for the Tock? . . . Where am I. . . ?'

8 a.m.

'Hello.' Voice a croak. Can't speak.

'I'll be down later on today, Jifda.' Minnow.

Terry with Teil. Pills very hard to manage. Injections soon. How many? Can't swallow, can't eat, can't. . . . 'Is Tick coming?'

'Later today.'

'Will you die too?'

'Your wife isn't going to die. Your wife is going to live!'

'How long?'

'Long enough to do what we want me to do!'

10 a.m.

Where's Bean? 'I have something to say!'

'I'm just ringing Worthing. So I can test the pump.'

'Peter Worthing?'

'He's coming down tomorrow to show me what to do.' Why isn't she here with me? 'Just coming, honey. The pump has a fault!'

'I have something I want to say. Why aren't you listening? It's important!'

'I'm sorry, honey. The manufacturers shut at ten-thirty for the weekend. I've got to get it straightened out.'

'I have something important to say! Listen to me. I have something to tell you!'

'Just coming. They're sending another one by tomorrow morning.'

Sits by the bed, preoccupied with the damned pump. 'It's just dawned! It's a syringe driver – we'll need a syringe. I don't know what type or size.'

I'm dying. She's not here. Soon I won't be. Then I can't give her details for the Diary. Want her to take notes. Extensive records. So she'll know. Want . . . explain . . . communicate . . . will she manage . . . keep reminders. . . . 'Listen to what I have to say!'

Noon

'Hello, Tom!'

'Hello, Jeremy!' Startled. Expects me to lie here like a log. Thinks I'm comatose. Mistaken as usual! Rotten doctor, nice man.

'How are you?' Ask a doctor how he feels. Always gets them on the wrong foot. Thinks it's none of one's business. They're the ones who do the asking! 'Hear you've been ill. Any better?'

'Not too bad. But what about you?'

'Am I dying?'

'We all have to die, Jeremy.'

'Yes, you're dying.' Teil. Annoyed with him. Equivocates. No good. No use at all. Sophistry at a time like this. Prevaricates in the face of death! She'll not deny the truth.

'Are you good at machines? Could you look at this pump? It's not functioning, is it?'

Tom's happier fiddling with the gadget. 'It isn't working, no.'

'I think it's the battery.'

'I'm sure you're right.'

Battery, nattery. Flattery, scattery. Cattery, battery. Bats. Am I going bats? Where am I? Where's Teil? 'I gather there's no one here.'

'I'm coming, honey. Just phoning Ayliffe to bring a battery.' Bats. All bats! 'Mad's picking up syringes for me.'

'Mad?'

'They're all coming tonight. Cockle and Anna. Minnow's meeting the Tock at Heathrow. They'll all be here tonight.'

'Where am I?'

'At home, honey, with me by you. The children will be with us soon.'

'They'll all be here? All of them?'

8 p.m.

'I'll always come and help. Don't give them to him on your own.' Terry.

'The night nurse didn't come. We managed.' Letting Teil down. Said they'd support her!

'I may be ten minutes late or so. But I'll be here.' Terry's back to support Teil. Always liked her. Sympathetic. Concerned.

'Worthing is coming at ten. So's Dr Quigley.'

'Would you mind if Nurse Kalmett and I come, too? We haven't seen a pump in action. It would help us.' Don't ask *my* permission. Talk across me. Do what they like.

'I'm sure my husband won't mind. Just two of you. There'll be so many people already. I've got to be there. And my daughter-in-law – she's a doctor – in case she has to take over.'

Tomorrow the pump. The end.

10 p.m.

'Hello, Cockle. Hello, Anna. Good of you to come.'

'Hello, Dad.'

'Hello, Minnow. Hello, Tick. Lovely of you to come.'

'Thanks for asking me.' Tick's here now, from Boston. Must be it. Richard's here. Must be dying now. Richard. . . . 'Love all of you.'

'We love you too.'

6 a.m.

'Isn't it rather early for you?'

'It may be the last time we'll be alone together.'

'How am I doing?'

'Well. You're doing very well. Are you in pain?'

'No. How will I live if I dry up?'

'Don't worry about it. No point. I'll do everything I can. I'll see they do everything that can be done.'

'Thank you for being such a wonderful companion.'

'Thank you too. I've always loved you, right from the start, the moment I first saw you.'

'Yes, I love you too. You've been a wonderful helpmate for so long. I'm sorry I can't make it much . . . much longer.'

'You've given me many wonderful years. As you said, few people have had a bond like ours. I'm grateful to have had you at all.'

'I shall always be with you – never fear.'

'I know.'

'As you'll always be with me, thank God.'

'Yes, I will. I'm sad I couldn't help you more. Sorry we couldn't defeat this awful disease.'

'Is it time now?'

'A few days yet.'

'D'you think *you* would want to live? In my position? Now?'

'I shouldn't think so.'

'Things being as they are?'

'Not really.'

'Do you mind?'

'I mind for me. I prefer it for you.'

What will she do? How will she survive? Will I kill her with my ghastly cancer? 'How will I live if I dry up?'

'I'll look after you.'

'How will I be if I live?'

'You'll be as you were before this infection.'

'I can't live *according to them*.'

'I know, dearest.'

Always pretending they know what's going on. Don't know anything. If I wanted to live, I would. Don't want to. Can't. Too difficult. I'd kill Bean. Can't do my work. No point now. Things being as they are. Have to leave Bean. Worst of it. Have to go . . . love them all . . . leave them all . . . depart. . . .

7.30 a.m.

'Sorry, Minnow, I keep falling asleep. I'm trying very hard, but I keep . . . asleep . . . falling. Messages . . . I . . . want . . . to . . . send . . . messages . . . for . . . people. Take . . . it . . . all . . . down. As notes.'

'Yes, I've got a pad and I'm taking notes.'

'Tell the boys . . . the twins . . . I adore them.'

'I'll tell them, Jifda.'

'You, too. I adore you all . . . love all of you . . . I'm definitely going. Is Bean well? . . . Bean? Sorry about leaving her. Tell her. I can't stay.'

'I'm taking it all down. Teil's here now.'

Standing beside me, leaning over the bed. Can still see her. Touch her. 'Will you . . . be . . . strong enough?'

10 a.m.

'Send love . . . to . . . Ruthi . . . Certainly love Ruthi. . . . David. Thank him . . . for . . . coming. Coming to see . . . me. Good of him. Tell him so . . . tell my brother . . . my brother David. . . . Like my nephews and nieces. Don't know them . . . very well. Like them very much.'

'I did my first production, Jif. It's turned out well.'

'Well done. Jolly good. Could I do that . . . d'you think I could do that?'

'Of course. If you'd wanted to.' Teil. Thought it was Mad. 'You did what you wanted to do in life.'

'With your help. You helped. . . .'

'. . . can you see? I've brought some photos for you. Little Jeremy . . .'

'. . . I'd like see him . . . not too much trouble . . . trouble. . . . If it's not too much money . . . only if it isn't bad for . . . bad for little Jere . . . Jeremy. Not bad. . . .'

'Baby? You can't bring a baby here!' Tom's here again.
'Hello, Tom.'
'Hello, Jeremy. Any pain?'
'No.'
'We're just going to insert the syringe driver needle into a vein, so we needn't bother you with pills.'

After all this time. Tom Quigley, in at the kill! Crowds of them. Come to see the play – Worthing, Terry, Nurse Kalmett, Teil, Anna. All here. Tom's the one who's got to do it. To get the needle in. Doctor in charge. Not Anna. Not Worthing. Tom. Tom Quigley. How odd of God! And he does it with a flourish. Can't feel anything.

'The pump's working, honey. Are you comfortable?'
'I'm fine.'
'Good. Anna will brief me before she leaves.'

Teil will see me through, just as Medora said. Stand by me to the end. Can rely on her. See . . . to . . . the . . . end.

6 p.m.

'Am I alone? Is someone here?'
'It's me, Jifda.'
'Say the names. So that I know who's here . . .'
'Richard.'
'Tock. Hi, Tock. I love all of you.'
'We love you too.'

'Why can't I live? Why do *I* have to die? why *me*?'
'Your body doesn't want to live.'
'Why not?'
'It's very ill.'

9 p.m.

'Names. Tell me the names!'

'It's Minnow, Jif. I'm taking down the messages.'

'Message to Gissel. Liked her. Admired her . . . admired her for getting things together . . . still working . . . nearly eighty. . . . Respected her.'

'Read David's letter to me, Mad. . . . Yes. Good. Well done, David!'

'Hi, George. Liked George . . . still do like George . . . not been in touch for ages now . . . my fault really . . . well, not entirely me . . . not altogether me . . . circumstances . . . the force of circumstances . . . pity. . . . Sorry I . . . haven't . . . sorry . . . George . . . like to see him . . . wished I'd seen him . . . George . . . more . . . liked him . . . didn't see . . . much . . . of him.'

SUNDAY, 8TH JUNE

6 a.m.

'Where are we?'

'At home, honey. We're all with you.'

'Col? Is that you, Cockle?'

'Yes, Dad.'

'You . . . put . . . pictures of ancestors . . . only two . . . look like Warburgs. . . . I'm like John Warburg . . . never knew him . . . never knew my grandfather . . . just like Jeremy Hillier . . . like little Jeremy.'

'Put down the detail . . . so we know . . . need to know . . . detail . . . when you're . . . talking . . . say . . . names . . . can't tell who it is . . . talking to . . . me. . . .'

'Time to prime the pump, honey. Are you all right?'

[246]

'I . . . suppose . . . sup . . . so . . .'

'Anna's teaching me. I can do it.' Heroin addict now. 'Try to swallow the tranquillizer.' Nothing but drugs. Introvenous feeding. Heroin pumping through the blood vessels. Pump it through. Pump life through . . .

'Ice-cream. I'd love a taste . . . of . . . ice-cream.'

'Of course. I'll get you some. Apricot?'

'Ice . . . cream. . . .' Not apricot. Vanilla. Can't speak fast enough. They get the wrong idea. I d e a. . . . 'Phone call . . . message from . . . f r o m . . . message . . . I have previous knowledge. . . .'

5.30 p.m.

'We're all here. Teil and Mad and Col and Tick. Everyone's here.'

'Ack . . . now . . . ledge . . . ments. Will . . . you . . .'

'Of course, honey. I'll see to the acknowledgements.'

'*Macro Factor* . . . acknowledgements.'

'We'll see to it.'

'Diary . . . acknowledgements . . .'

'We'll see to it, Jifda.'

'*Call* . . . acknowledgements . . . for *Call*.'

'Any more messages?'

'Dealt . . . with . . . messages. . . .'

'. . . ack . . . now . . . ledge . . . ments. Teil . . .'

'She's gone to have a bath. She'll see to it, Jifda. We'll all see to it. More ice-cream?'

'. . . knowledge . . . knowl . . .'

'We know. Any other messages to write down?'

Don't understand. Can't make them comprehend. Need to have it all acknowledged properly. How else can I live on?

9 p.m.

'The big fight . . . fight the big fight . . . tomorrow. The big fight's tomorrow, isn't it? . . .'

[247]

'Don't fight too hard, honey. Don't struggle all the time.'

Fight the big fight with all your might. My right. With all my might. Have to fight. Otherwise I'll die. Fight. Why shouldn't I fight?

'If I take . . . take . . . liquid . . . and ice . . . cream . . . s'cream. . . . If I take . . . them . . . together . . . strength. They'll give me . . . strength . . . i . . . s'cream . . . to fight.'

Flight. Right. Lost sight. Fading . . . light.

'Good night, honey. We're taking it in turn to stay with you. First the Tock. Then Cockle. Then Minnow. I'll be here first thing in the morning. Night!'

Night. Dark night. Black night. The night has come.

MONDAY, 9TH JUNE

3 a.m.

'Is it time?'

'It's three o'clock. In the morning.'

'I'd love some ice-cream. Is it time?'

'Time for what, Jif?'

'What day is it?'

'June 9th.'

'I want some ice-cream.'

'Do you want Teil?'

'. . . have sight . . . have a sight . . . Vicarage. . . .'

'Go back to bed . . . you'll get exhausted. . . .' She'll never be OK if she stays up. Didn't ask for her. '. . . proof . . . I have proof . . . prior evidence . . . of a stroke . . . prior evidence that I'm going to have a stroke.'

'I've known for ages . . . decades of ages . . .'

'D'you think you're dying, now?'

'I'm not prepared to go that far.' Not yet! Not yet!

'Mad. For the Diary. Put it down for the Diary . . . Diary . . . for our Diary . . . interesting . . . something you . . . would . . . like . . . to . . . know . . . about.'

'We all love you.'

'I know that . . . lovely of you all. . . .'

'. . . stroke . . . or similar . . . evidence . . . a stroke . . .'

'Are you in pain?'

'No.'

'Shall I fetch Teil?'

'No.' Must look after her. Must cherish her.

'Minnow's with you, Jif.'

'I know that . . . thank you . . . lovely of you . . . thanks, Mad.'

'Interesting event . . .'

'What is?'

'. . . event . . . interesting . . .'

'You mean for the Diary?'

'Maybe.'

'Always remember . . . lean over . . . by the bed . . . if . . . you . . . can . . . not too . . . near. So . . . you . . . can write. Write it down. . . . Sorry to be so long. So . . . long. . . . EVEN TE DO DE LA LEUR.

'E V A N . . . T E . . . D O . . . D E . . L A . . . . L E U R.' Teil understands me . . . knows . . . what . . . I'm . . .

'E V A N . . . T E . . . D O . . . D E . . L A . . . L E U R.' I want her to do the Diary . . . I WANT TEIL TO DO THE DIARY!

I WANT TEIL TO DO THE DIARY!

EPILOGUE

Jeremy Warburg died on Monday, 9th June 1986 at five-thirty in the morning, his wife and children around him.

The body lay at The Old Vicarage until Wednesday, 11th June, 'So Teil can have a little time with me. Adjust, so to speak, to my dead body rather than my live one.' Nothing was done to the body; it was left as his wife and children had arranged it. The remains were taken away and cremated, and the ashes returned, that Wednesday afternoon.

Widow, daughter and sons climbed Glastonbury Tor later the same evening, carrying the simple casket containing the ashes. 'That's all that will be needed for scattering my ashes from the top of the Tor. That's what I have in mind, by those of my children who are present and up to the task.' St Michael's tower cast a long finger of shadow on to the ancient mound. The scattered ashes rose on the wind, high into the brilliant blue sky, then drifted slowly down over the fertile 'pastures green' of the Somerset Levels.

A mass of remembrance was said in Somerset, and another in London.